W9-AYH-100

The Free Press
A Division of Simon & Schuster, Inc.
1230 Avenue of the Americas
New York, N.Y. 10020

Printed in the United States

printing number

6 7 8 9 10

Library of Congress Cataloging-in-Publication Data

Lewis, Jordan D.
    The connected corporation : how leading companies win through customer-supplier alliances / Jordan D. Lewis.
        p.   cm.
    Includes index.
    ISBN 978-1-4165-7336-4   ISBN 1-4165-7336-4
    1. Industrial purchasing—United States—Management—Case studies.
2. Strategic alliances (Business)—United States—Case studies.
I. Title.
HD39.5.L48   1995
658.7'2—dc20   95-4617
                                                     CIP

For Lynn

THE CONNECTED
CORPORATION

THE
CONNECTED
CORPORATION

*How Leading Companies Win Through
Customer–Supplier Alliances*

Jordan D. Lewis

 THE FREE PRESS

CONTENTS

TABLES AND FIGURES

INTRODUCTION

Alliances are powerful tools for building competitive advantage, and they have long been a compelling subject for me. Yet I wondered why, in view of their growing use, they were not more often applied in the vital area of customer–supplier relationships—the most common and important intercompany links in business.

The answer struck me while I was speaking to *Fortune's* annual meeting of the CEOs of America's 100 fastest-growing companies. During my talk on alliances, I asked the executives whether their companies supplied other firms, as opposed to consumers. I then asked those who responded positively if they had true alliances with those customers; only a handful did. Certainly, I thought, something was wrong. An alliance is literally the best way to get close to a customer, which is every company's goal. Why, I asked these executives, did so few of their firms have such relationships?

Several explained that they wanted to have alliances with their customers—and that many customers described their relationships as alliances. Beyond the rhetoric, however, it was business as usual. Pressed further, the executives said that customers did not trust their firms. Nor did customers share information needed to improve their firms' performance or plan for the long term. Customers also failed to respect their margins, and dropped them without notice for others offering lower prices—even though this often led to higher total costs. Most telling, I thought, was the comment that relationships were often adversarial. I then asked the CEOs whether their companies had true alliances with their own suppliers; only two said yes. Why, I asked the rest, did they not have such relationships? The consensus: Suppliers cannot be trusted.

As the reality of this statement sunk in, there was a growing collective embarrassment. What the executives were saying, in effect, was that they were not willing to give their own suppliers the trust they wanted to have *as* suppliers. This insight and my belief in the value of alliances convinced me to write *The Connected Corporation*. I hope it will help managers everywhere build effective alliances with their customers and suppliers.

The Research Agenda

My research for this book began with discussions at Motorola and with other clients in Asia, Europe, and North and South America. I also talked with journalists at *Business Week*, the *Economist*, the *Financial Times*, *Fortune*, the *New York Times*, and the *Wall Street Journal* who covered a broad array of industries. With more than two decades of deep involvement with a wide variety of alliances, I was looking for best practice in customer–supplier relationships. This led to a list of potential candidates, followed by face-to-face interviews with these firms.

During the interviews, I asked each company to describe its results and how they were achieved. I also asked for introductions to its top customers and suppliers, and I inquired about the extent to which each firm had benchmarked best practice in this area, in any industry worldwide, and for the names of other companies that it knew to be proficient with these alliances. This information led to a revised list of potential candidates and a second round of interviews. My discussions with some designated suppliers were particularly enlightening: Several of them worked with more than one of the companies on my list of customers, and saw clear distinctions among them.

In the search for best practice I was guided by a desire for a broad scope. If I could meet that objective, I believed, this book would be most useful to a wide variety of readers. Much of what has been written on supply relationships reflects methods used in the Japanese auto industry; I wanted to understand and describe practices in other manufacturing sectors and in the services, as well as in industrial-goods businesses. Including these four categories—manufacturing and the services, consumer and industrial goods—would cover all major sectors of an economy. I also wanted to describe smaller firms' experiences. Most business books overlook this dimension, perhaps because readers are attracted by examples from large, well-known companies. Yet in industrial economies, small firms account for well over half of all economic activity.

These considerations, plus the networking described earlier, produced a list of about forty companies in Asia, Europe, and the United States that were the initial focus for my intended in-depth research. To be on the list, a company had to have customer or supplier alliances that had produced major benefits which were continuing to get better over time. Most companies were willing to share their experiences with me on the record. Five agreed to interviews but asked that no information they shared be attributed to them.

Following another round of interviews I further narrowed the list, developed an interview guide, and spent the next four years conducting in-depth discussions with scores of people at all management levels of both customers and their suppliers. Many interviews required several meetings. Many companies also shared internal documents with me, to help me better understand their activities. One company shared a large set of benchmarking studies it had recently completed on the supply practices of selected American, European, and Japanese firms. I also accepted invitations to sit in on meetings between customers and suppliers, which gave me valuable insights into how they conducted their relationships.

In total, more than one hundred individuals, ranging from sales and purchasing people to mid-level managers and corporate chief executives, participated in the research. Many of my typed notes from a single interview exceeded fifty single-spaced pages. (Completed interviews were approved by the respective firms.) The interviews were complemented by descriptions of customer–supplier alliances culled from the business press.

During my research, I found that each company was ahead of the others in some areas. When I described the differences I saw, the people I spoke with were eager to know who to contact for more information. This led, for example, to a joint benchmarking meeting between Motorola and Philips Consumer Electronics Company (PCEC), and to Motorola sharing its quality audit process with Marks & Spencer (M&S). As is typical with excellent companies, the lessons learned were quickly put into practice. Not surprisingly, this passion for learning was a hallmark of the companies on my short list of best practice firms. It was a tremendous help for me, because it made my interviews mutual explorations rather than tedious one-way interrogations.

Key Firms: Motorola, Marks & Spencer, Chrysler, and Philips Consumer Electronics Company

As my research progressed, it became clear that many aspects of best practice are common across all firms and industries. Further, the methods needed for high-performing customer–supplier alliances involve an exceptionally wide range of activities at the interface and within each firm. Only an in-depth description of all these activities, and how they tie together, would meet my objective of giving this book enough detail to make it a practical guide for most companies. This need for depth caused me to increase my research focus on Motorola, Marks & Spencer, and several of each company's suppliers. Motorola, which has been using supply alliances for more than a decade, has built in many of the practices needed to succeed in such partnerships. M&S has had alliances with its suppliers for several decades, so its techniques have even deeper roots.

To build a picture of best practice across a wide variety of settings, my research on M&S, Motorola, and their suppliers was complemented by interviews with other outstanding practitioners whose situations or techniques were unique and important. This included, for example, the Kodak–IBM data processing outsourcing alliance, a temporary employee recruitment alliance between Hewlett-Packard and Reed Personnel Services in the United Kingdom, how suppliers link with Ford's new global structure, and aspects of PCEC's work with its supply partners.

At the time I began my research, decades of hostility had created severe difficulties between American and European auto companies and their suppliers. As a consequence, the automakers' costs, quality, and cycle times were so bad that observers were predicting the collapse of some companies. This is significant, because automakers are major factors in an economy (in the United States, they purchase more than $200 billion in goods and services each year). Toward the end of my research, it was clear that Chrysler had made the greatest advances in reversing the situation, even to the point where Motorola and other alliance leaders were benchmarking its practices. Because key aspects of auto companies' supply relationships are unique to them—and because I was encouraged by people at Motorola to visit there—I arranged to conduct interviews at Chrysler as well.

Obviously, no research is ever complete. There are always more questions to be asked, other companies with superior practices, more details to be described. Even so, because Motorola and M&S have been using customer–supplier alliances longer than other Western firms, their work in this area has more facets, is more deeply imbedded in their organizations, and has given them more substantial results. Clearly, there are marked differences between an electronics manufacturer and a food and clothing retailer. Even so, the methods these companies use to gain their results are remarkably similar to those employed by PCEC and Chrysler, many of these companies' suppliers with *their* own suppliers, and other firms that have succeeded with customer–supplier alliances. What is striking is that, regardless of whether a firm is in manufacturing, services, or consumer or industrial goods, best practice in these alliances is essentially the same in many ways.

These observations, plus exploratory interviews in Asia, gave me some confidence that my research had gone well past the point of diminishing returns in terms of my objectives for this book. As I applied these understandings to my consulting practice and to lectures and courses worldwide, my insights were validated.

Because of the importance I have given to Motorola, Marks & Spencer, Chrysler, and Philips Consumer Electronics Company, a brief description of each firm follows. While these companies are proficient at supply alliances, some of their suppliers say the relationships do not work as well as they might, and some parts of these firms are not as advanced in their use of alliances as other parts. Still, they are acknowledged leaders whose levels of excellence set a useful benchmark for others. That is the focus of this book.

ABOUT MOTOROLA

Motorola is the global market leader in cellular phones, pagers, two-way radios, and microchips used to control devices other than computers. The company is a world leader in quality, having reduced its defect rate in manufacturing by well over 99.5 percent. As a leading innovator, Motorola produces an average of four new or improved products each day. Intense competition—the firm's pager prices fall an average of 8 to 12 percent a year, and its cellular phone prices drop 25 percent a year—and the investment needed to stay ahead keep Motorola's profit margins razor thin. Still, with sales growing faster than 25 percent annually for several years, Motorola's earnings (now in excess of $1 billion) are sufficient to fuel its continued growth.

Motorola has been a pioneer in many key management areas, including self-directed work teams, training, and business process reengineering. In the early 1980s, the company began transforming its supply relationships into alliances, and it has reaped dramatic results. Chief executives of the prestigious Business Roundtable rank Motorola as America's top practitioner of total quality management. Says

Anthony Langham, a NatWest securities analyst who has followed Motorola for twenty-six years: "This company is just on a tremendous roll. They are very, very good at everything they do."[1]

ABOUT MARKS & SPENCER

British retailer Marks & Spencer has consistently been the most profitable firm in its industry. M&S has 17 percent of the domestic clothing market, and the clothing it sells represents 25 percent of the U.K. garment industry's output. The company's food sales make up 5 percent of the British market.

M&S is a world leader in offering high-value fabrics, clothing, home furnishings, and foods. Together with its garment suppliers, M&S constantly innovates in design; extends the frontiers of quality; shortens cycle times; and pulls together technologies in fibers, spinning, weaving, knitting, dying, printing, finishing, and manufacturing literally from around the world. In food, M&S and its suppliers are equally adventurous—and successful—at the frontiers of ingredient technology, bacteriology, processing, delivery, and fast response.

M&S owns retail food and clothing chains in Japan and North America, and is rapidly expanding with new company-owned stores,

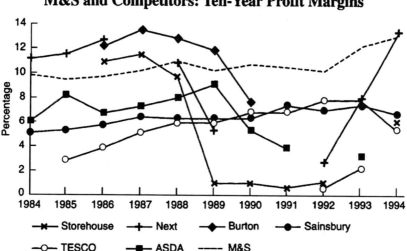

M&S and Competitors: Ten-Year Profit Margins

franchises, and joint ventures in Asia and Europe. In its most recent full-year results, 13 percent of Marks & Spencer's turnover and 7 percent of its operating profits came from outside the United Kingdom.

In 1994 a survey of 2,000 chairmen, CEOs, and finance officers from more than 600 major European companies (undertaken by the *Financial Times* in association with Price Waterhouse) identified M&S and Asea Brown Boveri as the two most respected companies in Europe. The figure shown compares the growth and pretax profits of M&S with other major retail chains in the United Kingdom.[2]

ABOUT CHRYSLER

In 1989 Chrysler suffered record losses of $664 million. It had fallen to fifth place in the American car market, planned to cut a third of its capacity, and was close to bankruptcy. In 1994 the automaker launched the Neon—a car described by its Japanese rivals as having "designed-in cost savings that were unprecedented in an American car"—and recorded annual earnings of $3.7 billion.

In addition to the Neon, Chrysler developed a new range of medium and small cars (collectively known as the LH) with a fresh design that put them well ahead of the competition. Working with unprecedented efficiency, Chrysler produced these cars in just three years instead of the usual five, employing only one-third of the engineers needed to produce the previous range. The story of Chrysler's transformation, told in a book by Paul Ingrassia and Joseph White and later summarized in the *Economist*, makes fascinating reading.[3]

One key to Chrysler's rebirth was eliminating from its organization the traditional industry structure of "functional chimneys." Rather than designers overlooking the engineering aspects of converting their drawings into cars—and engineers ignoring the design implications of their work—Chrysler brought designers, engineers, and other functions together in "platform teams." Each team now cooperates in making a car, beginning at the concept stage and continuing through production to final delivery.

This arrangement not only avoids problems caused by misunderstandings between functions, but allows workers to spot and solve problems quickly. It has also produced a much leaner organization, with only five levels between top management and shop-floor workers. Another key to Chrysler's transformation was the conversion of its supply relationships into true partnerships, making all relevant suppliers full members of the platform teams.

About Philips Consumer Electronics Company

PCEC is the American unit of Philips Electronics, N.V., a $36 billion company whose products include lighting, semiconductors, medical systems, consumer electronics and (through the Polygram subsidiary) entertainment software.

PCEC manufactures and markets a wide range of consumer electronics products under the brand names Philips and Magnavox. In the mid-1980s, PCEC began a concentrated effort to gain market share after years of stagnation and, by 1991, had grown substantially but with marginal profitability. The parent firm, Philips Electronics, was faced with similar problems and in that year declared a loss of $2.5 billion including restructuring charges. The entire corporation, in an effort to dramatically increase profitability, began a focused effort to recreate itself through redesigning the basic business processes from product creation through customer service.

Two important initiatives that were foundations of this corporate transformation were an increased focus on the customer and improved supplier relationships. The goal was to break down the traditional barriers between elements of the supply chain to improve time to market, efficiency, and margins. At PCEC, a better understanding of consumers' needs led to new products with features that provided sales growth without price erosion. Time to market was improved by working closely with suppliers and involving them very early int the product creation process. By working with its suppliers and focusing on its customers, PCEC was able to substantially increase market share and became solidly profitable. The improvements from these initiatives were recognized by retailers such as Wal-Mart, which named PCEC its supplier of the year in 1993.

Benchmarking Customer–Supplier Alliances

Customer–Supplier alliances in Japan have often been cited as a model of best practice for such relationships. However, a brief review of some of these alliances weakened my confidence in that model. As has been widely reported, Honda and Toyota appear to have generally outstanding supply relations. Still, some large, well-known independent Japanese suppliers in the auto and electronics industries told me that because they were not members of their customers' *keiretsu*, they were free to sell to any customer. Consequently, they enjoyed larger volumes and could afford more R&D than *keiretsu* members, which generally sell to no other customers.

But, they said, this independence came at a price. Their less secure links to customers often gave the independents weaker integration with those firms than *keiretsu* members enjoyed. By contrast *keiretsu* firms, with lower R&D budgets, were less important innovation sources. Further, many *keiretsu* companies traditionally had very weak margins, reflecting a cultural paradigm described to me by Akio Morita, then chairman of Sony, as the contrast between a samurai and a farmer. The samurai, he noted, is expected to eat well and live well; the farmer only has to survive.

These differences, I was told by others in Japan, create a lower-class social status of *keiretsu* suppliers compared with their final-assembly customers. At the suppliers, salaries and perquisites are both lower. In addition, customer executives who have peaked in their careers are often outplaced to first-tier suppliers. Similarly, first-tier executives are often outplaced to second-tier firms, where salaries and benefits are even lower. These factors were described as causing patterns of information flow for new ideas that tended to be more from customer to supplier than vice versa.

Such differences suggest that there may be a flaw in Japanese supply relationships as these are commonly understood to work. On the one hand, *keiretsu* suppliers have the close ties needed for effective integration, while the independents do not. On the other hand, the independents may be more important sources of innovation, yet may be hampered in this role due to weaker links. I chose not to pursue this further because, in the early 1990s, Japanese industry began a transformation that was driven by the country's steep economic downturn. Many *keiretsu* firms started selling to other customers to survive, and a growing number of customer companies began sourcing outside Japan in order to get lower prices.

The alliances featured in this book do not have this apparent flaw and may thus provide better benchmarks of this practice.

How to Use This Book

I have tried to make *The Connected Corporation* a useful guide for companies that are involved in customer–supplier alliances and want to improve their performance, as well as an overview for others that are contemplating such alliances. In either case, different readers will want to use the book in different ways, so some guidance may be helpful.

Readers who want a quick overview may skim the book and the table of contents. Those who want more depth can use the book selectively, rather than read it from cover to cover like a novel. There are three reasons for this. First, the subject has considerable breadth and depth; to cover it adequately required extensive detail that might overwhelm a page-by-page reader. Second, some aspects of customer–supplier practices (such as reducing the supply base, then creating focused competition) are step-by-step in nature; others (like building trust and value chain management) must be conducted in parallel, or as ongoing tasks. Third, companies tend to be proficient at different things. Some practices described may already be part of a firm's skills, while others may not.

To use the book selectively, I suggest referring to the table of contents as a first-cut guide. As another guide, I have included a list of tables and figures immediately after the contents pages. Each chapter typically has two or more of these, which summarize key lessons.

I sincerely hope you find *The Connected Corporation* to be useful, and not just because I put a lot of effort into it or because the companies that shared their experiences invested a great deal of time as well. Most important for me, the world is becoming a challenging place for all of us to live and work. Daily news reports describe growing friction among racial, religious, ethnic, and national groups, and even between the sexes. Certainly the ability to cooperate with others has become an essential skill for everyone; helping people understand how to do that is my greatest motivation.

THE CONNECTED CORPORATION

1

CUSTOMER–SUPPLIER ALLIANCES: UNLOCKING THE POTENTIAL

Our first reaction was to get angry and say, "Why didn't you do this before?" They said, "Because you didn't ask."

Rolando Anderson, global purchasing head of Asea Brown Boveri, after a supplier made a part at 30 percent lower cost when ABB gave it design responsibility[1]

We now realize that the people who make these components know a lot more about it than we do.

Ronald Woodard, president of commercial airplane production, Boeing[2]

Imagine that some firms could double their competitive resources—and greatly improve their costs, quality, cycle times, technology, customer satisfaction, and more—usually without added expense. Who could ignore the chance? In fact, this prospect has always been nearby for most firms. Yet most have rejected it, perhaps because of a mistaken desire to avoid becoming dependent on others.

Until now, virtually the entire art of business strategy has focused on how a firm could wring more from its own assets. Relationships with suppliers were at arm's length, confined to an exchange of terms from the customer and price from the supplier. By withholding all other data about its plans and processes, the supplier thought it was guarding its margins; the customer believed it was avoiding reliance on the supplier, which might exploit this dependence to win a higher price.

Such narrow relationships prevent joint creativity. Firms that refuse to share knowledge limit what they can do together. Confining the possibilities also encourages a transaction attitude: What each firm gets from suppliers depends on its bargaining power alone. A transaction mentality, though, assumes an endless line of suppliers— for every one discarded, another is waiting to serve. This logic over-looks the possibility that an unbridled use of power will damage sup-pliers or drive them away. It also ignores the full potential of what suppliers can do, and it guarantees that a customer will get little more from its suppliers than what others get.

By contrast, working with suppliers to create unique value adds them to a firm's distinct competitive resources. Since suppliers get one-half of a typical firm's revenues, cooperating with all of them *doubles* its competitive resources.[3] And that is just the supply side of the picture.

Companies have long recognized that success requires getting close to customers: Only by better serving customer needs can firms outflank their rivals. Remarkably, this celebrated paradigm of market-ing is incomplete. No firm can get close to a customer unless the cus-tomer wants this.

Every firm is both a customer *and* a supplier. It is not consistent to seek closer ties with one's customers while refusing to build the same kind of relationships with one's suppliers. Yet many firms that make great efforts to partner with their customers do just this, forcing suppliers to take risks alone and demanding price concessions and other actions that weaken suppliers' commitments and even the firms themselves. In a time of savage competition, such practices are self-defeating.

As might be expected from increased competencies, close collabo-ration can produce dramatic results compared with arm's-length trans-actions:

Higher Margins. British retailer Marks & Spencer (M&S) has consis-tently been the most profitable firm in its industry, and its suppliers have enjoyed above-average profits as well. "M&S has depended very largely on the partnership approach, which has made possible our outstanding values and, in turn, excellent sales," says chairman Sir Richard Greenbury.[4]

Lower Costs. Chrysler began using supply alliances in 1990. Between 1991 and 1994, higher motivation of suppliers and their better integration into Chrysler's operations led them to *propose* cost savings totaling $1.1 billion. In the 1994 model year alone, more than $500 million in savings were achieved. Because about 69 percent of the total cost of producing Chrysler's cars are managed by its suppliers, these savings were a major reason why Chrysler had the lowest costs and highest profits per vehicle of any automaker in North America. And Chrysler is still in the early stages of building supply alliances.[5]

More Value for Customers. M&S and its suppliers are constantly pushing the frontiers of value, and often break important new ground. Together, they created the easy to iron cotton shirt, machine washable silk, and machine washable lambswool knitwear. For piece dyed knitwear, M&S and its suppliers cut the time between factory order and store receipt from twelve to sixteen weeks to a few days. In foods, M&S is a widely acclaimed source of fresh, attractive items, made without preservatives and yet totally safe, some with a shelf-life of just one day. An example was the development of pre-cooked rice, which requires extreme care to produce the taste and texture that appeal to consumers, while totally avoiding bacteria—for which rice can be a breeding ground.

Larger Market Share. Motorola's Paging Products Group (PPG), which has won 60 percent global share of its markets, could not have done that without cost, quality, cycle time, technology, and other advances made by its suppliers.

Underlying such benefits at Chrysler, M&S, Motorola, and other firms are more specific gains from customer–supplier alliances:

- *Ongoing cost reductions* that can double those possible through market transactions
- *Quality improvements* that exceed what individual firms can possibly do alone
- *Design cycle times* 50 to 75 percent shorter than those in traditional relationships
- *Increased operating flexibility,* which in some firms has yielded an economic lot size of one—the ultimate in flexible manufacturing
- *More value for the customer's customers,* including faster and better responses to new needs and opportunities
- *Enhanced leverage with technology,* including earlier access to new concepts and more control over technological change

- *More powerful competitive strategies*, gained when a customer adds its supplier's expertise to its own

The techniques described here are generally applicable to all firms, regardless of size or industry. Best practice in customer–supplier links is largely independent of whether the activity involves materials, parts, equipment, or services. In some cases, however, such as risk sharing with suppliers, the methods to use depend on whether the customer is a retailer or distributor, or whether it sells directly to other firms.

Competition Is Driving Firms to Integrate

Commerce has traditionally involved a chain of independent firms, each adding separate value to items bought from others. Typically, each link in that supply chain has been an arm's-length pact. Buyers shopped for price and performance in the open market. Whenever the marketplace offered a better deal, one supplier was left for another.

These arrangements are regarded as central to the success of market economies. This notion is faulty, for they also impede economic growth. In fact, supply firms cite poor relations with their customers as one of the most critical barriers to their improved competitiveness.[6]

For example, U.S. and European automakers long suffered from high costs relative to their Japanese rivals. A main obstacle to reducing these costs was the firms' hostile relationships with their suppliers, which are only now being turned around. Similar problems troubled the computer chip business. Sematech, the nationwide semiconductor alliance, was launched to perform R&D on a scale that would save firms that make chip manufacturing equipment, which had grown dangerously weak. Yet the creation of Sematech did nothing to address a crucial cause of the problem: longstanding adversarial relations between chip producers and their equipment suppliers. Sematech members, representing 80 percent of U.S. chip volume, did not involve suppliers in their planning, nor did they share data on equipment performance. Business relations were conducted purely on short-term considerations, although today the situation is changing.[7]

Driven by brutal competition, supply chains in every industry are moving toward integration. The demands on individual firms have become too vast to be met by each one acting in isolation. For a company to deliver maximum value to its customers, it must receive maximum value from its suppliers. Moreover, no firm working alone can differentiate its products as much as is possible with suppliers' help. Nor can it have lowest costs if its suppliers do not, or top quality without their support, or shorter cycle times than theirs, or more generally obtain their best efforts on any task unless they choose to apply them.

No contract or amount of bargaining power can create these benefits. They can be gained only in an environment of cooperation and mutual commitment. To distinguish the new, integrated arrangements from typical arm's-length supply chains, the former will be referred to here as *value chains*.

Hallmarks of Powerful Customer–Supplier Alliances

By definition, a strategic alliance is a relationship between firms in which they cooperate to produce more value (or a lower cost) than is possible in a market transaction.[8] To create that value, they must agree on what it is, need each other to achieve it, and share the benefits. Without a shared objective, meaningful cooperation is not feasible. Without mutual need the firms may have the same objective, but each can reach it alone. If they do not share the benefits, they cannot expect the commitments required for cooperation.

For alliances with customers and suppliers, the closeness implied by these conditions is manifest in an elaborate web of joint tasks, which in turn are governed by a set of key principles.

Objective: To Beat The Market

There are two paths by which alliances add value. One is to produce more for the customer's market than is available from other sources. This path spawns healthier revenues and profits for partners to share. The second path leads to lower total costs. For instance, rather than reducing each firm's costs separately, between 20 and 30 percent of the savings in successful customer–supplier alliances comes solely from the efficiencies of cooperation. Such savings help partner firms offer market-beating prices without damaging suppliers' margins.

ADD A NEW OUTLOOK TO STRATEGY

Traditional competitive strategy matches a firm's internal abilities with its market opportunities. Because supply alliances add an entirely new set of resources, they create a new, powerful frontier of strategy. To identify supply opportunities, scanning and benchmarking current and potential suppliers, plus a continuing dialogue with them, become ongoing tasks as vital as marketing research and competitive analysis.

CUSTOMERS: CREATE A STABLE BASE OF FEWER SUPPLIERS

Having fewer suppliers makes it easier to build the mutual understandings, trust, and close coordination essential for continuous improvement. Moreover, one element of obtaining the lowest costs is to provide suppliers with the best possible scale economies, which occur when there are fewer suppliers. Infrequent changes in suppliers are also important. Change adds costs through higher overheads, lost learning curves, and less efficient investments by suppliers. The need for stable relationships is one factor that makes partner choice so important.

PARTNER CHOICE IS CRITICAL

It is not realistic for any firm to seek alliances with all of its major customers. Partnering calls for specific organizational norms that are not present in all firms. Similarly, in selecting suppliers to be alliance partners, it is best to emphasize organizational traits rather than surface attributes like best price.

Because alliances create more value than market transactions, and because competitive markets keep increasing the benefits they offer, alliances must stay ahead of the markets they serve. For a customer in a price-competitive market, a supplier's price tomorrow must be better than its price today.

Many of an organization's greatest strengths are ingrained in its culture. For example, a keen ability to cut costs is manifest in attitudes and practices that are widely accepted across a firm. Such links with corporate culture affect any improvement—such as in quality or cycle time—that depends on organizational processes. For best performance, the process of supplier choice must locate firms with internal norms that support the same continuing advances sought by the customer.

That is why supplier selection criteria at Chrysler, Motorola, Marks & Spencer, and other leading firms emphasize organizational culture rather than the current best offer.

ALLY WITH ALL RELEVANT SUPPLIERS

For maximum benefit, it is essential for a firm to cooperate with all companies in its supply base whose products, parts, materials, or services affect its costs or performances. Motorola's Paging Products Group, for example, spends a small fraction of its total purchases on production equipment. Yet work with equipment suppliers has dramatically increased PPG operating flexibility, at times reaching the ultimate goal of economic lot sizes of one unit. That is a tremendous advantage in a market where success often favors the most agile firms.

Another reason for alliances with the whole supply base is that it is difficult to build trust with some suppliers while continuing traditional animosity with others. The practices needed for each style are polar opposites; they cannot be sustained in the same organization. Further, there is no way to know what ideas that might significantly affect one's business are being withheld by suppliers that have not been included in an alliance.

FOR BEST PERFORMANCE: CHALLENGE AND COMMITMENT

The essence of customer–supplier alliances is to create more value for the customer's market than the same firms could do in an arm's-length relationship. Because the objective is the customer's market, the customer must set the alliance course. Further, producing more value imposes a demand on both partners for superior performance. Should the supplier slip badly, or if another firm is well ahead with desired performances, the first supplier may lose the business. Those conditions create destructive tension in a relationship. For an alliance to function, they must be offset by other forces that encourage supplier commitment. In short, how hard a supplier works for a customer depends on what it gets back: The more a customer meets its needs, the more the firm will stretch.

The most obvious supplier needs are stable and growing revenues, healthy margins, and credible opportunities for new business. Another is to be treated fairly. When a supplier has problems, for instance, the best course for the customer is to help solve them rather than go to the expense of developing a new supplier. Besides, the experience of Motorola, Marks & Spencer, and other firms indicates that suppliers' problems often have roots in how customers manage the relationships.

Also important—but often overlooked—is the need for advanced competitive skills in areas like quality management, improved design, lower costs, and better service. It is clearly easier to develop such competencies in the cooperative framework of an alliance than to do so alone without feedback or guidance. In fact, suppliers that enjoy alliances with Chrysler, Motorola, Marks & Spencer, and other leading customers regard gaining such skills as one of the most valuable benefits of their relationships.

Just as a supplier must keep winning its customer's business, so too must the customer win its supplier's loyalty to get the most value from that firm. Providing exceptional benefits to suppliers is essential to high-performance alliances.

INTERFIRM LINKS ARE BROAD, DEEP, AND UNIQUE

The greatest value from cooperation comes from integrating each firm's separate processes into seamless operations. Instead of lowest price from the supplier, the emphasis is on lowest total cost; rather than seek fastest separate response times, the goal is shortest combined cycle time; and so on. By focusing on shared processes, both customer and supplier recognize that the traditional practice of separately optimizing each firm's performance often compromises their joint effort, just as poor functional integration within a firm raises costs and slows reactions.

The more value sought from suppliers, the more they must be involved in the customer's business. Achieving lowest total cost, for instance, requires attention to all cost drivers, many of which involve several business functions—design, quality, logistics, technology, and marketing among them. Each of these may be influenced by suppliers, and each affects how suppliers work. So the most productive customer–supplier interfaces require multifunctional teams, which must be involved in depth. For example, cooperation at the pre-concept stage offers the best opportunity to leverage design and quality of the customer's product or service.

The greatest benefits of customer–supplier alliances come from continuous improvement over the long term. Such improvement calls for ongoing alignment of firms' priorities and resources, which requires top-to-bottom connections at all relevant policy and operating levels. If decisions on matters like capacity and technology development are made separately, partner firms may evolve away from meeting each other's needs. Further, to create the most value, a supplier must adapt its organization for each customer interface, reflecting the need for resources, structures, and practices that are unique for each situation.

REPLACE CONTRACTS WITH STRONGER COMMITMENTS

It is not possible to write contracts about the extensive interfirm activities customer–supplier alliances require. There are too many tasks, too many connections, and too many uncertainties. None of the high-performing alliances depicted here involves traditional detailed contracts. Indeed, many function without any contracts at all.

Alliances are sustained by mutual need, a common objective seen as important enough to dominate any issue, a willingness to share the benefits, and a trusting relationship. To an important extent, alliances are between people. When adjustments must be made, only people who trust and understand each other can make them in a way that maintains commitments. Only people who share a vision and the enthusiasm to make it a reality will invest the efforts needed for an alliance to succeed.

BEST PRACTICE REQUIRES SPECIFIC ORGANIZATIONAL NORMS

Customer–supplier alliances work best in firms with continuous-improvement cultures, long-term views, and root-cause attitudes toward issue resolution. Other requirements are a high degree of internal trust, robust team processes, substantial delegation and empowerment, and a genuine openness toward outsiders. The very best customer–supplier alliances involve companies where people at all organizational levels understand and support the goals of the firm. This alignment promotes the wide support of alliance objectives and avoids the conflicting priorities that hinder many firms.

The ability to sustain small ongoing improvements (what the

Japanese term *keizan*) facilitates a constant flow of ideas between companies so they can continue to create more value together. Similarly, comfort with long time horizons supports the joint planning that keeps firms' performance on the cutting edge.

A root-cause attitude—a preference for getting to the bottom of problems and eliminating their origins—is needed to resolve issues between companies without animosity, and to build new understandings needed to sustain continuous improvement.

Teamwork (including horizontal processes that easily span internal boundaries) is essential for alliances with customers and suppliers. One reason is the multifunctional nature of these alliances. Another is that the greatest benefits of such alliances require cooperation across business units.

Without trust, information is not shared, and commitments are withheld. If a company treats its employees fairly, honestly, and with trust and dignity, they will be more likely to treat others that way. Further, the multifunctional interfaces needed for customer–supplier alliances are most effective at firms that have mastered teamwork on the inside. And since value creation may be at several organizational levels—including the lowest—firms that have succeeded in empowerment and in delegating authority into the depths of their organizations get the most benefit from such alliances.

All these behaviors also go hand in hand with a constant drive for total quality in all aspects of a business. It is no coincidence that firms like Motorola and Marks & Spencer, which excel at supplier alliances, have just such a drive.

EXECUTIVE LEADERSHIP IS ESSENTIAL

In marketing, it is common for a firm's top executives to take a lead role in building customer relationships. Yet suppliers typically do not get such attention, although they receive about one-half of the average firm's revenues, which puts them on an equal footing with a firm's internal activities. Further, the tasks involved in supply alliances are as complex and demanding as any other aspect of business. To deny them top management attention is tantamount to senior executives ignoring the inner workings of their own firm.

Moreover, the organizational transformations required for supply alliances will not occur without top leadership. In fact, firms with the most effective supply alliances enjoy ongoing visible support from the highest corporate levels.

LINK ALLIANCES IN VALUE CHAINS

Alliances between customers and their direct suppliers are the first step in building a powerful network that reaches far up the value chain to deliver the most possible value to the final customer. Because suppliers account for about one-half of the average company's costs, *their* suppliers represent one-half of *those* costs, and so on going back up the value chain. Further, every company in the chain innovates within its scope of expertise. A customer that effectively manages all of those costs and leverages all of that creativity builds a tremendous competitive advantage for itself, compared with rivals that still regard suppliers as firms whose goods they buy through arm's-length, price-dominated transactions.

Common Myths and Misunderstandings

It is not true that only large, rich firms like Chrysler, Motorola, and Marks & Spencer can be effective in these relationships. Even small businesses—and others with limited resources—have built powerful alliances with their customers and suppliers. Consider that, like many other small companies, Craftsman Custom Metal Fabricators, a 135-employee sheet metal firm near Chicago, has successfully converted its trading links with suppliers and customers into effective alliances. Targ-It-Tronics, a small Florida-based producer of flexible electronic circuits, has grown dramatically through such alliances. Desmond & Sons, which began as a small clothing manufacturer in Northern Ireland, has grown tenfold through such alliances.

All alliances do not deserve that label. Some firms mistakenly regard any long-term relationship as an alliance (the term partnership is also used). Such beliefs are dangerous, because they create a false sense of security. That a relationship may persist for some time is not necessarily related to whether it sustains continuing improvements, as is the case with true alliances. In competitive markets, the only safety is in creating more value than one's rivals: Here, alliances have a demonstrable edge over arm's-length transactions.

Another common misunderstanding about supply alliances is that an increased reliance on fewer sources is risky, because it makes a firm vulnerable to their quality and dependability problems. Nonsense. Attitudes about poor reliability in supply relationships stem from practices that discourage commitments and inhibit longer-term investments needed for quality and other improvements.

Some people believe that having an equity stake in suppliers is essential for close relationships. This attitude stems from observations about Japanese supply *keiretsu* where large firms in the automobile and other industries have such arrangements with their suppliers. In Japan, however, those suppliers in which customers own equity appear to be financially and technologically weaker than the independent suppliers with which they compete. By contrast, supplier independence is a source of strength and a benefit to supplier and customer alike. The Western firms that have succeeded with supply alliances hold no equity in their suppliers.

Pitfalls on the Road Ahead

Crossing the bridge from conventional customer–supplier relationships to alliances is not simple. Often a history of adversity must be overcome, and habitual attitudes and routines changed—dramatically. To be sure, immediate cost savings (on the order of 10 percent) may be possible simply by shrinking a firm's supply base. Yet several years may be needed to bring about the deeper changes and build mutual trust that support ongoing improvements and produce the most powerful results.

There is a sharp contrast between having alliances with only one or two selected suppliers and having alliances with all of them. Stand-alone deals to pursue specific opportunities typically bypass problematic internal processes; leveraging the entire supply base cannot. Further, it is one thing to build trust with a few people in one firm for the life of a project. It is an entirely different matter to nurture durable, trusting relationships with many firms.

This difference is where most initiatives to form supply alliances bog down. Overlooking the needs for substantial changes in management and organization styles, and for broad and deep interfirm links, many companies assume the process is a mechanical one: Just reduce the supply base, establish a supplier rating system, mandate cross-functional teams, and everything is set to go. This assumption is wrong. Only a consistent long-term commitment from top management to wide-ranging transformations leads to the best results.

Just as significantly, suppliers must be seen in a wholly new light. As the authors of a landmark study of the automobile industry, *The Machine That Changed the World*, wrote: "Progress remains blocked by an unwillingness to give up the power-based bargaining firms have relied on for so long. In our interviews with customers and suppliers we found strong evidence that everyone knows the words of the song but few can hold the tune."[9]

2

GETTING STARTED

As long as there is better expertise on the outside, to succeed we must use that.

Thomas Natale, vice president for operations, Philips Consumer Electronics Company

It isn't a matter of putting a gun to a guy's head. It is a question of whether we are all following the same signals from the marketplace. Those who cannot go down the same quality curve with us take themselves out of the game.

Tom Slaninka, director of sector sourcing, Land Mobile Products Sector, Motorola

In the early 1980s, Motorola's paging business was threatened by a major loss of market share. Motorola had invented paging, and Bob Galvin, the company's chairman, was determined to keep the business. Galvin knew that in order to do this, the company needed a better product with a lower selling price and healthier margins. All relevant functions—product design, manufacturing, and purchasing—had to contribute. For its part, purchasing asked suppliers for a 10 percent price cut. Suppliers, however, viewed the initiative as only helping Motorola; in essence, the message they heard was, "we'll keep you around if you give up some profits." Because Motorola was not offering anything in return, few suppliers took the program seriously.

Disappointed by the lack of results, and in concert with new people taking key positions in its communications sector, Motorola quickly changed its supplier effort to a mutually beneficial program. One facet was quality: Motorola had concluded that advances here could yield lower costs and better margins for itself and its suppliers. The firm was willing to share ideas to reach these objectives, and also to share in the business growth it believed would occur. Ron Schubel, then president of the commercial products division of Molex, a supplier of electrical connectors, describes the time: "We started on the partnership path together by working on tasks that clearly offered near-term benefits to both firms."

Still, a history of arm's-length, sometimes adversarial relationships had created an atmosphere of low trust. To set a new course, Motorola management met for two days with top executives of important suppliers. Helped by an outside facilitator, the participants developed a list of more than 100 issues that concerned the suppliers. Motorola publicly committed itself to resolving them, which it did.

Bob Galvin drove the entire change, constantly talking about how each side had to work to earn the relationship. To reinforce what he knew would be a demanding process, Galvin began visiting suppliers just as he did important customers, later discussing the visits with his organization and insisting his direct reports do the same. These actions sent a powerful message to the suppliers and to Motorola that they were highly important to its future. On one occasion, Galvin attended a supplier advisory board meeting and asked members to comment on being a Motorola supplier. The message he got—that Motorola could be hard to work with—reinforced his commitment to change.

To realize his vision, Galvin also won the strong support of several paging executives, including Ray Farmer, Bob Growney, Mort Topfer, Bob Hall, and George Fisher. Farmer, Growney, and Topfer later became Motorola sector presidents; Hall, a group general manager; and Fisher, chairman and CEO of Motorola, Inc. Today, Motorola's top management, its infrastructure, and the clear benefits from its supply alliances all reinforce the process Galvin began.

Bob Becknell, an early director of Motorola's sector sourcing function and later a vice president in the Paging Products Group, is credited with having played a key middle management role in transforming the supply relationships. Becknell recalls that the single biggest task was convincing legions of people who had always dealt with suppliers in an adversarial way to adapt a cooperative partnership style. Supported by higher management, his first step was to find a group of middle management people who truly believed there was a better way to work with suppliers. They then proved this vision really worked through early small-scale successes with a few suppliers.

Clearly, any meaningful change must be championed by one or more people who have the skill and credibility to cut through traditional ways and encourage new ones. At Philips Consumer Electronics Company (PCEC), Bill Kennedy, then vice president of purchasing, was the force behind the shift from adversarial supply relations to partnerships. Like Motorola's Bob Galvin, Kennedy understood that to win converts and reinforce the new process, both his firm and its suppliers would have to see near-term benefits. For that reason, the first purchases under his new regime were connectors, for which PCEC had many suppliers. By substantially reducing the number of suppliers, Kennedy could offer the remaining ones more volume while reaping the cost benefits of greater scale economies for his firm.

Both Galvin and Kennedy knew their efforts were first steps on an endless path. They viewed improved relationships with suppliers—like those with customers—as an ongoing process that would produce more benefits for as long as the alliances were nourished.

Suppliers, like their customers, must also stretch for alliances. When IBM was forming its alliance with Kodak, two IBM executives—Harry Beeth, vice president of finance and planning in the service division, and Irv Schauer, vice president for service quality—were key champions of the opportunity. Frank Palm, IBM's top executive directly involved in the alliance, reported at first to Beeth and later to Schauer. "Irv was always in my corner when I needed him," says Palm. "Harry controlled the IBM business, which gave me the freedom to develop the alliance as was needed. At the same time, Irv controlled a lot of the technology resources, and gave me his full support. The alliance was a new kind of activity for us, and he was also an important sounding board for me. When I wanted to talk something through, he was the guy who understood both the technical and relationship parts of the opportunity."

In addition to championing the concept and sharing the benefits, early steps in building customer–supplier alliances include setting objectives, deciding when to use alliances, choosing firms to partner with, determining what to allocate to suppliers, and reducing the supply base.

Objective: More Customer Value

In the early 1990s, consumer markets in the industrial world experienced a shock when high-priced brand-name products came under attack by moderately priced goods of comparable quality. The revolution gained visibility when Philip Morris—one of the most venerated brands—dropped its prices in response to nonbranded competition. In retail markets throughout Europe, Japan, and North America, better informed consumers increasingly bought goods on the basis of highest value (a combination of quality, style, timing, availability, performance, and price) rather than the imagery of brands alone. Only in emerging economies, where brand names still represent an assurance of value, do such products seem secure at present.[1]

A similar drive for more value is accelerating in commercial and industrial markets, spurred by growing competition and rising demands for more value from companies that serve consumers. (Consider that, in industrial economies, consumer purchases account for about two-thirds of gross domestic product.) This emphasis on value promotes the integration of every step in every value chain leading to final customer satisfaction. For each company in a chain to deliver maximum value to its own customers, it must receive maximum value from its suppliers.

One corollary of this integration, however, is that as the performance of a value chain advances, each firm in the chain benefits as well. For example, because of Marks & Spencer's objective of giving its customers maximum possible value, its suppliers have gained handsome rewards. Listen to Chris Haskins, chairman of Northern Foods, a firm in Hull, England, that has worked with M&S to create chilled premium foods and up-market groceries, all developed to sell at reasonable prices: "Our business would not be where it is now without Marks & Spencer. We began as a tiny family dairy in Yorkshire. Now we are one of the most profitable businesses in the U.K. food market, with between 4 percent and 5 percent market share." This emphasis

Alliances Versus Market Transactions			
	Market		Alliances
	Fixed contract	Incentive contract	
Behavior	Meet fixed terms	Supplier stretches	Both stretch for continuous improvement
Results determined by	Market	Supplier's skills	Both firms' skills
Use when	Market-paced improvement is acceptable	Customer wants more value than market offers	Customer wants greatest possible value
		Supplier controls improvement	Both contribute to improvement
Relationships	Arm's length	Arm's length	Partners—high trust

on value has helped Northern to reach high levels of product quality and to compete on innovation and service rather than low price. It has also fended off retailer pressures to cut prices, a fate that other food companies have not escaped.[2]

Suppliers can affect many aspects of the value a firm offers its customers, so the objectives the firm gives suppliers must be comprehensive. For example, when PCEC was considering connector suppliers for its television sets, Molex and a rival were equal on quality, delivery, price, and innovativeness. But because PCEC competes in part on its ability to respond rapidly to changing demand, it also required fast service from suppliers.

This included responsiveness to requests for quotes, order changes, samples for design engineers, and design assistance. It also required immediately available personnel for problem solving and salespeople who understood the parts they were selling (since much time would be wasted if they had to ask the home office for answers). It would be even better if they could work directly with the PCEC design engineer to find the best part for the application. Because it was clearly better on all these dimensions, Molex won the business. Largely as a result of its quick response ability, supported by Molex and other key internal suppliers, PCEC won Wal-Mart's prestigious "supplier of the year" award.

When to Use Alliances

Alliances create more value than market transactions and require the efforts of both firms to gain that result. They are distinct from incentive contracts, used when a customer wants timing, performance, or some other value that exceeds what is available in the market; when the supplier alone controls the improvement; and when an extra payment or other incentive will elicit that behavior. By contrast, alliances join the skills of both firms to offer the greatest possible value. These points are summarized in the figure shown.

Alliances add value to virtually any customer–supplier arrangement, from simple parts like electrical connectors to large, complex projects which, traditionally done as market transactions, foster add–ons, overruns, and other ills that contribute to high costs, low quality, and slow timing.

To illustrate, for the design and construction of a 730,000–square–foot, $300 million paint finishing plant—one of the world's largest—attached to its Oakville, Canada, car assembly plant, the Ford Motor Company sought substantial reductions in capital investments and time to completion. Further, quality had to be exceptionally high because an automobile's finish is a vital part of the consumer's purchasing decision. Rather than follow the usual practice of first developing a specification and then requesting bids from contractors, Ford formed an alliance with Asea Brown Boveri, the Swiss–Swedish multinational.

With Fluor Daniel adding construction expertise as an ABB partner, Ford and ABB combined their engineering talents to develop a better plant design, agreed on a way to share cost savings, took early steps to build trust, and created a joint management structure that maintained this trust and kept the whole project on course. The result was an innovative, low-risk plant that cost about 25 percent less than it would have normally, was completed in near–record time, and did not compromise (and in some areas exceeded) Ford's performance expectations.[3] Such behavior is impossible in arm's-length contracts even with incentive terms, because they limit information sharing and deny each firm the benefits of the other's full expertise.

Alliances should be used whenever cooperation will make a meaningful difference, compared with arm's-length relationships. For example, Motorola uses electronic data interchange (EDI) to share logistics data with its suppliers. EDI, like the telephone, only transmits information. Issues that arise based on that information—unexpected schedule changes, misunderstandings, and so on—require a partnership environment to be resolved effectively. Further, to get the most value from EDI, the operations in each firm that it connects must be adjusted to work better together. For that, people have to be comfortable with each other and open to raising issues and making changes.

Dale Kelsey, a senior buyer in Motorola's Plantation, Florida, plant, notes that in his weakest supplier relationship, the supplier gets data via EDI, but he gets little feedback on the information he shares. By contrast, in his best relationships, both firms discuss the data and change their processes together.

Choosing Customers for Alliances

Suppliers allocate their resources according to where they can receive the greatest benefits, and not all customers are equally effective with alliances. These facts make partner choice a key early step for suppliers.

It can be awkward to push a customer farther into an alliance than it is willing to go. Some retailers, for instance, have complained that Procter & Gamble salespeople, wanting to create partnering relationships, took too much time collecting information about activities in which the retailers did not want them involved. The customers' attitude, says industry expert Walter Williams, was, "I don't want to work the way you tell me. I'm going to tell *you* how *I* want to buy."[4]

LOOK FOR ALLIANCE BEHAVIOR

Targ-It-Tronics, a producer of flexible electronic circuits in Melbourne, Florida, excels at bringing major cost savings to customers by cooperating on better designs. For example, Targ engineers joined one customer's design team and changed the firm's original specification for a 35-cent Targ part. The change led to a substantial productivity improvement for the customer, which was able to take seventeen people off its assembly line. Such results, says Targ president Larry Groves, "require a partnership environment," because cooperation takes an open exchange of ideas and sensitive information. His firm has walked away from prospective customers who were unwilling to listen to Targ ideas or made unrealistic demands.

The need for an alliance atmosphere can be equally important when problems arise, as they often do. "It is difficult discussing problems with a customer," says Chris Nunn, managing director of Hunter Plastics, a pipe manufacturer based in London, England. "But if something is going wrong in production or delivery, it is better for the customer to know."[5] Unfortunately, because some customers use such data to punish suppliers, the latter, anticipating such a reaction, withhold the information. Both firms then forfeit the opportunity to solve problems together.

NOT ALL CUSTOMERS ARE POTENTIAL PARTNERS

It is worth being careful when choosing customers to be partners. *Purchasing*, the leading professional journal, found in a recent survey of its editorial board that "most purchasing executives' talk about partnerships is skin deep. It is just so much 'sweet talk' that disappears when times get tough. Top corporate executives are twisting the arms of purchasing managers to get across-the-board price cuts while talking up partnering to the press. Suppliers who fell for the partnering message and invested in capital improvements have been left holding the bag by greedy customers demanding progressively greater price cuts."[6]

As a supplier, PCEC's Bill Kennedy concurs that not every customer behaves in a way that encourages alliance-like conduct. To determine how to work with a customer, PCEC must learn whether it understands the nature of an alliance and actually practices that. In some firms, Kennedy says, senior executives "say all the right things and do all the wrong things." Examples that prevent the building of trust include a lack of continuity at the interface (such as buyers being rotated annually) and people failing to deliver on their commitments.

For customers with unpredictable non-alliance behavior, a supplier is forced to pick those areas where it can win while guarding itself elsewhere. Ironically, though, when a customer causes a supplier to defend itself, the customer loses. One typical protection tactic is to add risk premiums to prices, which cost the customer more than it would otherwise pay. Another tactic Kennedy describes is used with companies that have a deal mentality. He notes that some customers win favorable terms by telling PCEC there will not be a rival supplier, and then another firm "comes in through the back door. Or a customer may say they will buy 50,000 cases in April, but you do not put it on the schedule because you know they may decide to buy from a low-ball firm at the last moment. That can lead to shortages for the customer."

Despite these observations, Kennedy notes that "just because a customer does not behave the right way now does not mean they are not trying. You have to think of the future relationship as well. The biggest problem is when people are not honest in their intent. Then, one must be opportunistic and decide whether to go into a project or not. Some customers have made a conscious decision that they will treat suppliers poorly. In those cases we have to allocate our best resources to others. For example, some firms have used our quality products to attract consumers into their stores, and then use all their sales efforts to push lower quality products where they make larger margins."

Frank Palm, the IBM executive who led the early formation of his firm's successful outsourcing alliance with Kodak, concurs that it is not always possible to form alliances with customers. Like Bill Kennedy, Palm says alliance prospects must be prequalified. One criterion is whether a firm demands a lot of specific detail in an agreement. The more of that, the less trust is likely to be present. Another criterion is whether the acceptance of change is built into a contract. A third is

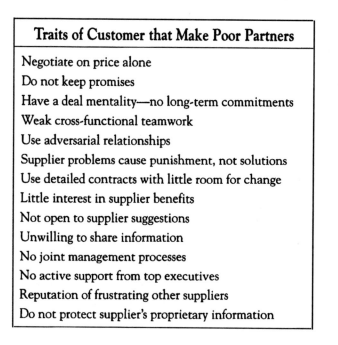

Traits of Customer that Make Poor Partners

Negotiate on price alone

Do not keep promises

Have a deal mentality—no long-term commitments

Weak cross-functional teamwork

Use adversarial relationships

Supplier problems cause punishment, not solutions

Use detailed contracts with little room for change

Little interest in supplier benefits

Not open to supplier suggestions

Unwilling to share information

No joint management processes

No active support from top executives

Reputation of frustrating other suppliers

Do not protect supplier's proprietary information

whether the firm uses joint management processes to guide such change. If it does not, any adjustments may be at the customer's whim.

These and other characteristics of customers that perform poorly as alliance partners are summarized in the table shown. For instance, a customer that has not achieved cross-functional integration will emphasize price with suppliers because purchasing is traditionally driven by price considerations, while other functions (such as engineering) do not participate effectively in supplier selection, negotiation, and management. More detailed criteria for selecting customers and suppliers as alliance partners may be found in Chapter 13.

Partner with Leading-Edge Customers

One great benefit of being a supplier to firms like Marks & Spencer and Motorola is the advanced practices that develop in those relationships, which are shared. Such firms have earned their leading positions through sheer excellence. They stay there, in part, by finding and working with outstanding suppliers and, together, advance the state of the art in quality, product development, and other areas that bring more value to the customer's markets.

Listen again to Chris Haskins of Northern Foods: "M&S took us beyond milk into quality standards and other products such as pies, cakes, and prepared foods. The know-how we gained in quality standards enabled us to move into these product areas, and all was encouraged by M&S. Our skills in the milk business and theirs in retailing have created a totally new enterprise for both of us."

Partnering with leading-edge customers can mean looking outside the usual set of companies.[7] For example, auto seat belt use was mandated in Europe several years before it was in the United States. So demand for advances like belts with shoulder harnesses that automatically retract in a crash appeared first in Europe. American seat belt firms took advantage of this opportunity by forming early links to European customers. By contrast, Japanese software firms ignored U.S. computer users, which started switching from mainframes to networks of personal computers—and to the software that works with them—long before the Japanese. As a result, mainframe programs still accounted for 90 percent of Japanese software sales at a time when they had become virtually inconsequential in the United States. By staying with their traditional customers, the Japanese lost the opportunity to build a global business.[8]

What to Allocate to Suppliers

Reed Personnel Services, a British temporary employee placement agency, formed an alliance with Hewlett-Packard (H-P) in the United Kingdom to provide office support people to H-P. The tie-up, which allows H-P's personnel group to concentrate on recruiting and supporting higher-level staff, is jointly managed by the two firms for continuing improvement in temp employee quality and faster responses to filling vacancies. Since Reed specializes in recruiting and training temps, it can do a better job than H-P could.

Similarly, Eastman Kodak outsourced its data processing to Integrated Systems Solutions Corp. (ISSC), a unit of IBM, allowing Kodak to focus on its core skills in the imaging business while freeing itself from investing in and maintaining computer centers. Further, compared with data processing service firms like ISSC, Kodak could not offer information technology professionals the same career opportunities. That made it hard to attract and keep the best staff, which inhibited Kodak's centers from reaching their full potential.

As these examples suggest, there are advantages to allocating work to whichever firm is best qualified to do it. One constraint on this observation is that a firm must hold on to activities that are part of its core competence—that set of abilities with which it delivers unique value to customers, and that are difficult for others to duplicate.

Choosing Supply Sources		
	Internal Suppliers	**Outside Suppliers**
Activities	Core competencies	Non-core activities for which robust suppliers exist or can be developed
	Internal suppliers perform significantly better than outside ones, which cannot easily be developed	For alliances, suppliers meet partner selection criteria
Benefits	Pursue excellence where it matters most	Often more scale, expertise, innovation, and more experience than is possible on the inside

Mounting evidence shows that firms which focus on a few core competencies outperform their rivals. One benefit of a sharp focus is that rather than trying to be excellent at everything it does, a firm can more easily maintain investment scale in a few well-chosen areas. A related benefit is that focused firms pressed by rapid change have a better chance of staying near their most critical frontiers. Flexibility is another advantage. New products can be introduced faster if a firm is not bound by the capacity requirements—and the need to sequence—many different operations.[9]

Conventional wisdom holds that vertical integration—the polar opposite of concentrating on a focused core—eases coordination along the production chain. Yet the extra hierarchy needed impairs flexibility and innovation. Also, notes Sir John Harvey Jones, formerly boss of Britain's ICI and now chairman of the *Economist*, "The capital spend [of vertical integration] forces you to sell what you can make rather than the other way around."[10] Perhaps most important, internal supply units that are insulated from direct market pressures perform poorly compared with independent suppliers in the same business. As cost centers, they lack the profit motive and fear of failure needed to drive advancing performance.[11]

Consider that Chrysler's major North American rivals, and PCEC's global rivals, are all far more vertically integrated than either of those firms. This gives both of them advantages in being able to pick and choose world-class suppliers. "As long as there is better expertise on the outside, to succeed we must use that," says Thomas Natale, PCEC vice president for operations.[12]

These observations, which are standard practice at leading firms, are summarized in the table on the facing page. Motorola, for example, defines its core competence as the ability to integrate product and manufacturing technologies with the best possible set of product features, costs, size, quality, and availability. In those areas, Motorola focuses on being better than anyone else. Outside that scope, its suppliers focus on the rest. Motorola internal sources are used for items that are part of the core competence of a product offering, or when costs are much lower because of scale or quality efforts. Another reason for internal sourcing is when Motorola cannot find a supplier to provide critical inputs—such as short responses on key items or particular frequency characteristics of radio crystals.[13]

The decision to outsource must be seen as a way to focus on excellence for the best interests of the firm. Even when appropriate suppliers are not available, if the needed resource is not part of their core skills Motorola, Marks & Spencer, and other companies make the effort to develop outside sources so they can devote their own energies to what they do best. Significantly, the high degree of internal integration of functions and processes found at Motorola and M&S is a rare organizational skill. It sustains excellence and renewal, and is central to their core competencies. Both firms view outsourcing non-core activities to well-chosen supply partners as critical to maintaining those internal competencies.

British Airways (BA) attributes its healthy bottom line in part to an effective use of outside partners. In one situation, BA helped two firms set up local distribution centers to provide parts for the airline, rather than run its own parts centers. BA procurement executive Clive Mason says the new suppliers "used their expertise to offer an attractive package" compared with what BA could do itself. Denis Bobker of Bobker Bearings, one of the suppliers, adds that "the payoff has been quick and measurable. It has been an extremely gratifying way to do business."[14]

Choosing Suppliers for Alliances

Unlike some other alliances, those between customers and suppliers should be regarded as long term. Like a team that keeps getting better as it successfully works through new challenges, the greatest benefits from these alliances come from ongoing improvements that parallel the continued development of close working relationships.

Short-term relationships cause high costs. They require more overhead at the customer to deal with a constant flux of new suppliers and higher selling costs for suppliers that are passed on to the customer one way or another. They also discourage suppliers from making long-term investments that are unique to a relationship, and inhibit the integration and growth of shared understandings that are the basis of constantly advancing value creation.

Transitions to new partners are thus lengthy exercises, with the costs of finding and qualifying new ones being quite high. For this reason, Chrysler, Marks & Spencer, and Motorola select suppliers with great care and start them with low volume. This practice gives each firm a chance to learn about the other and adjust before major dependencies develop.

To illustrate, one of the biggest and best-known knitwear suppliers in the world, located in the Far East, wanted to do business with Marks & Spencer. M&S was interested because it saw a chance to add to its product offerings. But the courtship took a year to find the right product and agree on distribution, quality standards (which were higher than what the supplier was used to), and other matters.

In alliances, customers and suppliers need the same attributes: the ability to form trusting relationships, a focus on continuous improvement, skills in using cross-functional teams, and a willingness to achieve long-term alignment and encourage partners' commitments. The methods for qualifying potential partners are necessarily different.

Because the customer defines the objectives for an alliance and pays for what suppliers deliver, it has the right to probe prospective suppliers' abilities to determine how well these match its objectives. For this reason and due to the high costs of changing suppliers, supplier choice for alliances must be managed as a process, in contrast to the arm's-length bidding used with market transactions. Such bidding does not elicit the breadth of information needed to make partner selection decisions. Nor does it start both firms on the important path of building understanding and trust.

Visits from potential customer partners need not be one-way discussions. These are good times for suppliers to begin learning how the other firms work. Customers interested in building real alliances will be happy to talk about their negotiation and problem-solving styles, give references to other suppliers, and answer questions based on the partner selection criteria noted earlier. Further, observing customer representatives' behavior—such as whether they meet with the supplier as a team, and discuss questions constructively and with evident interest in the supplier's well-being—provide more useful insights into the potential for an alliance.

A Critical Decision

These considerations make choosing the right partner "the single most critical element in working with suppliers," says Tom Slaninka, an early champion of supply partnerships at Motorola and director of

sourcing in its Land Mobile Products sector. Like Motorola, Marks &
Spencer regards the caliber of supplier relationships as so crucial that
it goes to great lengths to keep its current suppliers, offering substantial technical assistance and management guidance when they have
problems. Both firms take pride in the low turnover rates of their suppliers. Among its clothing suppliers—all of which it constantly challenges to innovate in fashion, fabric, and style, as well as improved
quality—M&S loses only about one or two a decade.

Recruit the Best Firms

Supplier selection is not just a matter of choosing from a number of
applicants; even the most attractive customers must take the initiative. Whenever it needs new suppliers—for capacity, proximity to a
new plant, or other reasons—Motorola has learned from experience
that it has to search for and recruit the best, rather than hope that
such firms will approach it.

   In one case, a team from the Paging Products Group made a trip
to find more suppliers of printed circuit boards and liquid crystal displays. Companies were located whose skills were as good as those of
current PPG suppliers, and they were added to the supply base. This
extra capacity allowed PPG to develop a new product with the new
suppliers.

Ally with All Relevant Companies

Conventional wisdom holds that suppliers are those firms already in
the business of selling the desired goods to others. While true, that
view can be too narrow. The more intense competition gets for any
firm, the more it pays to look for expertise beyond traditional sources.
For instance, when Motorola wanted to develop a wristwatch pager
(rather than learn how to do what others already knew), it formed an
alliance with Timex, which supplied the needed understandings.

   For maximum benefit, it is also essential to cooperate with all traditional suppliers whose products, parts, materials or services affect a
firm's costs or performances. At Motorola, PPG spends a small fraction
of its total purchases on production equipment. Yet work with equipment suppliers has dramatically increased PPG operating flexibility,
which at times has reached the ultimate goal of economic lot sizes of

one unit. That is a tremendous advantage in a market where success often favors the most agile firms.

THE SELECTION PROCESS

Given the pivotal nature of relationships and continuous improvement, both of which depend on hard-to-change organizational cultures, those factors must carry more weight in supplier selection than purely technical items such as price or product.

To illustrate, among suppliers in a competitive market, current prices are likely to vary within a narrow range. For customers facing a steep price curve in their own markets, a supplier's price today is not as critical as whether it has the internal skills and drive to keep lowering its costs and offer better prices tomorrow. Many of Motorola's communications products, for example, compete in markets where prices are falling more than 10 percent annually. That is why, in selecting suppliers, Motorola emphasizes organizational attributes that affect key cost drivers like quality.

Because alliances typically require sharing sensitive information, an understanding of how a firm protects such data must be developed in the process of selecting a partner. One of the first things Motorola looks for in a new supplier is whether the firm is in any way revealing sensitive information from its rivals. If that happens, Motorola concludes that its own information might be similarly disclosed, and the supplier does not get the business.

Since the in-depth examination needed to qualify a supply partner is expensive, the selection process involves a series of increasingly rigorous steps:

Step 1. Derive product or service objectives—in terms of projected price, cost, quality, technology, and other performance curves—from benchmarking, competitive analysis, and market research.

Step 2. Develop, from scanning and benchmarking, a list of potential suppliers of parts, equipment, materials, software, and services that in any way influence those objectives.

Step 3. After determining their interest by phone (and, possibly, by reviewing product samples and quotes), one person should visit the most promising candidates. The visit should cover a brief assessment of management, operations, quality systems, and development abilities. The purpose is to assess if the long-term potential seems realistic.

Step 4. Dispatch a team to narrow the field. If serious mutual interest develops, the team should revisit candidates to make quality audits, judge the firm's management and financial strengths, learn about its other customers, and otherwise deepen the understandings gained earlier.

Candidate suppliers are judged against quantitative measures of quality, capacity, technology, and delivery cycle time from manufacturing start, as well as their process abilities—the demonstrated skill to perform as a firm says it does. For suppliers that must keep up with technological change, R&D abilities must also be considered. Approved firms that are inadequate here will eventually be dropped as they fall behind important frontiers.

Also used are qualitative measures of service, management, organizational style, and commitments to continuous improvement. A firm's potential in these categories is as important as how well it meets current requirements. Motorola, M&S, and other firms such as Chrysler, Ford, and Honda that put a premium on quality look for a strong internal desire and ability, manifest in effective quality organizations, to pursue the same objectives they themselves embrace. It is also helpful to learn if a potential supplier's current major customers have similar high expectations. (The kinds of measures used to judge potential suppliers are discussed in Chapter 7.)

In essence, finding firms with a true commitment to improvement is a matter of cultural values—choosing those firms that really want to march in the same direction, as contrasted to being held to specific targets. Says Motorola's Tom Slaninka: "Supplier selection and management are not a matter of putting a gun to a guy's head. It is a question of whether we are all following the same signals from the marketplace. Those who cannot go down the same quality curve with us take themselves out of the game."

A TEAM EFFORT

Because supply alliances typically include multifunctional teamwork with the customer, partner selection must be a team process involving all relevant customer functions. Leaving out key activities gives a supplier mixed signals from different parts of the firm, which defeats an alliance.

At Motorola, the choice of new suppliers is based on consensus decisions in commodity teams composed of buyers, quality engineers, and designers from each division. Before visiting with potential suppliers, the Motorola team decides what it wants the new supplier to do, and how it will compare the candidate with current suppliers. Going to a new supplier used to require a waiver from a division general manager, and some managers still insist on this. But consistent with Motorola's constant drive to delegate more authority deeper into the organization, approvals are increasingly being given by division sourcing. At Marks & Spencer, supply decisions made by the selector (buyer), merchandiser, and merchandising executive are ratified by the division director.

EVALUATING ORGANIZATIONAL COMPETENCE

The only way two firms can reach their highest potential together is if, within the scope of their mutual interest, everyone in both organizations is committed to the same goals and both firms' cultures nourish open, candid team relationships.

Carole O'Beirne, senior selector in ladies' tailoring at Marks & Spencer, says one key consideration is "whether the supplier will argue. Some just take orders; M&S needs suppliers that will express their own views, which is the only way to get the best from both firms." Adds Alan Lambert, a divisional director, "M&S looks for people who think like us—product improvement processes that start with the customer, a concern for quality with a capital Q, and the same operating principles. We want to see evidence of this in how they work in their factories and offices. It is all about management and relationships with people. We will be put off by evidence of adversarial relationships with employees."

Although they are in vastly different businesses, M&S and Motorola are strikingly alike in their emphasis on people and style in supplier selection. At Motorola, each commodity manager (the executive with lead responsibility for supplier relations) understands that while he or she may find an outstanding supplier, cultural differences can inhibit effective relationships. For example, a firm may have a superb product but an inflexible culture that prevents it from staying on the improvement curve. In such cases, the opportunity is declined.

Listen to Ron Vocalino, a regional sourcing manager in Land Mobile Products: "We try to get suppliers that we believe have the same strategies, goals, and drives as Motorola. While our judgments are partially subjective, we do look for aggressive goals for improvement and work force empowerment—needed to drive continued improvement—including clear evidence of work teams in the factory." Motorola people learn a lot of about these matters by walking around a factory, talking to people on the shop floor, and looking for charts on the walls that indicate ongoing work team efforts.

Of course, cultural considerations are also important in selecting supply partners abroad. In Hong Kong, whose culture is heavily oriented toward short-term trading, it can be difficult to interest suppliers in long-term alliances requiring continuous improvement. Singaporean suppliers, by contrast, have a more typical Asian interest in long-term matters and tend to be much more adept at such relationships. As another example, when it was looking for a plastics supplier in Japan, Motorola wanted a firm that had worked well with North American customers because the mutual learning curve would then be shorter.

SUPPLIERS OF ASSEMBLED GOODS

Compared with most parts or materials, assemblies—such as a complete door for a car, or operating equipment—tend to be more complex, with more relevant parameters. In alliances with suppliers of such products, the combination of stretching for continuous advances and overall optimization to meet the customer's needs is more difficult, and the selection process takes more effort.

By definition, assemblies integrate a variety of parts and subsystems, many of which are obtained by suppliers from other firms. The process of choosing supply partners for assemblies thus requires adding steps to those used for less complex goods. One such measure is to talk to other users and make site visits when possible to learn about reliability, service, program management skills, and other key parameters. Another step is to probe a candidate's relations with its own suppliers to learn how much control it has over purchased components. In its clothing business, for example, Marks & Spencer pays as much attention to firms that supply fibers and textiles to garment makers as it does to the garment firms that assemble the goods. This helps ensure that its final suppliers can produce quality products, with the latest technology, on time.

LOW-VOLUME AND SERVICE SUPPLIERS

A full set of quantitative measures, including thorough quality audits, may not be feasible in assessing suppliers of low-volume items or some services. One reason is that quality audits based on statistical processes do not apply in these situations. Another is that objective measures for a number of services are not available.

Motorola's Paging Products Group is illustrative. While piece–part suppliers are chosen with the help of comprehensive quantitative and qualitative procedures, the measures employed to select equipment suppliers are less stringent when volume is low. Besides assessing a firm's financial health, PPG gives substantial attention to performance, delivery, and reliability. For high-volume equipment purchases, such as those made by Motorola's Semiconductor Products Group, the selection procedures involve the full set of quality and management audits.

Competitors as Supply Partners

It may seem illogical that rivals should cooperate. Still, by nature, they have more complementary skills than any other sets of firms. That is why, in response to competitive pressure to find the best possible outside resources, Ford and Nissan cooperated to develop a minivan, Coke and Schweppes did the same in soft-drink bottling, and many other rivals have formed links that have been successful for each firm.

At times, rivals may be the *only* sources of some needed inputs. While Philips Consumer Electronics Company competes intensely with Japanese consumer electronics firms, "we cannot always get away from their internal suppliers, which do a good job for us," says Tom Natale. So the question is not whether to work with rivals, but when and how.

The first test of a prospective alliance between rivals is whether the people who must work together are or can be separated from those who are paid to combat each other in the marketplace. That condition can be met, for instance, when sales or marketing efforts are not involved.

The second test is whether the benefits for each firm exceed the risk of giving the other an undesirable advantage. Knowing this requires both firms to do a competitive analysis of the pros and cons—how a relationship would add to each one's know-how, capacity, and so forth. Two beverage firms, for example, have an alliance that supplies them with distribution services and gives them substantially lower costs than working alone. The firms compete mainly in marketing, with distribution being a secondary factor. But at a time when price competition with other drinks firms has become significant, the alliance helps both of them.

The more that critical items are involved in these relationships, the more awkward they become. Natale says his Japanese rivals "get a 'first look in the kitchen' on new developments from their internal suppliers, which can be a disadvantage for PCEC. There is a general feeling here that when we go to the consumer electronics show or similar events, our Japanese rivals are getting favored treatment by those suppliers. It is like walking a tightrope. However, since the Japanese are vertically integrated, they must use their own internal suppliers. None of them has an absolute edge, so we can pick and choose among them to balance those factors."

When PCEC works with a Japanese supplier, "we do not want them to use the know-how gained from our TV people," says Natale, noting that this is achieved partially with a nondisclosure agreement, and more so if PCEC pays for the work and owns the result. "But even when we just share concept information with such suppliers, we suspect it flows to their production people. Still, this is not necessarily a major issue because we feel we move faster in this market." When it does become an issue, PCEC has changed suppliers. At one time, chips for its TV sets were supplied by Mitsubishi Electric, a rival in the TV business. When the performance of those chips became a critical factor in its sets, PCEC switched to Motorola to supply that part.

Working with Internal Suppliers

A firm may have internal suppliers for a product or service that is part of its core competence, or because acceptable outside suppliers are not available. Whatever the reason, they should be held to the same criteria as any outside firms. Being required to buy from internal suppliers that cannot pass this test forces the buying unit to compromise its performance, and hurts the supplier by shielding it from market forces. This has been a critical weakness of American and European auto firms, which were highly vertically integrated and allowed captive suppliers to operate without meeting the same standards imposed on outside sources.

For example, while other Motorola units have capabilities relevant to the needs of its Paging Products Group, they are not always chosen as suppliers. On printed circuit boards, the internal cost may be prohibitive, especially on lower-cost items. Motorola units hold internal suppliers to the same expectations as they do outside firms. Backdoor politics cannot be used to cover up issues such as supply quality, because corporate quality goals dominate. When significant performance issues have appeared, internal suppliers have been told that they will get no more orders until those are fixed. More generally, the communication and coordination practices between internal Motorola buying and selling units are the same as those for outside suppliers.

Philips Consumer Electronics Company also has internal suppliers (for tuners, picture tubes, and other components) that are treated like external suppliers. At one time, for example, Philips Nijmegen (Holland) supplied PCEC with signal processors that did not work as expected. PCEC said it would switch to Mitsubishi unless they were fixed by a specified date. When this did not happen, PCEC did just as it promised, despite political pressure. Not until two years later, after the arrival of new people on both sides, were communications resumed. PCEC told Nijmegen what had to be done to reestablish the relationship. The changes were made, the supply link was rebuilt, and Philips gained a stronger internal unit from the experience.

Committing to the Long Term

Following Motorola's supply partnership initiative in what was then its communications sector, it took several years before the firm and its suppliers could talk openly—and proudly—about their relationships. Even so, no one believes they have reached their full potential. Molex, the connector firm, is working with Ford and Chrysler toward alliances it expects will be similar to those it has with PCEC and

Motorola (which date from the mid-1980s). Richard Black, vice president and general manager of Molex's automotive group, notes that the two auto firms started on the alliance path only a few years ago and are working to transform their entire supply bases. So they are not as far along as PCEC and Motorola with respect to building trust, understanding, and clarity of joint processes.

Both customers, says Black, are still concerned about whether they will get a world-class price if they have true partnerships with their suppliers. The firms have not collaborated long enough to share all information—including being candid about costs—that would be mutually productive to share.

Alliances, like marriages, do not work just because promises are made. They keep getting better only if people on both sides make a continuing effort toward that goal. "They even used the word *love*," says Robert Wahlstedt, president of Reed Precision Manufacturing, about his firm's relationship with Xerox, for which Reed is a highly rated supplier. But in the end, he notes, it took about five years for reality to catch up with Xerox's idealism.

The kinds of massive changes—and substantial benefits—that customer–supplier alliances bring must be seen as the fruits of a long-term process. While early gains are available and should be sought in order to fortify the effort, the greatest value comes from a persistent commitment to an endeavor that yields more benefits as long as it is nourished. "We are slowly moving away from one-night stands and adversarial relationships," says Dennis Hiser, corporate director of procurement for Texas Instruments. "But there is a lot of history we have to overcome."[15]

3

CONDITIONS FOR HIGH PERFORMANCE

Our people are always wanting a monopoly with Marks & Spencer, but it is not good for them. When another supplier comes up with a winner in our product area it is healthy for us—it pushes us into new areas.

Chris Haskins, chairman, Northern Foods

Vaughn Hovey really stretches me to provide better service and be more competitive, which makes me distinctly more viable in the outside marketplace. We have refined service level management to a high art.

Frank Palm, IBM's lead executive for the Kodak alliance, on his counterpart at Kodak

It is not from the benevolence of the butcher, the brewer, or the baker that we expect our dinner, but from their regard to their own interest.

Adam Smith, *The Wealth of Nations*

In 1992, ten years after Motorola began converting its supply links to alliances and was reaping vast benefits from them, General Motors made headline news. Under the leadership of J. Ignacio López de Arriortua, its newly installed purchasing chief, GM was demanding double-digit price cuts from suppliers, breaking long-term contracts, and sharing the firms' proprietary know-how with rivals in a quest for lower bids. No one doubted that GM, like other auto firms and their suppliers, needed a painful readjustment. Costs, quality, and cycle times were far from the norms set by their Japanese rivals. And while López cut ample costs from GM's purchasing bill, the fallout—if GM stays the course—will cost it far more.

One immediate effect was that suppliers began withholding their newest developments from GM. Typical was a comment by James J. Mahoney, a marketing manager at National Steel, who said his firm chose not to share a stamping technique that would have reduced the automaker's scrap metal by up to 75 percent. National, he said, feared that GM would pass the information to a rival. "Why should we risk telling them our good ideas?" comments Mahoney. "At GM there is no certainty." Timothy D. Leuliette, head of ITT Automotive, echoes that sentiment: "If there's anything that sends a supplier through the ceiling, it's taking our information to our competitors."

Another consequence was that firms shifted their brightest engineers to work on projects for Ford and Chrysler, which take a partnership approach with their suppliers. An inevitable result of such moves is that it will cost GM more to fix future quality problems, and innovation will suffer. In a survey of the supplier industry at the time, GM ranked dead last on supplier relations among the twelve automakers with factories in the United States.

By emphasizing price alone with its suppliers, GM won immediate savings—and ignored total cost. At GM's plant in Arlington, Texas, an ill-fitting ashtray from a new, substandard supplier caused a six-week shutdown of Buick Roadmaster production. At another plant, GM managers had to beg for help from a supplier López had rejected in favor of one that bid 5 percent less. One-half of the low bidder's parts flunked quality tests. Within four days, the other supplier geared up to make parts that it flew to GM by charter plane. "My guess is that their 5 percent savings turned into a 15 percent loss," says the second supplier. By early 1995, growing discomfort among suppliers was inhibiting GM's plans to reduce its own tedious bureaucracy. When GM tried to get them to take on much of the development work for new components that was being done in-house, it was resisted because the parts companies complained that the automaker was unwilling to include the costs in its pricing.[1]

As links between GM and its suppliers were polarizing, Chrysler was on a different path with many of the same firms. During the first three years of the program, cost savings *proposed* by suppliers helped Chrysler become the lowest–cost, highest–profit per vehicle automaker in North America, as noted in Chapter 1. These are cost eliminations, not the cost avoidances that some firms count when they discuss benefits. Further, many of the same parts companies that resisted GM efforts to outsource development work were happily doing the same work for Chrysler. And Chrysler, compared with Motorola and Marks & Spencer, is still in the early stages of building supply alliances.

Most likely, General Motors will recognize it started on the wrong path and change its ways. But its ordeal emphasizes a central feature of relationships between firms. High performance cannot be mandated; it must be earned. Just as a supplier must keep winning its customer's business, so too must the customer win its supplier's commitment to get the most value from that firm. Reaching that stage requires a set of conditions, constructed from an understanding of the customer's and supplier's needs, that encourage each supplier to do its best. As always, it is appropriate to start with the customer.

Using Focused Competition

Customers seek alliances with suppliers to get more value than is possible from market transactions. This does not mean that competition is abandoned, however, because there is no more powerful force than rivalry for continued improvement. Best practice in supply alliances is to raise competition to a higher level between carefully chosen suppliers. Such competition is focused on whatever costs or performances are most critical to the customer.

Motorola and Philips Consumer Electronics Company buy the same kinds of parts for their products. Motorola uses focused competition between its supply partners to drive down their costs, as well as improve their quality and cycle time. PCEC does not use this technique at all. Motorola's supply costs have been dropping at a consistent annual rate ranging from 8 to 10 percent. By contrast, PCEC's supply costs have been falling at about half that rate, or close to the average decline in market prices for the electronic parts both firms buy.

Based on data collected from its supplier audit process and general process evaluations of new suppliers, plus experience with focused competition, Motorola has found that less competition between suppliers leads to smaller cost reductions. Other major contributors to annual supplier price reductions at Motorola are volume, including corporatewide supply contracts; ongoing quality improvements; work on cost drivers via early design participation and technical assistance; and formal supplier training through Motorola University.

Such focused competition involves a small number of firms that supply similar goods—such as skirts in the case of Marks & Spencer's ladies' clothing department, or printed circuit boards for Motorola. Many companies use the term *commodity group* to describe all such supplies having closely related characteristics.[2] In the retail business, *product category* and *product range* are used in a similar way.

Driving Suppliers to Excel

"Our people are always wanting a monopoly with Marks & Spencer," says Chris Haskins, chairman of Northern Foods, "but it is not good for them. When another supplier comes up with a winner in our product area it is healthy for us. It pushes us into new areas." For example, Haskins observes that it was United Biscuits rather than Northern Foods that became the first supplier to develop sandwiches for M&S. Such rivalry, he says, "puts our people on their toes. In this case, it prompted Northern to create different flavors and kinds of sandwiches to win some of the M&S business."

Focused competition—along with shared learning, cooperation on tasks like quality improvement, and the launch of new joint processes—is specifically aimed at motivating suppliers to excel for mutual gain. It is by no means a tactic to weaken or intimidate them. The experience of smaller firms that are suppliers to Marks & Spencer and Motorola supports this idea. Perhaps because they tend to be more innovative, such suppliers form a substantial part of each company's supply base. Unlike conventional market relationships, where the bargaining power advantage of size can weaken small suppliers or send them away, the long-term alliances M&S and Motorola have with smaller firms have been quite profitable for them. Suppliers to M&S, for example, enjoy above-average profits from their business with it, compared with others in their industry.

Take the example of Desmond & Sons, based in Londonderry, U.K. Desmonds, with annual revenues of about £100 million, makes jeans, trousers, nightwear, and leisurewear (such as sweatshirts and T-shirts) for Marks & Spencer. It ranks fifth in size among sixty suppliers that are responsible for about 80 percent of the clothing M&S sells, and it supplies about 70 percent of the retailer's jeans. Denis Desmond, the firm's chairman, says that competition for shelf space at M&S is an important source of pressure for the constant improvement M&S expects from its suppliers. Because M&S has selected and nurtured the very best suppliers to support its goal of continuously advancing consumer value, rivalry among them leaves no room for complacency.

For each Marks & Spencer department it serves, Desmonds wants to have at least 20 percent share, but is not up to that level in all cases. The challenge, says Denis Desmond, is to increase market share at M&S via better value and quality, product development, and innovation in raw materials. Through cooperation with its own suppliers, the company used this strategy to go into women's jeans, displacing another M&S supplier. Desmond thinks it will take a long time to reach the firm's goal, however, because of rivalry among suppliers.

In cases like men's jeans, where the company already has a large share of a department, Denis Desmond wants to expand his firm's volume by helping M&S increase its own market share. To do that, Desmonds has to look at the overall market, understand relevant trends, and spot opportunities. Such efforts, along with those of M&S, have contributed to a doubling in the retailer's share of the British jeans market.

Desmonds has an extremely strong balance sheet; it performs consistently in the upper quartile of the U.K. clothing industry in return on net assets and on sales. While many clothing firms in Northern Ireland, its home base, have closed over the past thirty years, Desmonds has grown from a staff of 300 to 3,000 at present. The company sells only to M&S and is privately held. But that is not a major feature of the relationship. Publicly held firms (including Dewhurst, another garment maker) also have exclusive relationships with M&S. Significantly, Desmonds is not a sole-source or even a single-source supplier to M&S. The company must compete with others to win the business it gets.

As another example, consider Craftsman Custom Metal Fabricators, which makes sheet metal parts for customers in the electronics industry. Before Motorola's supply alliances began, Craftsman won business there on price alone. Craftsman now competes with a small set of selected Motorola suppliers by working to improve its performance against

Motorola's objectives of quality and cycle time. Says Bruce Bendoff, president of Craftsman, which has benefited handsomely from the relationship: "I believe strongly in Motorola's having more than one supplier to maintain competitive pressures. It is in the best interest of the partnership to have that element of rivalry."

TARGET SPECIFIC PERFORMANCES

To be effective, focused competition among a firm's suppliers must emphasize whatever behavior is essential to the firm's competitive advantage. For example, since Motorola competes intensely on price and cycle time, it focuses its suppliers on cost and other factors that affect these variables. By contrast, Marks & Spencer, in its prepared fresh food lines, competes not on price alone, but on the quality and value—in terms of taste, freshness, and other factors—of products developed with its suppliers. To support that objective, M&S designs its focused competition to drive suppliers toward improving value while discouraging direct rivalry purely on price.

For example, M&S might say to its strawberry yogurt sources: "Supplier XYZ's raspberry yogurt is doing quite well. How will you improve your strawberry yogurt to keep up?" That kind of competition moves the whole prepared food line forward. By contrast, other retailers favor direct competition among suppliers of the same products. That causes an emphasis on price, distracts their attention away from value creation, inhibits the retailers' ability to offer the most value, and contributes to price competition and eroding margins in the retail sector.

Guy McCracken, the M&S joint managing director who heads its food business, believes the M&S use of competition among suppliers of high-value items is important in the continued drive for better products. When there is an opportunity to create unique value in the product, he says, M&S wants to encourage its suppliers to innovate in that direction. In more basic product areas (such as certain types of fresh produce) price competition is important and M&S works with suppliers to ensure that they are correctly positioned in the marketplace.

Always Have a Market Benchmark

As a complement to focused competition, or as a partial substitute when conditions favor a more exclusive supply relationship, having a market comparison helps ensure that an alliance does what it is supposed to do: stay ahead of the market. Benchmarking is a way of learning about specific costs and techniques from selected practitioners.

As an example, to develop its new Cirrus and Dodge Stratus pick-ups, Chrysler benchmarked 280 features on all rival autos and trucks and sought to match or beat every one of them. Chrysler also benchmarked 250 competitive vehicles on quality and set the ambitious goal of having even better quality for new models coming off its production line than it had achieved after long production runs with the previous line. That is something no auto company—and probably no other firm—has ever achieved.

Kodak's outsourcing alliance with IBM, as another example, is a sole-source relationship designed to give IBM good reason to reach for continuous improvement. One incentive is the revenue growth and acceptable margins that will come from more penetration of Kodak. That, in turn, requires ongoing advances in customer satisfaction ratings so the alliance keeps ahead of the market: Any Kodak business unit may take its business to others if the alliance does not deliver higher service levels than could be obtained by going outside. IBM has not won all the Kodak business it sought. Still, Frank Palm, IBM's lead executive for the alliance, says: "Competition is very important to our energy level and creativity. In spite of our close relationship, Vaughn Hovey [Kodak's lead executive] uses the availability of alternatives to ensure that I do my best job, and I respect that. I have better people and better processes because of it."

Because they are important complementary tools for alliances, it is useful to compare benchmarking with focused competition. On the one hand, since benchmarking can be done with any firm that is willing to share its data, the technique can cast a wide net to find the best prices and practices, as well as learn about interesting new frontiers. However, because benchmarking requires an investment of professional time, except in highly critical areas it can be done only occasionally—perhaps every few months. That can be a serious disadvantage in fast-changing areas.

Focused competition, on the other hand, produces data from suppliers that can be collected with far less expense and thus can be done more often. This can be an important advantage in fast-changing areas. Further, since suppliers involved in focused competition are working in the same customer context, data about their costs, delivery, cycle times, and other performances that tend to be unique in each context

Comparing Benchmarking and Focused Competition		
	Benchmarking	Focused Competition
Data about	Best price, practice New frontiers	Activities in customer context, and are thus directly comparable
Age of data	Average can be months	May be one week or less
Inherent advantage	Monitor outside world	Better data in fast-changing areas Better cost reductions

are directly comparable. That is not always possible with outside benchmarking. These distinctions between benchmarking and focused competition make both practices worth using together. They are summarized in the table shown above.

Sole, Single, or Dual Sourcing?

Alliances work better when a firm reduces the number of its suppliers to a select few. This creates scale economies, gives each remaining supplier a better chance to win more of the customer's business, and facilitates closer working relationships.

One factor that determines the lower limit on the number of suppliers is that a firm needs enough suppliers to sustain rivalry within each commodity group. A related point here is that since all suppliers in a commodity group do not have the same technology, some may not be able to make a particular part. In setting limits, then, a firm must balance these considerations. Second, a firm needs enough suppliers to ensure it has a backup source in case a supplier has quality or other problems, or changes its priorities and becomes less committed to the alliance.

Sometimes, however, scale economies, low volume, integration requirements, a need to encourage innovation, or a supplier's unique position favor working with just one firm for a particular good or service. Then focused competition may suffer, and backup can be a greater challenge.

All of these factors lead to three kinds of supply relationships: sole source, single source, and dual (or sometimes multiple) source, which are defined in the table shown on the next page. Alliances may be used with each kind of relationship.

Sourcing Definitions	
Sole source	Cannot buy from others due to special conditions
Single source	Can buy from others but choose to buy from one
Dual source	Two suppliers concurrently provide the same item

In general, the distinction between sole and single sourcing is a matter of timing. In a sole-source relationship, no other supplier can perform as well as the current supplier on all dimensions that are important to the customer. However, given enough time (which may be several months or more), it is often possible to develop another source. By contrast, with single sourcing, other suppliers could meet the customer's needs in a shorter time frame. These distinctions are sharpened in alliances, which depend on close working relationships that take considerable time to develop.

USING SOLE SOURCING

Some people maintain that sole sourcing has broad natural advantages over single or dual sourcing because it promotes greater commitments and closer relationships. One interesting aspect of this view is that it seems to be more strongly held by firms as suppliers than by the same firms as customers. A typical attitude is that of a sales executive at a firm that prefers to be a sole-source supplier: "When you have all of the business you can handle with a customer, there is more pressure to constantly do your best, because you are aware of the great responsibility to them." Adds a purchasing executive at the same firm: "We have a lot of faith in our supply partners, but no company is free of problems, and we can't afford to take those risks. Besides, rivalry among them is healthy for all of us."

Many firms that use sole sourcing keep an eye on the market to be sure the supplier is giving them the best price. Even so, price is too narrow a benchmark for alliances, which deliver more value than that through focused competition, cooperation, and other ways. In fact, because of quality, cycle time, and other factors, lowest price may not mean lowest total cost. Further, holding a supplier to market standards is not as effective as subjecting it to direct rivalry with the very best firms in terms of the specific performances that are most critical to the customer.

At Philips Consumer Electronics Company, where Molex is the dominant connector supplier, periodic discussions are held with a leading Molex rival. These talks are aimed at benchmarking Molex, giving the other firm a chance to show what it can do, and alerting Molex of its need to stay ahead of the competition. Still, because the second firm has not won any business, it has become wary about meeting with PCEC since preparation is time-consuming. That reduces benchmarking inputs to PCEC and relaxes the pressure on Molex, which is an ongoing issue.

Another argument in favor of sole sourcing is that it facilitates bringing the supplier into new programs early, which can be an advantage in reducing design cycle time. Then, because the supplier has virtual certainty that it will get any new business it can handle with the customer, it can commit its engineering, plant, and other resources at the earliest time in the cycle. This logic is defeated by experience. Chrysler, Motorola, and others often discuss new projects at the concept or even preconcept stage with two or more supply partners. In that way, whichever partner best meets the needs of the situation is chosen for early design participation, permitting that firm to commit its resources at the best time. Further, having to contend for such opportunities helps keep firms at the cutting edge.

Sole sourcing makes it difficult to have a backup plan, which can create problems. At PCEC, some parts—such as chips, large TV tubes, and projection TV lenses—substantially leverage the design and cost of PCEC products, driving the company to seek unique designs for those parts. But because the suppliers are sole source, a supplier problem can shut down a PCEC factory. Says Gordon Couch, a PCEC component applications engineer: "Backup is a serious issue. We do a lot of sweating if a supplier has a plant failure; we have to rush to find the part from someone else." While backup may be provided by a multiplant supplier, or by tooling adequately, that is not yet formally done. PCEC has not had the resources to develop full backup plans.

For chips and TV tubes, a new supplier would need twenty-six weeks to develop the required artwork and dies, and its part may still not function the same as the one being replaced. In general, PCEC owns whatever tooling suppliers use that is unique to its parts, and has the right to transfer the tooling to another firm should the relationship end.[3]

With PCEC's lens supplier, that firm owns the tooling, which (along with the lenses it sells to PCEC) contains substantial proprietary know-how. Further, the technology is so unique and the volume so low that having another supplier ready and able to provide backup is not feasible. So in case of problems, PCEC must make a go/no-go decision, or have past designs to which it can turn. Says PCEC's Bill Kennedy: "It would be a huge problem for us if their plant burned down."

Sole Sourcing for Unique Attributes. Despite these drawbacks, there are specific situations when sole source is the best choice. One requirement is that backup risk must be low. For example, in certain product areas, such as high-value Italian foods, Northern Foods may have a sole-source supplier of Italian flour because the firm cannot get the same quality or value elsewhere, and those attributes are critical to the success of its products.

Sole Sourcing for Innovation. Another reason for sole sourcing is to foster supplier innovation. For instance, M&S wants to encourage its food suppliers to innovate in unique high-value items and protects their investments by granting them sole-source status. That continues until and unless the products lose their uniqueness (which is rare), capacity limits arise, or quality drops. Says Guy McCracken: "If a supplier has developed the product, made the investment, and built the business, why should we undermine it? If a supplier cannot capitalize on its idea, that reduces its incentive to invest in new ideas. If the plant goes out, we lose that product for awhile. Of course, if it goes out often we would have to rethink."

In Marks & Spencer's clothing lines, though, advances by garment makers come mainly from their design efforts and require less unique investment. Here, if a supplier develops something that gives it a differential advantage, M&S wants to make certain the supplier benefits from this. But the retailer also wants to satisfy its customers, which often requires more capacity than any one supplier has. To do this, garment makers that develop unique designs will be the sole source for an agreed time, after which M&S will bring in other suppliers.

Motorola, like Marks & Spencer, encourages its suppliers to innovate. It is concerned about growing too dependent on any one firm, however, because of issues related to capacity; supply reliability; a need to maintain focused competition (to achieve better quality, costs, and cycle time); and the chance that a supplier might gain unacceptable negotiating leverage. For these reasons Motorola has a backup plan for most critical sole-sourced parts, or in case a key supplier innovation fails. The plan may require redesigning an existing part or product, or creating the internal ability to produce the same part or equipment. As part of its backup strategy Motorola, like most companies, develops and maintains performance specifications that are used to communicate requirements to new or current suppliers.

On unique equipment developments, one backup is the fallback position to the last generation of equipment. As a partial safeguard, Motorola constantly benchmarks suppliers to know where to turn in an emergency.[4]

Another backup is to develop a new supplier. At one time, the Paging Products Group had sole sourced a key part from a supplier that subsequently demanded high prices and offered little service. In response, PPG found a small firm with the potential to make the part. PPG shared its quality system with the firm and helped it understand the part's critical functions as well as improve its own suppliers' processes. The firm then developed a unique and superior part that was interchangeable with the first supplier's part.

To promote innovation, suppliers of unique parts get the business for the first year or so, provided they meet PPG's quality, capacity, and other requirements. To avoid overdependence, PPG may tell a supplier that it wants a backup source but will not require the first supplier to share its unique design. Instead, PPG asks both firms to negotiate design or sharing, or has the backup create its own design. Having two designs does not necessarily create problems. For instance, when different suppliers designed separate vibrators for Motorola pagers, each was given a distinct part number.

Design sharing may not be an issue if the first firm is capacity limited. Usually, suppliers of critical parts will not share their designs. Because Motorola never expects a supplier to share key innovations, the supplier must decide whether to do so to earn goodwill. Motorola will not force the issue for fear of damaging relationships.

Sole Sourcing for Integration and Scale Economies. In some situations, a need for integration or scale makes sole sourcing unavoidable. Certain petrochemical plants, for example, require chemically unique feedstocks that are available only from specific suppliers, which requires sole sourcing.

The Kodak–IBM alliance is sole source because Kodak's long-term goal is to have a single integrated global data processing system, and the economics strongly favor having one global supplier. Further, the complexities of integrating two separate suppliers' data processing systems strongly favor sole sourcing.

For backup in the event of equipment failure, arrangements have been made to switch to other computer facilities. If Kodak and IBM decide to end their alliance, the firms' agreement permits Kodak to buy the data center operation back from IBM. While that is not ideal, since data centers are not a Kodak core competence, at least the centers would have been improved by the alliance. Other alternatives, such as finding another partner for Kodak, might also be possible. Still, given that many services provided by the alliance depend on close cooperation and trust between several levels in both organizations, it seems unlikely that any new Kodak partner would be able to reach the same level of performance in a short time frame.

The British alliance between Reed Personnel Services and Hewlett-Packard, which provides temporary office support and clerical people to H-P, is sole source because working with one agency was expected to improve communications and facilitate accountability. H-P's earlier practice of working with several agencies inhibited problem solving on issues such as the failure of staff to turn up or perform well. A sole-source arrangement also gives Reed a larger contract, with more to lose if its performance falls off. Hewlett-Packard's backup is in the marketplace. Although time would be needed to establish effective relationships, other temp agencies could quickly move in if that were necessary.

SINGLE AND DUAL SOURCING

In traditional arm's-length sourcing, a customer that buys undifferentiated goods assumes, absent scarcities, that any supplier is easy to replace. With alliances, the partner selection process and a desire for unique value make moving from one supplier to another a difficult, lengthy process, unless the second firm is already an accepted partner. The experience of Marks & Spencer illustrates.

Carole O'Beirne, a senior selector (buyer) in ladies' tailoring at M&S, notes that if the company had just one supplier for ladies' skirts and experienced a sudden surge in demand or a serious quality problem, or if the supplier slipped on design, it would take many months to bring an outside firm up to speed. While the outsider went through the M&S quality procedure and financial evaluations and learned other M&S ways, the season would have passed and the opportunity would be lost. By contrast, since M&S has more than one skirt supply partner, another could respond within weeks if one firm could not meet unanticipated growth requirements (as long as needed fabric was available). If there were just one supplier, O'Beirne says, that firm might use the power of its position to charge too much. Although those situations are rare, M&S still wants to protect against them. Overall, the company wants to maintain balance and competition among suppliers.

Single Sourcing. With single sourcing, a customer has other suppliers in the same commodity group that are single-sourced on other, closely related goods. The requirement that suppliers serve as backups if necessary limits how small a commodity group can get.

When a supplier can meet the customer's capacity requirements, single sourcing has scale advantages over dual sourcing, including easier communications, logistics, and inventory management. For these reasons, Motorola prefers to single source, except for critical items—typically a subset of unique parts developed jointly with the supplier, such as printed circuit boards for a high-volume product line.

For single-sourced items, the lead time needed to shift to another supplier varies considerably with the commodity. At Motorola, the lead time for capacitors or resistors is short, and part substitutions are readily available. In those cases where switching to the backup supplier cannot be done quickly, Motorola recently began requiring single-sourced suppliers to have their own backup plans.

Dual Sourcing. In most clothing lines, Marks & Spencer shares volume across manufacturers because no one firm can meet its volume needs. Sharing is also done for backup purposes: Unlike with food purchases, the consumer is often making an investment, and availability is more critical. For these reasons, M&S has more than one supplier for each kind of ladies' skirt in major lines.

While Motorola typically uses single sourcing, the company sometimes finds that capacity limits at a supplier are causing two of its business units to pull against each other to meet their volume needs. To avoid that, the company may limit volume at any one firm and use dual sourcing. More generally, dual sourcing is appropriate when any of the following conditions exist:

High Volume: One supplier cannot readily meet the customer's capacity needs.

Long Lead Time: Any one supplier may not reach full volume by the desired time.

High Risk: Customer or supplier is on the edge of a difficult new technology.

Conceptually, high volume and long lead time are straightforward. A hypothetical example illustrates the notion of high risk. Say, for instance, that Motorola is pushing the state of the art in some area (such as liquid crystal displays) and asks a supplier to stretch with it. The supplier may be willing to accept the challenge but says that because considerable risk may be involved, its ability to perform is uncertain. Motorola may then go to dual sourcing; another supplier may have a different technology that performs essentially the same.

Some suppliers ask Motorola to dual source their parts because failing to perform could risk their long-term business with the firm. Motorola has knowingly paid more—sometimes significantly more—for parts by dual sourcing to ensure the availability of adequate capacity. Dual sourcing critical parts (about twenty to twenty-five parts, out of thousands) has greatly reduced the risks of production shortages. It is not uncommon for suppliers to have occasional major quality problems or struggle to meet large increases in demand.

To support focused competition, and given available capacity, Motorola and M&S allot volume between dual- and multiple-sourced suppliers largely on the basis of their relative performance on designated parameters. Another allocation consideration for Motorola is a supplier's geographic proximity, which affects response times, shipping costs, and ease of communications. For M&S most suppliers are close by, which makes the issue irrelevant.

To avoid compromising a supplier's proprietary position, make certain that each supplier's goods can be identified, hedge against technical risks, or deal with variability, dual sourcing may require additional investment (for example, having separate part numbers for each item). Often, such costs are well below what would be required for backup if a sole or single supplier failed.

One argument against dual sourcing is that, for example, a 75/25 percent allotment with two suppliers (with the second in a backup role) makes the second firm unhappy with the arrangement and prone to submit below-cost bids (low-balling) to win more business. This argument is defective for two reasons. First, as discussed earlier, volume allocations should be based on each firm's relative performance rather than arbitrary quotas. Second, low-balling reflects a customer's poor management of supply costs. Any underbidding firm is going to have to raise its prices later to make up for the loss; an intelligent customer should know that and reject such bids.

Some firms have found that with dual sourcing both suppliers tend to be sloppy, because each believes that if something goes wrong the other will be there. These firms' experience has been that, when problems arise with one supplier, the second cannot be counted on to help. Motorola's experience, however, is just the opposite. Dual sourcing has saved PPG on several occasions when one supplier of critical parts had unexpected difficulties; the other firm in each case was ready and able to provide an immediate backup. Similarly, Marks & Spencer uses dual and multiple sourcing for many of its goods, and it rarely has had backup problems. The difference seems to be that both Motorola and M&S hold all suppliers to stringent performance standards. Suppliers to both firms know that weak performance may jeopardize future business.

Another issue with dual sourcing is the problem of variability: Goods made by one supplier somehow differ from those made by the other, and the customer cannot make substitutions without problems. Of course, the same thing can happen with one supplier, but once the customer has identified the problem, the supplier can resolve it by analyzing and correcting its own process variances.

The challenge to ensure consistency is obviously greater with two or more suppliers. In such cases, the customer may take the lead. For example, PPG found that tooling variations were the main causes of some part interchangeability problems; it solved those by having one supplier produce tooling for itself and the other supplier. PPG also evaluates dual-sourced parts more thoroughly to be sure they are interchangeable.

At Marks & Spencer, where dual (and multiple) sourcing is common, the firm uses what it calls specification buying to provide a high degree of uniformity among suppliers that make the same item. M&S and its suppliers agree on detailed specifications that describe every aspect of each garment, from the number of stitches per inch to dying and finishing procedures to the type of yarn and fiber.

When variability cannot be reduced, the customer must be ready to make those investments needed to accept the differences. For example, although PPG receives sole-sourced chips from Motorola's Semiconductor Products Sector (SPS), SPS is helping PPG develop another source. The SPS business is growing rapidly, and it wants to have more capacity available for other customers. Further, due to PPG's tremendous demand for chips, volume declines could harm SPS. Until it has a dual source, PPG maintains a backup plan in the event of a problem with SPS supply. Should PPG succeed in dual sourcing chips, it may have to write new software to reflect differences from SPS chips.

The table shown on the following page compares the attributes of sole, single, and dual sourcing.

Reducing the Supply Base

For reasons of scale economies, the lower costs of managing fewer suppliers, and better working relationships, alliances benefit from having the fewest number of suppliers consistent with the needs for backup, capacity requirements, and focused competition.

Outokumpu, the U.S. unit of the Finnish mining and metals group, makes copper and brass sheet, tubing, and strip products from a blend of refined mine output and scrap, which is less costly but often contains impurities. To lower the impurity content and its costs, Outokumpu reduced the number of its scrap suppliers from 186 to 50, of whom 9 are key suppliers. By improving the quality of purchased scrap through alliances with its remaining suppliers, the firm cut its "off analysis" (the amount of unacceptable impurities) in the furnace from 10 to 0.2 percent and reduced its cost of purchased materials as well.

Scrap quality was improved by showing scrap suppliers—typically small, unsophisticated firms—how to separate high-quality from low-quality items, which included teaching them how to use a spectrometer to check the chemistry of the metal. Thanks to these improvements, the volume of purchased scrap tripled. And with fewer suppliers, each had considerably more volume and experienced faster growth.

Kinds of Supply Arrangements			
	Sole Source	**Single Source**	**Dual Source**
Pressure to improve	Outside market	Focused competition	Focused competition
Relationships	Closest	Can be close	Take more effort
Backup	No direct substitute, must have alternatives available	Other plant or supplier, or internal arrangements by supplier or customer	Other plant or supplier, or internal arrangements by supplier or customer
Scale economies	Best chance for full scale	Best chance for full scale	Full scale if each supplier at scale
Integration	Easiest	Easy to moderate	Requires most effort
When used	Cannot buy from others due to innovation, scale, uniqueness, integration	Often best blend of improvement pressures, relationships, backup, scale	Capacity limits with single source
	Backup risk is acceptable		Fastest backup on critical items
			High technical risk
			Variability is manageable

STEPS IN SUPPLY BASE REDUCTION

The first stage in supply base reduction is to identify the needs of all relevant users. The second is to characterize the current supply base. When Motorola took these steps for the tens of millions of capacitors it buys each year, the company found 110 different capacitor suppliers for the communications sector, which had grown seemingly without limit. Opportunities for scale economies based on supplier volume were being missed. Costs were even higher because orders to the same firm from various Motorola units often involved different paperwork, procedures, and specifications. Further, individual firms that supplied several Motorola units often received mixed signals from them. People also found that 80 percent of the business was with a few suppliers. The others were filling niches or had longstanding relationships with individual buyers.

By eliminating clear redundancies, the number of suppliers was cut from 110 to about 25. Immediate cost savings in paperwork and logistics were so dramatic that they more than justified the costs of expanding the effort to other commodities.

Motorola next took a closer look at the remaining 25 capacitor suppliers and asked what would be required to meet all of its needs from a reliable supply base. On paper it seemed possible to end up with 3 to 5 firms, but getting there would be far more difficult than making the initial cut from 110 to 25. Design incompatibilities in Motorola products prevented part standardization, and suppliers that served Motorola's needs in each broad commodity category had varying abilities. Sorting through this "became a giant chess game" because of the number of variables, says Bob Becknell, then director of sourcing for the communications sector. A full year was needed to reduce the number of suppliers to about 15, and efforts are still under way to trim even more.

Commenting on the differences between surviving suppliers and others—and underscoring Motorola's emphasis on quality—Tom Slaninka, a participant in the process, says the losers could be divided into three groups: those "chasing fast-growth business" that were less concerned with quality, those that "got the message about quality but just did not get on with it fast enough," and those that were dropped because they were not concentrating on the same technology as Motorola.

One key step in reducing a supply base is to set up the metrics, logistics systems, and quality audits needed for partner choice and objective performance measurement—both to spot and resolve problems and as a basis for focused competition. Doing all that at Motorola for major commodities such as printed circuit boards, plastics, and semiconductors required full-time, analytically strong people. Once that was done, maintaining the process took less effort.

To further reduce its supply base, Motorola is encouraging its supply partners (it calls them "preferred suppliers") to broaden their product

product. To achieve the best cost and performance of each assembly, the user must understand the components and materials, as well as how they are integrated. If this expertise is not within the firm's core competence, however, better costs and integration can be often achieved by delegating the work to suppliers that specialize in the area.

Chrysler, for example, used to design and buy components for its car seats from more than two hundred suppliers, assembling the seats in its factories. Now, the automaker works with just three seating suppliers that do all of the design and assembly of complete seats. These firms in turn work with their own suppliers in areas where this is most cost effective. Making this change—and similar ones with other assemblies—has helped Chrysler dramatically reduce its supply base. Once, the company had thousands of direct suppliers; now, about 90 percent of Chrysler's purchasing volume is with 150 suppliers.

Comments Tom Stallkamp, vice president, procurement and supply, and general manager, large car operations: "We've arranged so many marriages among suppliers I'm beginning to feel like Yente, the matchmaker from *Fiddler on the Roof.*"

This reduction in supplier numbers is spreading up the supply chain. Allied Signal Automotive, a major first-tier company, cut the number of its suppliers from 2,400 at the start of the 1990s to 1,000 by mid-1994 and expects to reduce this to 900. Valeo of France, which had 3,500 suppliers in Europe in mid-1991, is expected to have just 1,000 by the end of 1995.[5]

The value of using tiered assembly relationships includes services as well as manufacturing. Consider that Philips Consumer Electronics Company used to buy fasteners (such as screws, eyelets, and Velcro) from many suppliers but changed to having Semblex, a screw maker, take full responsibility for making those purchases. Thanks to Semblex's greater expertise with fasteners—and despite a handling fee it charges—the total cost has been lower than when PCEC did the buying.

Because assemblies are typically major building blocks of the customer's product, and are the last stage in its supply chain, the firms that produce them are known as first-tier suppliers, with *their* direct suppliers being called second-tier firms, and so on. In general, the advantages of tiered supply arrangements for complex systems requiring substantial integration include the following:

Shorter Lines of Communication. Arranging a supply chain in tiers facilitates understandings and cooperation among firms whose parts
interact substantially.

Better Technology Focus. A tiered arrangement concentrates expertise
around relevant technologies, leading to enhanced performance,
cost, and quality through improved design and integration.

Shorter Order Cycles. An assembler that is an expert in its area is more
likely to have an inventory of parts relevant to the customer's needs
or close relationships with suppliers of those parts, either of which
can shorten the customer's order cycle.

Lower Cost. Each of the above benefits contributes to better costs, as
does the higher volume of an outside assembler compared with a
customer doing its own assembly.

Better Responses to Order Spurts. An assembler serving more than one
customer (or customer unit) with assemblies having common parts
is less likely to run out of stock on a part and can adjust to faster
order spurts from its customers.

Higher Motivation. Because an outside assembler has more visibility
with the customer and a larger role in adding value than suppliers
of individual parts, it has more reason to make its best effort.

In moving to a tiered arrangement, suppliers of assembly components change from direct relationships with the customer into second-,
third-, or lower-tier positions. If those firms have substantial leverage
on the customer's product, the customer may keep some direct ties
with them to ensure effective understandings and long-term alignment.
Chrysler forms direct links with any suppliers whose performance significantly affects the cost or value of its cars. One such relationship is
with GE Plastics, which is not a direct supplier.

As noted in Chapter 2, another requirement for an assembler is a
high competence in systems integration. One more needed skill is an
ability to manage its own supply relationships as effective alliances. To
ensure an effective supply chain, Motorola requires an assembly supplier that is new to the task to work with other preferred Motorola suppliers as *its* suppliers. Chrysler does not specify second- or third-tier
suppliers, because each first-tier assembler must be comfortable with

and take responsibility for relationships with its own suppliers. But, like Motorola, the automaker recommends a short list of approved suppliers to the assemblers.

In moving to a tiered arrangement for seating, Chrysler first outsourced the assembly work while continuing to do the component sourcing and helping the first-tier firms to develop their design capabilities. After those firms took over full design responsibility, Chrysler transferred component sourcing to them.

Because of the more stringent selection criteria for assemblers, and since the nature of their work often requires deeper understandings and more integration with the customer than is needed with suppliers of parts or materials, they can be harder to replace. For these reasons, alliances with assembly firms should be more stable than other supply relationships. To keep that stability, each assembler must be willing and able to work with other firms that offer new developments, even when those innovations would replace the assembler's own technology. This responsibility tends to cause assemblers to become masters of integration, while second- and lower-tier firms focus more on component and material innovation.

Earning Suppliers' Commitments

A customer's expectations for constant improvement by its suppliers create tension in relationships, which can be destructive. For an alliance to function, these demands must be offset by other forces that encourage suppliers' commitments.

Suppliers to Marks & Spencer, for example, uniformly describe the retailer as by far their most demanding customer. Yet while M&S and other High Street retailers design their products with many of the same suppliers, the very best design, liaison, and plant people are usually put on the M&S account. The suppliers do this because Marks & Spencer respects their margins in price negotiations and helps them stay at the cutting edge with the finest production and other systems in the United Kingdom. Says Carole O'Beirne, "When you talk to a woman on the production line, she is proud to be part of the whole M&S process." Although M&S owns none of these factories, they still consider themselves part of the M&S team.

How hard a firm works for a customer depends on how it is treated.

The more a customer meets a supplier's needs, the more that firm will stretch. The most obvious supplier needs are stable and growing revenues, healthy margins, continued independence, and credible opportunities for new business. Another is to be treated fairly. When a supplier has problems, for instance, the best course for the customer is to help solve them rather than go to the expense of finding and developing a new partner. Besides, it is not consistent with experience or a root-cause attitude toward problem solving to automatically blame suppliers' problems on them. Many such issues originate in how customers manage the relationships. Clearly, customers should also avoid behavior that could damage a supplier.

PROVIDE OPPORTUNITIES TO IMPROVE

Also vital—but often overlooked—is the need for advanced competitive skills and help in other areas that are important to suppliers. Just as a supplier must keep winning its customer's business, so too must the customer win its supplier's loyalty to get the most value from that firm.

In the scrap metal market, there has been more demand than supply for high-quality product. To encourage suppliers to favor it with their capacity allocations, Outokumpu has worked to meet their needs better than its rivals that also buy from them, and to seek creative solutions to their problems. Examples include teaching scrap suppliers how to separate high-quality from low-quality metal, always paying on time, giving suppliers better forecasts, and paying in cash when this is desired. Similarly, in addition to the volume and learning advantages suppliers get from working with M&S, they get more regular and prompt payments (usually within twenty days) than they do from most other customers, which helps the suppliers' cash flow.

With remarkable consistency, suppliers whose customers rate them highly credit the benefits they get from these alliances as a key source of their motivation to do their best. Consider that, on a volume basis, Motorola is not the top priority customer for all its suppliers. For that reason, it is constantly working to attract their attention by helping them improve their quality and understand their cost drivers, among other means.

One popular Motorola tactic is an annual competition for total customer satisfaction teams. Open to preferred suppliers, these events are unrelated to winning new business. Instead, they promote increased learning within and across the suppliers on processes (such as cycle time reduction) that are important to them and to Motorola's customers. More generally, an informal benchmarking network has developed among preferred suppliers in which they exchange data with each other to move ahead collectively. Says Ron Schubel, president of the commercial products division at Molex, "We are members of a shared learning community."

Motorola represents a small fraction of Molex's business, and meeting its needs takes extra work. Even so, that effort is justified by the skills Molex gets from the alliance. Schubel says his firm's partnership with Motorola "has allowed us to develop products and services that helped us move forward in the marketplace with other customers. Motorola is often pushing our product, process, and business systems envelopes. Thanks to what they have taught us about quality, we went from most of our products being inspected on receipt to virtually none. Further, when we see what Motorola is doing internally—such as using total customer satisfaction teams—we become evangelists in our own company."

The skills Molex gains from its work with Motorola, including lower costs from higher quality, yield better margins on other business. Schubel regards this as "a survival issue more than a marginal one." Profit margins on Molex's business with Motorola are *not* healthier than they were before their alliance; in fact, profit is a little lower. But Motorola's revenue contribution to Molex is much higher than before. Pressure on margins comes from Motorola, as well as from other customers.

Other ways that Motorola actively seeks to help its suppliers—and win their favor—include promoting new developments and assisting with volume declines. For example, the Paging Products Group worked with Seiko to develop a manufacturing robot. Since PPG needed only a few of the devices, it helped showcase the development for other firms that were potential buyers. As another example, if reducing volume for a particular part with a supplier will hurt that firm, Motorola tries to find something else that firm can make for it. "We really don't want a ramp-down," says Neil MacIvor, the strategic sourcing director. "We could lose capacity, and it could hurt our relationship with the firm."

For Kodak's Vaughn Hovey, who led the formation of his firm's alliance with IBM, helping IBM in ways that are valuable to the computer firm reinforces its commitment to Kodak. Frank Palm, IBM's lead executive, says that, compared with arm's-length relationships, his company's largest benefit from the alliance is the new skills and opportunities that have come from meeting Kodak's constantly advancing expectations. "Vaughn Hovey really stretches me to provide better service and be more competitive," says Palm, "which makes me distinctly more viable in the outside marketplace. We have refined service-level management to a high art. Our learning is generic to other customers as well." Other important IBM benefits from the Kodak alliance include a reduced need for marketing expenses, and a long-term revenue stream and profits.

Kodak has also prodded IBM to consider new activities that offer potential value. For example, Kodak asked Solution Center Rochester (SCR)—the IBM unit responsible for the alliance—to install two midrange computers for its use. When SCR declined Kodak approached Frank Palm, who also said no; he thought it would be more cost effective for Kodak to handle the two devices on its own. Then Vaughn Hovey pointed out that Kodak had installed many of the computers, and if Kodak had those needs it was likely other firms did, too. "Vaughn described the opportunity in ways I had not considered," says Palm. "He stuck his finger in my eye—he really pushed me hard to go after it." SCR now provides the service for IBM across the United States.

MAINTAIN SUPPLIERS' INDEPENDENCE

Every firm, as a supplier, hopes to grow and prosper by serving its customers, setting its own long-term course, and avoiding pitfalls not of its making. Customers benefit from this independence and should contribute to it, because it produces the strongest suppliers—and earns their highest commitments.

Limit Volume. One way to contribute to supplier independence is to limit the amount of business given to each firm. Motorola wants enough of a supplier's plant capacity to get the desired attention to quality, costs, and Schedule Sharing (its inventory management system). But it does not want so large a share that a downturn would damage the firm. Motorola has thus reduced its volume with some suppliers when it believed it was getting too much of their business. Another concern has been that a supplier could not handle major volume upturns.

For these reasons, Motorola prefers not to have more than 50 percent of a firm's business. While the figure may seem high, there have not always been enough competent suppliers. Further, Motorola's rapid growth in some areas has caused concern at smaller suppliers, because they have not been able to build comparable volume with other customers. In the longer run, this issue is resolved by developing additional sources.

Seasonal volume swings at Philips Consumer Electronics Company are more dramatic than business fluctuations at Motorola, so PCEC limits its business with each supplier to 15 percent of that supplier's annual volume. The TV set business is very seasonal, with the highest sales being around the Christmas buying season. A supplier therefore would starve from January to June, then have a feast in the fall if it were significantly dependent on PCEC. Further, not all suppliers can or want to meet PCEC's ramp-up and ramp-down requirements. PCEC likes to see room for capacity increase should that be needed, and thus feels more comfortable staying below 15 percent of a supplier's business.

Facilitate Learning. Another reason to limit a supplier's volume is to ensure that it benefits from wider experience. By serving the unique demands of other customers, a supplier gains understandings and perspectives that benefit all of them. Consider that, while Motorola helps its suppliers adapt best practices in quality and other areas, it is not concerned that many of those firms also serve its rivals, which benefit from those learnings. This is because Motorola also benefits from the experience its suppliers get from those other customers.

Marks & Spencer, by contrast, does not limit the business it gives suppliers. It is worth understanding why. First, because M&S is at the cutting edge of value in its markets and is the highest-volume clothing retailer in Britain, it has been able to offer suppliers more stability. Second, M&S has helped its suppliers stay at the forefront in technical areas like quality and fabric innovation, and has little to gain in those areas from suppliers' experience in serving its rivals. Further, in clothing, much of the innovation that propels M&S ahead is done by producers of fibers and textiles that are supplied to the first-tier firms, which in turn manufacture garments for M&S. The innovators do serve many customers and benefit from these experiences.

Desmond & Sons, the Londonderry-based garment maker, decided to sell exclusively to Marks & Spencer in the 1960s, when its sole product was men's pajamas. At the time, Desmonds was much smaller than it is today, and M&S offered considerably more volume—enough to take most of Desmonds' capacity. Additionally, other customers were less reliable than M&S. Observes Denis Desmond, "One must have the confidence to go into an exclusive relationship."

Respect Suppliers' Cost Structures. A firm's cost structure is another aspect of its independence. On this point, Chrysler, Motorola, and Marks & Spencer are of one mind. From joint value engineering, benchmarking, quality audits, and other sources, they may know each supplier's direct costs for a particular product. But they do not know or wish to know all aspects of a supplier's costs. Having that information puts the customer in the position of being able to use it. Every firm has its own cost structure and must be free to manage its costs and allocate its resources for its own benefit. Providing a customer with information about all costs thus may lead the customer to try to manage those costs inappropriately. "At the end of the day," says Northern Foods' Chris Haskins, "the supplier must be independent to stay competitive. Having independent suppliers is necessary to have competition among them."

Accept Separate Decision Making. To be independent, a firm must be free to decide all matters according to its own best interests. At both Motorola and Marks & Spencer, suppliers are free to decline business without any recrimination if price negotiations move into an unacceptable range. Similarly, it is up to the supplier to conclude independently whether it will support a new product idea, just as the customer must decide whether it will adapt a supplier's idea. Of course, independence can cut two ways. For instance, M&S tried to interest Northern Foods in producing chicken kiev, but Haskins said it would not sell well. M&S then got another supplier to make it; and the product became a spectacular success for that firm.

Avoid Damage

Customer actions over which suppliers have no control may cause harm and reduce their commitments. Such events can occur in negotiations if the customer pushes beyond reasonable limits, or in the regular course of an alliance. If they cannot be avoided, it is in the customer's interest to balance the situation.

In the Kodak–IBM alliance, for example, Vaughn Hovey and Frank Palm both recognize that neither firm can afford to do anything that would hurt the other. For instance, soon after a new Colorado data center to be operated by IBM came on line, Kodak's needs declined from initial expectations, so its share of the total cost was lower than had been budgeted. To balance the loss and keep IBM's enthusiasm, Hovey agreed to cover the difference until volume became consistent with the original plan. He did this because he was convinced IBM would bring more value to the alliance—which it did—and he did not want to discourage their commitment.

Share Appropriate Risks

To earn suppliers' commitments and best performance, each firm should be accountable for those actions over which it has substantial control. How Motorola, Marks & Spencer, and Chrysler do this reflects the differences in their businesses.

Because Motorola's suppliers directly affect its costs, quality, and timing, they are held responsible for meeting increasingly stringent objectives in those areas. Other factors that affect its marketing risks (including product design, development, manufacturing, and marketing), however, are largely under its control. For that reason, Motorola may pay for a supplier's unique capital equipment if that firm cannot use it for other purposes (given the risk that a product may not meet expectations). By the same logic, Motorola typically uses stepped pricing, wherein the price it pays for parts depends on their volume, which in turn hinges on Motorola's product volume. And if Motorola decides to lower its margins to improve its own product pricing, the firm may work harder with suppliers to reduce their costs, but will not expect them to lower their margins.

Now, consider how Marks & Spencer shares risks with its suppliers.

By contrast to the situation at Motorola, since M&S is a retailer its suppliers' goods are sold directly in the marketplace. While M&S has the final say on product design, the suppliers play a key role and, of course, are responsible for manufacturing. Further, M&S depends on suppliers' continuing ideas about how to improve the value of their products. If an item is selling poorly, M&S wants immediate counsel from the supplier about how to adjust the value or replace it with something better. These factors cause M&S to share virtually all marketing risks with its suppliers, a decision that gives them the greatest possible incentive to contribute to their products' success. For example, investments for new product lines are made separately by each firm, with the decisions being made independently.

Chris Haskins describes how M&S sometimes wants his firm to make a capital investment for a product, but Northern is not confident enough about the prospects, so declines the opportunity. Whenever possible such decisions are facilitated with product trials, but that cannot always be done. Still, Haskins notes that he has occasionally made the wrong decision—both ways. Similarly, although it sells exclusively to Marks & Spencer, Desmonds is free to decide whether to accept new oportunities. The pendulum has swung both ways, with each company rejecting or accepting the other's advice.

Unlike Motorola, Marks & Spencer does not use stepped pricing with its suppliers, which therefore benefit from increased volumes. Additionally, while M&S competes most intensely on value, when it wants to offer more attractive pricing to generate and retain more volume, it first looks for cost reductions in packaging, factory utilization, and joint value engineering. It may also negotiate margin reductions with its suppliers. Any margin reduction is shared by M&S as well. Suppliers are accustomed to the process and, occasionally, decline to go along.

Current practices in the auto industry further illustrate the principle of accountability and the merits of assigning it correctly. In every car, the design and functioning of most parts are so highly integrated with other components that should one part fail, it is not always possible to determine the source of the problem. In such cases, the automaker assumes the risk. In other cases, such as with tires and batteries, it is easier to attribute failure to the design or manufacture of those items, which is why they carry separate warranties.

In a high-trust environment, the customer and supplier will do a root-cause analysis together to identify and fix any problems. Doing that helps both firms move to higher performance levels. Risk sharing might then be used if the source of a difficulty can be clearly assigned, and if any penalty will not damage the supplier. Without trust, however, problem analysis often leads to finger pointing and attempts to avoid blame.

The different ways to encourage supply partners' priority attention, and the logic for appropriate risk sharing, are summarized in the tables shown on the following pages. Additional aspects are discussed in the following chapters.

REGARDING EXCLUSIVITY

Many firms would naturally prefer exclusive use of a supplier's unique, valuable developments, just as many suppliers would prefer not having to compete for a customer's business. Exclusive access by the customer is legitimate if it provided much (or preferably most) of the relevant know-how, or if it must protect unique investments made to capitalize on a supplier's development. Similarly, freedom from competition for a limited time encourages suppliers to bring a customer their new developments.[6]

In each case, continuing an exclusive relationship indefinitely can hurt both firms, by denying the benefits of focused competition, scale, and wider supplier experience to the customer, and the opportunities for larger markets to the supplier. The best way to resolve these issues is to discuss them at the start and to recognize that, in the longer term, non-exclusivity is often in the best interests of both firms. In fact, exclusivity is always temporary, because all know-how eventually diffuses to others or is surpassed by new practices. Finally, since customer–supplier alliances create unique value, they have the appearance of exclusivity. That may lead to friction with other trading partners, which believe they have been shortchanged.

The experience of an alliance between a North American retail chain and a consumer goods maker is illustrative. This alliance, one of many in the retail business, was producing clear benefits for both firms soon after it started. But the visibility of those results generated complaints from other retailers that the manufacturer was receiving too

Encouraging Suppliers to Excel	
Growth	Train in valuable new skills
	Provide benchmarking opportunities
	Help promote their new developments
	Spot new growth areas for them
	Grant reasonable exclusivity for new ideas
Operations	Give reliable order patterns
	Pay promptly
	Facilitate level loading
	Assist with volume declines
	Fill capacity when possible
Relationships	Apply root-cause approach in problem solving
	Honor their suggestions as equals
	Use objective measures in decisions
	Build long-term mutually valuable commitments
Independence	Permit acceptable margins
	Limit amount of business done with each
	Respect their cost structures
	Protect proprietary know-how
	Accept separte decisions know-how
	Accept separate decision making
Avoid damage	Use reasonable limits in negotiations
	Balance unexpected harmful events
	Share appropriate risks
	Cooperate to introduce new practices

close to this retailer. The others perceived that the retailer was receiving better prices than they were. In fact, the supplier had not lowered its prices. Costs were lower due to how the firms worked together.

Still, for many years, the manufacturer had nourished a reputation of being evenhanded with retailers, and the complaints hurt. To address the others' concerns, the firm explained to them that the prices it could offer its retail partner were the benefits of cooperation, not favoritism. That response helped, and it was later buttressed as the other retailers learned more about the benefits of alliances.

Risk Sharing By Customer and Supplier		
Supplier Attribute or Activity	**Supplier's Influence on Customer's Performance**	
	Low	**High**
Unique capital investment	Customer may help if supplier has no other uses	Supplier invests
Pricing	By volume	Volume independent
Margins	Risks not shared	Risks shared
Costs, performances	Moderate accountability	High accountability

Another response by the two partners has been for them to minimize exclusivity in areas where doing so did not seriously harm their alliance. For example, one system they developed was shared with other retailers. At first the retail partner resisted this move. But the manufacturer made a convincing case that sharing was necessary to get the scale economies needed to benefit fully from the development.

Probably the most important tactic has been to keep moving the alliance ahead while sharing past results with others. This emphasis on continued improvement reflects a mutual belief that only by staying at the value frontier can both partners keep ahead of their respective rivals. At the same time, each firm has been forming alliances with others and shares the results from those when it is appropriate. In the end, how much value each firm gets from its own alliances, plus its internal activities, will be the sole determinant of its well-being. In dynamic markets there is no safety in exclusivity.

4

PRACTICES FOR JOINT CREATIVITY

If our suppliers are going to bring their best to us, they have to understand what our customers want. We believe that by sharing information with them, Marks & Spencer will be a better business.

Barry Morris, director for men's clothing, Marks & Spencer

We have tremendous access to M&S internal information.

Denis Desmond, chairman, Desmond & Sons

To elicit suppliers' best work, alliances require focused competition and measures that earn their commitment. Also essential is a set of practices that encourage customer and supplier to be creative together. Although it may seem obvious, alliances are built on shared objectives. The failure of many such efforts can be traced directly to their absence.

Set Clear Objectives

Cooperation works best when everyone understands and is committed to the same purpose. A shared objective—such as a specific cost target—guides joint design efforts and is the basis for allocating and aligning resources, raising and resolving issues, and more generally for alliance management.

HAVE SHORT-TERM AND LONG-TERM PRIORITIES

Since customer–supplier alliances produce increasing value over time, a set of complementary short-term and long-term objectives are needed to facilitate current activities and support joint planning. Near-term objectives involve current performance and reflect the partners' existing abilities; for the longer term, objectives describe targets to be reached through continuing organizational and technology development.

Motorola, for example, constantly reminds its suppliers and its own people of its relentless long-term drive for "Six Sigma" quality, as well as its more recent commitment to reducing cycle times. (Six Sigma, a well-known term in quality management, means having no more than 3.4 defects for every million items produced.) Those long-term objectives are backed up by rigorously enforced performance measures for current internal and external activities, resource allocation for training and development, constant organizational renewal, and senior management attention to how well performance trends are moving toward the long-term goals.

Similarly, Marks & Spencer and its suppliers share a clear understanding of its objectives. "They are absolutely product driven," says Noel Jervis, chief executive of Courtaulds Textiles, a major supplier. "Creativity is their prime goal. They want to maintain dominance through offering consumers more product value than anyone else." Like Motorola, M&S and its suppliers heed short-term performance measures related to current objectives, and they target longer-term goals by constantly monitoring trends in consumer desires and technological possibilities.

OBJECTIVES FOR MULTI-PROJECT ALLIANCES

Alliances between two firms often require a way to set priorities among a large number of possible projects. One way to do this is with a total cost–performance model, which compares all projects to the same overall objective. A related approach is to develop a set of more specific subordinate objectives that clearly contribute to the overall objective, then weigh all projects in that context.

For instance, in one large North American alliance between a retail chain and a maker of consumer goods, the firms' shared vision is to build an integrated partnership that helps each of them better serve the consumer. Their scope is the creation and delivery of any product—from its conception to when the consumer uses it. To guide their many activities, the firms identified four objectives that support their overall vision: higher profits, increased market share, lowered costs, and simpler ways of doing business together. They agreed to judge each proposed project on how it contributes to one or more of those objectives for both firms.

Begin Early, Avoid Constraints

In traditional competitive bidding, a customer often asks suppliers to suggest new ways to meet its needs. Usually it is disappointed by the few, narrow responses it gets. Such frustrations are inherent in conventional bidding because the customer fixes its specifications at the start of the bid process, thereby discouraging creativity between customer and supplier. Neither firm has a chance to explore the other's thinking and expose its own partial ideas. As a result, there are change orders to the initial specification, costly redesigns, inevitable delays, unproductive misunderstandings, supplier innovations that are limited to those requiring minimal customer interaction, and a chance that the supplier's development costs may not be recouped. Each factor encourages suppliers to keep to the original specification. Consequently, customers do not get suppliers' best ideas, and suppliers are inhibited in their own progress.

By contrast, consider that firms like Marks & Spencer, Chrysler, Motorola, and Philips Consumer Electronics Company involve key suppliers at the concept stage in their product planning—long before any specification can be written—and reap the benefits of shared expertise. For example, given the chance to influence PCEC's thinking before other designs were set, Molex suggested innovative connector arrangements that avoided assembly and reliability problems in new TV sets. Similarly, in designing and building Ford's paint finishing plant in Oakville, Canada, the automaker and Asea Brown Boveri deferred setting the final price and specifications until they had fully examined the project, developed new approaches that better met their objectives, and finished a complete and definitive design. The result, as noted in Chapter 2, was dramatically lower costs and a near-record completion time.

Motorola's Len de Barros, a corporate vice president and general manager in the Paging Products Group, points out that it is a mistake to get locked into a specification before knowing what can actually be done. He illustrates this by describing a joint robotics development for PPG undertaken by suppliers Seiko and Automatix. When these firms told PPG that some things it wanted were beyond technology possibilities at the time, the plans were changed accordingly. Motorola accepts such limits statements from suppliers because it knows it is working with best-in-class firms.

To complete his point about being flexible on expectations, de Barros notes that if one picks excellent suppliers and gives them room to do their best, flexibility is not a constraint. He tells of the time when PPG decided to outsource robot tables (the rigid platform on which a robot is mounted) and simply handed the specifications to a local contract manufacturer. When the firm suggested improvements on the design, it was given direct engineering ties to PPG manufacturing and made part of the design process for robots. By applying its knowledge of robot tables in that process, the supplier cut development time and helped improve overall robot system accuracy—a critical factor in PPG's manufacturing agility. In turn, the skills this supplier has gained from its experience are used with other customers.

Just as early participation with the customer creates more value for it, so can early customer participation in a supplier's developments. For instance, traditional practice in the commercial airliner business has been for the manufacturer to offer its finished product to customers, then wait for comments based on their experience with the aircraft to make design changes in future generations. Anything more than modest changes around a standard design would require prohibitively expensive new tooling. To reach beyond that practice and create more value for its customers, Boeing asked three of them—British Airways, All Nippon Airways, and United Airlines—to participate in the final design of its 777 airliner. One result is that the 777 has the flexibility to allow an airline to move galleys, toilets, and seats whenever it wishes.[1]

Share All Relevant Information

Innovation thrives on knowledge. With that understanding, Marks & Spencer shares virtually all data about its business with its suppliers (except for personnel matters, internal margins, and data about other suppliers). That includes all qualitative and quantitative marketing research, its own sales, inventory, pricing strategies, raw material sourcing tactics, and information about design and technology. Suppliers see weekly M&S sales data for their goods and total product line volume, but not data on other individual firms. Just as important, M&S suppliers share all their relevant data with it.

Listen to Barry Morris, the M&S director responsible for men's clothing: "I would not feel constrained to share information if that helped develop our mutual business. If our suppliers are going to bring their best to us, they have to understand what our customers want. We believe that by sharing information with them, M&S will be a better business." Denis Desmond, chairman of a leading M&S supplier, echoes Morris by noting that his firm "has tremendous access to M&S internal information." He adds that performing well for M&S means not only responding to its needs but second-guessing what it wants and innovating beyond the frontiers it has defined. Both strategies require the clearest possible picture from M&S as to how it sees the world.

Similarly, Philips Consumer Electronics Company begins its product design process by sharing all relevant information with key suppliers whose parts leverage the cost or performance of its TV sets. Shared data include PCEC product performance goals, demand forecasts, market share, proprietary market research, installation parameters, field failure rates, consumer complaints, warranty problems, and confidential profit and loss data on relevant product lines. The latter is shared informally and helps PCEC suppliers appreciate the reality of competitive pressures on it. This kind of interaction, says one supplier, "allows us to give PCEC the maximum possible value for their money. Yet it is rare with other customers."

Aside from information about personnel, core competencies, and total cost structures, or items that might alert rivals—which may also be suppliers—to one's future plans, the more that is shared the better. To reduce joint costs, for example, firms must communicate openly with each other about what is affecting those costs. Significantly, the opposite is also true: Suppliers often add a risk premium to their pricing (thus raising the customer's costs) to cover nondisclosed or unexplored customer requirements or design flaws that may require later adjustments.

By not sharing relevant information, a customer defeats its own objectives. An executive at one supplier recalls that before Motorola shifted to supply alliances, its engineers often came to meetings and said they would not provide any program start-up information or describe what the supplier's parts would be interfacing with. As a result, the supplier could not optimize the parts; the executive says it was "like driving a car at night without the headlights on." His firm could not invest in needed tooling, and costly hand labor and redesigns were often needed to fix problems with the parts that were made.

The limits on what can be shared are determined by how much the customer and supplier trust each other, and by the number of firms involved. The higher that number, the greater the chances of a damaging information leak. To illustrate, while M&S has at most only a few suppliers for any given item, Motorola typically has several score suppliers for each of its products. Thus, whereas M&S shares sales data with relevant suppliers, Motorola's Paging Products Group does not. PPG considered sharing raw pager volume with suppliers, but rejected the idea for sensitivity reasons. Instead, suppliers get part demand forecasts.

Protect Each Firm's Ideas

Alliances require a solid understanding that neither firm will take an idea from the other and give it to that firm's rivals. Otherwise, information sharing would obviously be inhibited. Also required, when inventions are involved, is a set of practices that clarifies ownership and avoids conflict in that area.

"It is a cardinal sin," says Chrysler's Steve Zimmer, commenting on a supplier that leaks confidential Chrysler information to rivals. Fears about this happening raise an issue in the company, because its engineers want to show design models to suppliers, but the automaker's designers tend to be reluctant to do so. Still, if Chrysler ideas do leak out, it is difficult to find the source. Chrysler expects suppliers to protect its sensitive information by using separate facilities and other practices. Of course, it is acceptable for generic learning to flow to others, but not specific designs.

SAFEGUARD SENSITIVE INFORMATION

A typical way to protect sensitive information is to build "Chinese walls" within a firm to segregate the use of others' confidential material.

Some customers, including Chrysler, Motorola, and Marks & Spencer, require that suppliers dedicate a facility to them to help avoid inadvertent disclosure.[2] McCann-Erickson, the advertising group, has opened separate offices across the street from its main office in various cities to help prevent any inappropriate contact between employees working on rivals' accounts.

It is not always practical, however, to make these separations. In such cases, one has to rely on the integrity of people and their organization. Motorola's Paging Products Group works with a single supplier for any one part, except when there are capacity limits. If another supplier is needed, this firm must create its own design. To do that, PPG's product designers give it the same original data, updated, that they gave the first supplier. In no case does PPG share one supplier's designs with another. But PPG's designers could not do their job without having both firms' designs. Of course, the first supplier is also kept current with updated data.

Molex often provides critical parts to direct rivals, with the designs based on sensitive information each customer has shared. Sometimes the data are isolated in separate groups within Molex. But when both customers' parts must be made with the same unique process technology, one Molex employee may have the confidential information from both firms. Even so, there has never been a problem.

This need to rely on people's integrity is important for alliances. Food companies, for example, get proprietary ingredients from firms specializing in those substances. To avoid any health problems, food company toxicologists must have full disclosure of the makeup of the ingredients. Still, it is understood that such information does not go beyond them. As another example, when Kodak and IBM develop a list of joint projects, neither firm wants to share its relevant cost structure with the other. When this is necessary, two trusted individuals from each firm discuss them confidentially, agreeing on what pricing would be fair to both firms. Their conclusions are accepted by both firms.

Clearly, the know-how gained from another firm's proprietary information potentially could be used in other areas. This may be a sensitive issue. To maintain trust, it is best to check with the source firm. For instance, Molex asks permission before it shares with others a development achieved with Motorola, or any other customer. This is the mirror image of Motorola not taking one of Molex's custom designs to other suppliers. Of course, even if sharing is not a problem, when Molex develops a unique part for a customer, that firm wants to be sure its volume needs are met before Molex can sell the new part to others. In the IBM–Kodak alliance, IBM must have Kodak approval to bring in a new outside customer at the data center, because the presence of rivals of Kodak units might cause those units to leave the alliance.

CLARIFY INVENTION OWNERSHIP

Within a firm's core competence and in other areas where an invention can make a critical competitive difference, full ownership is best. Otherwise, deciding who owns joint inventions requires weighing competitive advantage versus scale economies. Of course, inventions made separately by each firm are separately owned—unless one firm helps pay for another's development, in which case negotiation may be necessary. Even then, other factors can be more important in settling ownership.

The best time to negotiate the ownership and use of joint inventions is before a project begins. Often, the customer wants to own such inventions because they may enhance its competitive advantage. However, that can damage a supplier's future strengths by preventing it from capitalizing on an advance it helped create. It may also raise the customer's costs by preventing the supplier from gaining volume sales. One way to resolve this issue is to give the supplier full ownership of a joint invention, with a time delay when needed to assure the customer a head start. Major issues regarding rights transfers to suppliers should go to the corporate level, such as a technology transfer review board, for final decisions. One reason for this is that an invention may have value for other parts of the company.

Even when suppliers can sell joint developments to the customer's rivals, that may not give the rivals an edge. Motorola, for instance, regards its core strength as manufacturing integration. Thus, in manufacturing, since Motorola is more adept than others at using technology, allowing the sale to outsiders may not cause problems. To illustrate, when the Paging Products Group developed a major advance in manufacturing vision systems with suppliers Seiko and Automatix, it chose not to call the new system an invention, because doing so would have restricted its marketing to others and significantly raised PPG's cost.

When it is likely that particular inventions may be worth owning separately, the question of joint ownership can be avoided through early development. For instance, Motorola pursues some projects internally to solidify its proprietary rights before it initiates a project with a supplier.

Regarding the disclosure of sensitive information, Motorola follows the same principles as Marks & Spencer, with a narrower scope. In its core area of manufacturing, the company shares future plans with equipment suppliers on a very general level. Manufacturing technology "road maps," which detail specific future milestones and requirements, are not disclosed. By contrast, relevant road maps are shared with parts suppliers, because parts are a non-core area. Future product plans are not shared in any way. If Motorola has a proprietary component it shares only the performance interface, not the specifics of how it achieves the performance.

These points are summarized in the table shown. Evidently, M&S shares more with its partners than Motorola does with equipment suppliers. One reason may be that many equipment firms are also Motorola rivals.

Build Interfirm Teams

The benefits of cooperation come from integrating each firm's separate understandings into a more valuable whole. For that, joint teamwork is essential. Such teams must have the authority to make decisions and implement their conclusions. In this way, people are more committed to the task, shared understandings are sharper, and issues get resolved at immediate contact levels. The alternative—making decisions at higher management levels in each firm—slows the process. Further, when people make decisions away from the interface, they lack the direct understandings and trust that are essential for effectiveness.

At Chrysler, Motorola, and Marks & Spencer, virtually all cooperation with suppliers is done through two-company teams, and some tasks involve people from three or more firms on a single team.

In the Kodak–IBM alliance, the partners agreed to a course of continuously improving service levels for Kodak. This has required very close

Invention and Disclosure Guidelines		
	Critical Areas	**Noncritical Areas**
Ownership of joint inventions	Avoid joint inventions by separate inventing before cooperation	*Both:* If each will benefit from separate use
		Supplier: If benefit of its scale exceeds that of customer's exclusive use
		Customer: If benefit of its exclusive use exceeds that of supplier's scale
What to disclose	Performance interface	Based on time horizon, need to know, whether firms are rivals

collaboration between Kodak's applications software people and IBM's data center people, because service advances come from creative blends of software, hardware, and work practices from both sides. One result from the partners' teamwork has been an applications availability (how often everything works when users turn on their desktop computer terminals) of 99.85 percent, an exceptionally high number under any circumstances.

Teamwork pays significant dividends even in short-lived alliances. To illustrate, Inland Steel and Edward Gray, an engineering construction company, abandoned the traditional adversarial roles of owners and general contractors to complete the relining of an Inland blast furnace. At the start of the project, Inland and Gray held a two-day, off-site partnering workshop, assisted by a facilitator, to engage in team-building activities. Participants also developed a partnering charter and formal dispute-resolution procedure. To complement the teamwork, the firms defined their relationship as having equal involvement, agreed to share the risks and benefits, and used open-book negotiations. Thanks to these efforts, the project was completed three days ahead of the thirty-three-day schedule and under budget by 15 percent.[3]

Share Applicable Experiences

The extensive customer–supplier interactions needed for high performance will be more effective if partners help each other to adopt best practices in related management areas. Chapter 3 noted how customers earn their suppliers' commitments by helping them develop new skills and opportunities, and in other ways. Suppliers can behave in similar ways with their customers.

Consider PCEC, which has made a high art of learning from its suppliers. Tom Natale, vice president for operations in PCEC's color TV business, says that his firm, like others, often solved problems by "putting a band-aid on it and assuming it was fixed." Thus, if there was a quality issue with a supplier's part, it would be put on incoming inspection and then forgotten in the press of daily business.

Knowing it could do better than that, PCEC asked Molex to explain its quality system. Molex did this, also mentioning the "Eight D" approach it had adopted from Ford. This strategy goes beyond a quick fix to flush out the root cause of a problem and resolve it permanently. Wanting to know more, PCEC asked Ford to give three one-day seminars on the technique.

PCEC also sought help from Molex to implement electronic data interchange (EDI), which the supplier had already mastered. One early step was having someone from Molex lead a discussion on the topic. Later, PCEC asked Molex for help in developing a new purchase order system. After Molex suggested one based on its experience, the firms then shared issues and resolved problems together to get the system installed and working effectively.

Kelly Howell, an independent sales representative who calls on PCEC for Molex, says these activities were possible only in a partnership environment. The firms shared information, ran trials, discussed best configurations, and optimized the system together. In a non-partnership environment, Howell notes, if a customer asks for such help, it may get it but with less candor. A supplier wants to be confident it will benefit from such extra efforts and to know the results will be used constructively in the firms' mutual interests. Further, Howell says, the efforts of PCEC and Molex require sharing confidential information, which takes a trusting environment.

In a comparable experience, Chrysler asked Dow Chemical for help in developing improved team processes for its small-car platform team, and the automaker was delighted with the results. Ron Parker, Dow's business director for Chrysler, says: "We want to be the best supply partner for our customers. That goes beyond buying and selling. We ask ourselves what do we do that our customers can use."[4]

Plan an Expertise Overlap

Cooperation between people in different disciplines is easier when they have some knowledge about each other's area of expertise. Such shared understandings have minimal value in arm's-length relationships, where the dialogue is limited to specification and price. Alliances, however, require much more.

Len de Barros says Motorola has learned that trouble often follows when suppliers lack sufficient understanding of how their parts will be used. Motorola has had problems when it was not sufficiently familiar with suppliers' processes. Such gaps inhibit effective design and integration.

From experience, de Barros says it is not possible to specify a part sufficiently to cover all aspects of its use in complex products. To illustrate, he cites the time when a PPG specification on a capacitor did not say anything about it being plunged into a cold liquid in the assembly process. As a result, the capacitor failed. Further, when a factory is being "tuned" for better performance, knowledge gaps inhibit the flow of process information back to the supplier. Such voids can result in failed parts and painful time delays.

For these reasons, and due to limits on how much know-how it could share with others, Motorola decided to designate one in-house expert in each commodity area to help integrate suppliers into its products and processes. The experts also spot issues from the perspective of the final use of the part in Motorola products. The switch expert, for instance, not only understands the switch manufacturing process but also knows how switches are used across Motorola.

Having expert knowledge of a supplier's practices within a firm is not the same as having a supplier assign its people to the customer's site. Unlike the customer's experts, the supplier's knowledge is more tightly focused on the specifics of the task. The supplier's scope is also limited because it cannot be exposed to highly sensitive data. Further, customer employees who are acknowledged experts are typically called on to consult at several sites.

Challenge Each Other's Thinking

In the most effective relationships, each firm adds to the other's ideas and is free to question its assumptions, thereby putting the joint efforts on firmer ground. Comments Motorola Paging Products Group vice president Bob Becknell: "Suppliers are encouraged not to follow us blindly, but to question and check at every interval. In many cases, they have pointed out bad assumptions on our part." He recalls an occasion when Motorola was about to introduce a radio for railroads, and a sheet metal supplier challenged the volume projections. Just one unit was needed for each locomotive, yet sales projections exceeded the total number of locomotives. Motorola dropped the product.

Think in Terms of Systems

When Chrysler bought a new part from Inverness Castings Group, willingly paying 30 percent more than it had for the original part, the auto firm recognized an obvious but often overlooked fact: Key variables like cost, quality, design, and timing are linked, often in several ways. To optimize performance, these connections must be recognized. In Chrysler's case, although the new part cost more, its design contributed to a lower total vehicle cost because its use saved time in assembling the car and improved quality as well.[5]

Consider that arm's-length bidding allows each firm to work on its separate costs, but not on joint costs—which can account for as much as 20 to 40 percent of the separate costs. Only by identifying all cost drivers in both firms, and understanding how they interact, can one reduce total cost to the lowest levels. By the same logic, rather than seek best quality or fastest response time alone, the goal is best quality or response time *together*—both of which are invariably superior to what either firm can do by itself.

The two figures shown contrast both ways of thinking about performance. In the first, each company works in relative isolation; in the second, interfirm links are considered and managed as a combined whole. The latter approach is the path to greatest possible value. The second figure suggests the high degree of integration required—both within and between firms.

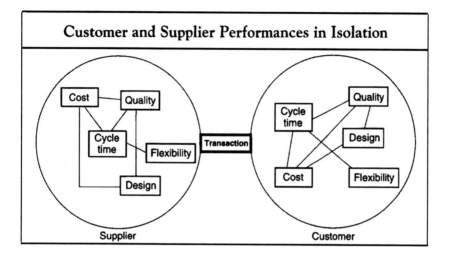

Customer and Supplier Performances in Isolation

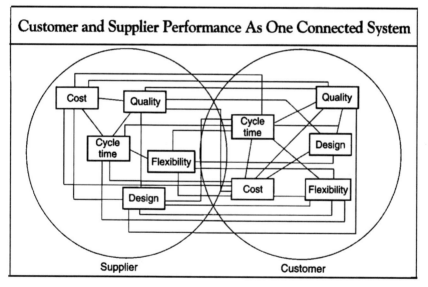

Customer and Supplier Performance As One Connected System

Define a Clear Interface

Cooperation should not mean a loss of identity for people or their organizations. Many decisions are still best made separately by each firm to avoid duplication, ensure clarity, and maintain independence. Further, people are most likely to do their best if they know their work will be used. For those reasons, Ford, Motorola, Chrysler, and Marks & Spencer give their suppliers performance guidelines, expecting those firms to produce the actual designs for what they will make. This

Practices for Joint Creativity	
Have clear objectives	Guides joint design and is the basis for allocating and aligning resources, raising and resolving issues, alliance management
	Long-term objectives for planning, short-term for specific activities
	Objectives hierarchy for large, multiproject alliances
Begin early, avoid constraints	Share thinking at concept stage; set specifications later
	Adjust objectives in light of new information
Share all relevant information	All data about objectives, marketing, pricing, sales, design, trends, warranty experience, customer problems
	Exclude only data about personnel, cost structures, core competencies, and that which would significantly benefit rivals
Protect each firm's ideas	Ensure nondisclosure to others
	Resolve invention ownership before cooperation
Build interfirm teams	Best results come from creatively joining both firms' expertise through empowered teams at the interface
Share applicable experience	Help each other adapt best practices in related management areas
Plan an expertise overlap	Understand each other's processes
Challenge each other's thinking	Legitimize each partner's questioning of other's assumptions
Think in terms of systems	Firms' cost, quality, timing, performance, other parameters are often interdependent, and best optimized together
Define a clear interface	Clarify separation of responsibility and authority between firms
Build trust	Essential for all else

practice also reduces not-invented-here attitudes, by depriving customer designers of the opportunity to create their own competing specifications.

Charlie Ross, Ford's director of strategic planning and process improvement, illustrates the need for a clear interface. When Ford has shared design responsibilities with suppliers, he says, it has been difficult to determine who is responsible for what task. Although Ford has the lead for integrating a component design into the overall vehicle, sharing the design responsibility on the same component creates confusion about who has the lead in that specific area, and designers from each firm often find themselves duplicating each other's work.

The practices discussed here that endow joint creativity, including the obvious need for trust described in Chapter 9, are summarized in the table shown.

5

COOPERATING FOR
MORE VALUE

*The more we do together in design, the better the design
and the less time needed to complete it.*

Gordon Couch, component applications engineer, Philips Consumer
Electronics Company

In any market, key sources of joint value creation include
better quality and design. To achieve the most value it is
essential to regard customer and supplier as one interconnected system,
and to examine how all value sources interact (see Chapter 4).

Value-adding practices may be initiated by either the customer or
the supplier. PCEC, for example, has working sessions with key customers to define how it can create more value for them. In those gatherings, PCEC personnel from marketing, sales, advertising, production,
quality, and finance are joined by customer representatives who have
the authority to commit their firms to agreed actions. Meeting over the
course of several days, people examine all aspects of their relationship,
resolve misconceptions, and jointly pursue beneficial projects to
improve how PCEC can deliver more value to the customer. Bill
Kennedy says that the first three of these meetings led to business
increases that, on average, *doubled* prior volumes.

Quality Is the Foundation

Quality across all aspects of an organization is a major determinant of cost, cycle time, product reliability, and customer value. The cost of poor quality—in terms of rejects, repairs, inspection, and returns—greatly raises an item's final costs. Many of Motorola's preferred suppliers, for example, do not offer the lowest price but are lowest in total cost. Neil MacIvor, director of strategic sourcing, Americas, notes that the Paging Products Group could buy virtually any part it uses for less if it chose to do so. But using lowest-price firms often results in higher total costs because of the need to fix quality problems, as well as the inability of these firms to provide the delivery or service required to meet business demands.

Alliances with suppliers can reach quality levels exceeding what even the best firms can do alone. Take Hewlett-Packard's U.K. temporary employee staffing alliance with Reed Personnel Services. Here, the combination of Reed's expertise in recruiting temporary help and the deeper understanding of H-P's needs that the alliance affords sharpen Reed's focus on serving its customer. This produces far better results than Reed could achieve for H-P in an arm's-length relationship or than H-P could realize by itself.

Motorola's relationships with its suppliers provide another insight. In these alliances, a key source of higher quality is better understandings—stemming from early design cooperation—about how suppliers' parts affect the quality of Motorola's products and how its requirements, in turn, influence suppliers' ability to make these parts. Such mutual learning leads to improved designs and processes, and total quality that is better than what Motorola could achieve alone.

To illustrate, the proposed design of a Motorola pager involved a printed circuit board that had much of its copper—which is used in the circuits—in one location. The board supplier knew a concentration of copper would make a board warp when it was warm, causing quality problems. Understanding the pager might be exposed to heat, it suggested an alternate design; Motorola accepted the suggestion and redesigned the board.

Customers can also help suppliers through quality audits and by sharing experience data with them (for example, on part fallout from manufacturing or warranty problems). Recognizing the tremendous leverage quality has on cost and other value sources, Motorola further helps its suppliers improve their manufacturing processes; it also requires them to take relevant courses at Motorola University, a fully accredited institution. Molex's Ron Schubel says Motorola's in-depth quality audit process, which gauges a firm's ability to meet Motorola's increasingly demanding requirements, "has been a tremendous catalyst" for change at his company and continues to have great value. He illustrates this by noting that Molex has requested more audits.

Combining for Design and Development

The process of cooperation in design depends on the customer's market and product, as well as its suppliers and the goods they provide. Several factors are important here: whether the customer is a retailer or distributor (so that its suppliers' goods sell directly in its market), the nature of competition in that market, the complexity of its product or system, and the expected life cycle of that product. Those factors are illustrated by how Marks & Spencer and its suppliers design clothing together, by the approach Philips Consumer Electronics Company uses to design TV sets, and by the process Motorola's Paging Products Group employs to develop manufacturing equipment with its suppliers. In each case, cooperation involves extensive information sharing and in-depth interactions that begin well before designs are crystallized.

CLOTHING DESIGN AT MARKS & SPENCER

M&S designs are driven by a combination of blue-sky creativity, a deep understanding of consumer needs, and advancing supplier innovations. The following describes the process in clothing; it is much the same in foods and household furnishings.

Pre-Concept Shared Learning. Due to development lead times— about eighteen months before product line introduction and long before product concepts are clarified—M&S designers and suppliers begin experimenting with colors. Their work is based on ongoing color development activities of the suppliers and Marks & Spencer's color standards group. Next, they determine which fabrics work well with those colors. All of the designers make inputs from their own experience, as well as from consumer research firms, on colors and styles for the coming season.

M&S wants a lot of sharing and mutual exploration during this early phase. Designers and M&S selectors (buyers) meet sometimes daily and at least weekly. Typically, they have worked together over the years and know each other well. Once there is agreement on the color palette, technical people in the M&S color lab standardize the color and provide specific guidelines to all suppliers.

In general, M&S buying departments begin considering garment concepts one year before their introduction. Meanwhile, technology people may be looking well beyond that—at advances in fibers and sewing methods, for example. Often, suppliers are ahead of M&S in considering emerging technologies. All information about garment concepts, consumer needs, and technological possibilities is shared by M&S and its suppliers. As a technology attracts interest, the suppliers follow it more closely and eventually move it into product development. New fibers, for instance, are introduced in small ways and then evolve with fabrics, changes in consumer trends, and growing know-how regarding manufacturing with the new fiber.

Twice a year, designers from leading manufacturers are invited to briefings by individual M&S product groups. These meetings, which are a step toward developing the next season's design, are a forum for discussion and feedback leading to an M&S decision for its design briefs. Each meeting typically lasts half a day and includes twenty to thirty manufacturers and about twelve people from M&S.

Formalizing the Concept. Each year, based on the earlier brainstorming and experimentation, M&S assembles a design brief—a conceptual document that narrates the desired mood and key look for the coming season. Sparked by the M&S internal design group and discussed with individual buying departments, the brief reflects color, fabric, and styling trends for each product range. Following internal discussions, manufacturers are advised of the design brief and product mix, and respond with their own views on ease (or difficulty) of production and consumer demand.

To illustrate how these interactions lead to final product selection, consider the process in ladies' tailoring. Once a season, Carole O'Beirne (the M&S selector in that department) and her team meet with their suppliers as a group to discuss the design brief and get them started for the next season. The suppliers have their own ideas about where fashion trends are going—shape, color, style, and so forth—and are vocal in saying so. O'Beirne and her team make the final decision on the product range that will satisfy the customer base.

Later, all suppliers respond to the design brief with a variety of designs to cover the range of products sought by Marks & Spencer. The supplier's designs translate the broad concept that has been agreed upon into product specifications. From those suggestions, M&S chooses what it believes best responds to its brief. Approved design specifications are followed by sketches and fabric presentations, and then prototype garments. Everything is iterated over time, with an ongoing debate between M&S buyers and supplier salespeople and designers. Because Marks & Spencer regards these inputs as crucial, it wants its suppliers exposed as much as possible to the marketplace. "I don't want to make slow sellers," remarked a supplier as he was visiting stores to learn how a product he made was selling.

All proposals are made separately by each firm, to protect its interests. When a significantly unique design is submitted and M&S decides to market it, the supplier is allowed to provide it on an exclusive basis for at least one season. After that, the design may be shared with other suppliers. Since M&S works with the same firms over the years, everyone understands and accepts the practice.

Every supplier takes part in the design process, with the involvement varying by product since some goods require more innovation than others. Each M&S clothing product goes through the process to identify possible opportunities. Sometimes changes may be small, say, adjusting the width of a skirt waistband.

Because it is constantly pushing consumer value frontiers, Marks & Spencer is intimately involved in design. For instance, M&S, rather than the garment maker, chooses the lace design for brassieres, where such design has a great effect on value. Other retailers do not get involved in those decisions for the goods they sell.

Carole O'Beirne offers an example of how suppliers have the freedom to push hard on M&S. One day, a firm approached her department and insisted that Marks & Spencer buy a particular print skirt. It was not being sold anywhere else, and had been developed for M&S based on a design the supplier picked up in Paris. M&S said it was not interested, because the skirt was too expensive. But the manufacturer persisted—and prevailed. When the skirt became a big success, M&S was forced to rethink its pricing policy for print skirts.

O'Beirne says such stories can be found throughout Marks & Spencer. Most suppliers push M&S in this way; the company does not yield every time, but often it does. "This practice is part of our life," O'Beirne says. Invariably the supplier will have done its homework—in terms of fabric, costing, styling, timing for when the product can be in the stores—and will come in with the skirt in hand and knowing it is in the correct phase of the M&S selling cycle. Such events are discussed widely within the buying group and with suppliers, so that everyone is aware of what M&S regards as best practice.

Managing the Value Chain. Noel Jervis, chief executive of Courtaulds Textiles, says that an essential difference between Marks & Spencer and his other retail customers is that M&S is involved in the entire textile supply chain, while most others are not. He explains that M&S is uniquely interested in the source of its garments, from the quality of raw materials to the financial and other strengths of its supply routes. Due to its involvement with the value chain, except at low price points, M&S brings a considerable difference in benefits to consumers. Its competitive prices are achieved through scale economies, attentiveness to design, and stringent standards that ensure consistent high quality—all of which require close relationships along the full vertical chain.

By contrast, Jervis says, one of the biggest problems other retailers face is getting decent raw materials needed to meet acceptable quality levels (based on standards less exacting than those of M&S). Clothing manufacturers that buy their materials in the Far East, a common source, affect style only through their specifications. Not having an upstream influence beyond that limits quality as well as innovation—most of which, in the clothing business, is in textiles.

DESIGNING TELEVISION SETS AT PCEC

Like that at Marks & Spencer, product conception at Philips Consumer Electronics Company begins with marketing research, an understanding of technological possibilities, and informal discussions with suppliers about future needs and capabilities. After that, cooperation follows a different course, since PCEC's suppliers (unlike those for M&S) do not sell directly in its market. Consequently, they join in the design process according to how their parts leverage the cost and value of the PCEC television set.

PCEC products are more complex than clothing in terms of the number of parts and their interactions, so design optimization there is a more involved process than at M&S. PCEC also faces substantial price competition, which has an important influence on its design relationships with suppliers.

At any one time, PCEC is actively working on three product generations: one in production, one in final development (for which major changes are not acceptable), and one at the concept generation stage (which is where new ideas enter). During an earlier preconcept phase, all marketing and technical information is integrated to define cost/performance objectives for the product over a three-year time horizon. Those objectives—related to improvement targets for stereo output, picture quality, display features, set reliability, and other attributes—are then shared with the suppliers to guide their own developments.

Phased Design Participation. At the formal start of the design concept phase, PCEC people representing all functions involved in design, manufacturing, and supplier relationships, as well as a manufacturing line worker and a buyer, meet with their counterparts from the suppliers. PCEC shares all information with this team, including proprietary data that might help suppliers perform. Because such information is not shared with suppliers that also compete with PCEC, they are not invited to join these teams.

The timing of these meetings, and of each firm's entry into the process, is determined by how it influences PCEC product design. Optics, which affects overall TV set design including set size and performance features, comes in early. Next is electronics, because it hinges on the optics design. After that comes packaging, including cables, chassis, connectors, and the cabinet. Each stage must be flexible enough to support the design from the prior stage. This is not a purely sequential process; it involves some concurrent development by each group to account for interaction complexities. For projection TV sets, the optics, electronics, and cabinet groups start together because all three affect product size, which is a major competitive variable.

Molex used to come in late in the concept phase because its connectors were the last item people considered. Then, when PCEC was developing a new TV set, it proved hard to assemble and posed potential reliability problems. These issues were not recognized until the product was close to manufacturing start, which caused considerable anguish at PCEC. Molex observed that if it had been involved at the concept phase, it could have seen the component layout in the proposed product, probably recognized the connection problem, and been able to suggest alternative layouts. Starting with the next product generation Molex participation began earlier, and it has had the solutions when they were needed.

Following the product concept meetings, suppliers launch their own design efforts, which lead to part specifications. To ensure continued alignment and support design iterations, contacts between PCEC and its suppliers are virtually continuous. Prototype parts are developed to support ongoing design discussions and further refinement with PCEC.

At product range start, a PCEC milestone, all new ideas and technologies from suppliers have been gathered by PCEC. Up to this time, the firms have been working together continuously through all stages. By now there must be working prototypes of all parts, or relevant developments must be postponed to the next year. No more inventions are needed or acceptable; the next steps are design release and manufacture.

Team Continuity. PCEC's design process dovetails into a long-range joint planning effort with its suppliers. Designers who participate in this exercise belong to a team that continues from planning through design and interactive problem solving to final products being shipped. The constant makeup of the team supports easy raising of issues, shared understandings, and fast decisions. While new people occasionally enter the process, total continuity is essential during the final design iteration. The firms understand this and adhere to it as an unspoken agreement.

Design for Cost Reduction. With about 70 percent of PCEC's revenues going to its suppliers, their work has tremendous leverage on the firm's final costs. For this reason, and because it competes intensely on price, PCEC wants to use as many standard, catalog-available parts in its products as possible so that it can benefit from scale economies.

Since PCEC also competes by offering advanced performance in its

TV sets, it has a list of critical parts that leverage those attributes. All such parts are involved in the early design process, where trade-offs are made according to how the parts affect final product cost, quality, features, size, and so forth. In general, custom designs are sought when standard parts will not meet the final product's design objectives.

Focus on Major Functions. For complex products or systems composed of many interacting parts, optimizing overall performance by considering one part at a time can be difficult. A better way to approach this goal is to focus on improving key subsystems that leverage total performance. PCEC does that though what it calls "town meetings."

Lasting for two or three days, each of about ten annual town meetings is organized around a major product subsystem (such as the TV display, high voltage, and cable and connectors). Meeting participants from PCEC and the relevant suppliers represent every function involved in designing and manufacturing those aspects of the TV set: engineering, factory and warehouse people, supplier logistics, and PCEC finance. A third-party facilitator participates as well; rival suppliers are not involved.

Each meeting, consisting of about twelve to fifteen people, is given a cost or performance objective, such as reducing the cost of an assembly by 10 percent over two years. Samples of PCEC TVs and competitive products are available for examination and comparison. Over the course of the meeting the group, helped by the facilitator, develops into a team focused on the stated objective. Ideas are surfaced, issues are raised and resolved, and an action plan is developed, along with estimated benefits, costs, time frames, and individuals responsible for implementation.

At the conclusion, PCEC's management team, which sanctions the town meetings, comes in for a presentation on the action plan. A key element here is for the management team to indicate, at that time, what items it approves or disapproves. A typical result from one year's town meetings is the identification of $35 million in potential savings, with about two-thirds of that amount actually being realized. For example, color TV sets with wood cabinets are a rapidly declining segment of the market. Given this shrinking demand, aggressive cost cutting is needed to stay competitive. A town meeting team recommended reducing PCEC's twenty-five cabinet styles to eight. The team also suggested changing cabinet construction to match a rival's more cost-effective method and to using alternate materials proposed by a supplier. In total, this single town meeting identified close to $1 million in savings that could be implemented in one year.

Bill Kennedy, who launched the town meetings when he was vice president of purchasing, says that while many new ideas surface in the meetings, others have been proposed before. Often these were rejected not on merit but because of politics, insufficient data, or resistance to change. Such ideas have a much better chance to bear fruit in the context of a multifunctional forum that is made up of people who understand the relevant parts and processes, is sanctioned by top management, and is focused on a specific objective to which the ideas contribute. Further, suppliers' ideas—which often never get to the right person in the firm due to poor communication and bureaucracy—get needed attention in the town meetings.

Kennedy also points out that the presentations to top management bypass the normally endless chain of memos and internal meetings that too often kills ideas. The need to make these presentations also creates an immediate objective that can be met only if the group cooperates. Fast feedback from the executives reinforces the process, as do follow-up presentations the team makes to the same executives four to six months after the town meeting. At these meetings, discussions cover how the top management team can help remove roadblocks to implementation.

DESIGNING MANUFACTURING EQUIPMENT FOR PPG

Suppliers are important sources of new technologies that may significantly affect the customer's costs, quality, timing, and other value sources. The process of integrating such know-how into a customer's goods or services begins with the location of new value-creation opportunities at relevant market and technological frontiers. To guide this process, it is useful to know where to look in the supply chain, as well as to understand the pace of innovation, development risks, and the degree to which supplies leverage the customer's final product.

These parameters are illustrated by the process Motorola's Paging Products Group follows to develop new manufacturing equipment with suppliers. The example also shows how PPG pinpoints those specific developments in highly complex systems that will best serve its marketing objectives.

As with supplies for less complex goods such as clothing or TV sets, those for factory operating equipment should support the user's competitive objectives. To the extent that any equipment might affect these objectives, alliances with suppliers can create unique value for the customer. For example, by knowing what parameters to stretch on which pieces of equipment, and succeeding with the relevant developments, PPG has achieved exceptional flexibility—economic lot sizes of one—in its manufacturing, with a cycle time of fewer than two hours from order through manufacturing and testing to a finished pager ready for delivery. For a product offering some 20 million possible feature combinations, that is unique competitive value.[1]

Unlike the situation with less complex goods, finding the right equipment parameters—and technologies—that leverage one's competitive objectives takes some effort. Any plant has many pieces of equipment, and the plant is linked to the firm's market objectives only through the products or services it creates. Further, for much equipment, technological change is rapid, development risks can be high, and considerable innovation occurs outside the current supply base.

For effective alliances with equipment suppliers, these factors require the continuous monitoring of the outside environment; an analysis of how each piece of equipment leverages the firm's competitive objectives, pinpointing development priorities; and sharing development risks. PPG has been a successful pioneer on these frontiers.

PPG finds equipment development opportunities through its planning process, which seeks the best possible set of product features, cost, size, quality, and availability given the limits of product and manufacturing technologies. The company follows two simultaneous paths in this process. Product planners define desired products through market studies, competitive analysis, and technology forecasting. At the same time, manufacturing planners define future factory attributes on the basis of quality, cost, manufacturing lead time, and flexibility. They also draw on an intense ongoing benchmarking and forecasting effort of relevant manufacturing technologies. The product and manufacturing planning groups meet frequently to keep abreast of each other's progress, promote cross-fertilization, and ensure effective integration.

Because unique equipment is costly to purchase and maintain, PPG wants to stretch with its equipment suppliers only in well-defined, high-leverage areas. Otherwise, says Sunil Lakhani, director of advanced manufacturing technology, it prefers to buy standard off-the-shelf equipment. This makes service far easier, because there are no problems with getting extra parts or unique service know-how. For these reasons, specific developments often involve customizing standard equipment, typically by designing needed controls or data interfaces so that it can be integrated into PPG operations.

Constant Benchmarking Helps Set Development Objectives. At PPG, a seven-person team works full time benchmarking equipment and process developments and doing competitive analysis to keep abreast of the rapidly expanding manufacturing frontiers of cost, cycle time, and other areas. In addition to outside help from analytic and modeling people, some thirty other people add functional expertise as needed. Disciplines involved include automation, materials science, surface analysis, electrical engineering, computers, and physics.

Twice yearly, all relevant benchmarking data for key performance and business parameters are joined in two sets of pictorial documents that summarize the analysis and are the basis for specific plans. One set consists of technology road maps that describe timing targets for the evolution of key parameters at plant and individual equipment levels. The other documents, known as "spider charts" (see figures on the following two pages), are used to plan factory performance. These display key parameters as spokes on a wheel, arranged to show current and projected performance envelopes of PPG rivals plus its own desired envelope.

At the factory level, sets of spider charts show parameters like factory development cycle time, cost, and other important variables. At lower levels of aggregation—such as for individual pieces of equipment—spider charts display different parameters. Among these are reliability, accuracy, speed, computer integrated manufacturing compatibility, service (whether a firm has local engineering resources in case PPG needs help quickly), controls system capability, and spare parts availability.

All equipment spider charts are integrated into those for the total factory, with factory parameters like development cycle time being spokes on individual equipment charts. Factory simulation models connect equipment parameters to overall factory performance. Cost models that reflect actual experience plus projections tie costs together at equipment and plant levels as well. In general, the manufacturing technology road maps are developed directly from future product needs, and these are then used to generate the spider charts. There is, however, some iteration between the two sets of documents.

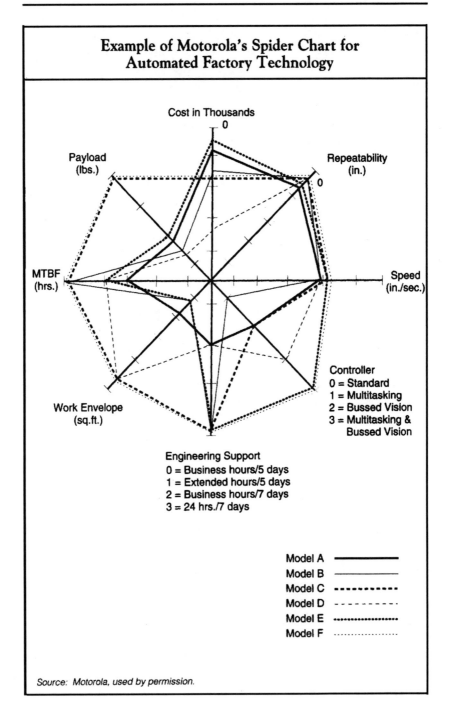

Example of Motorola's Spider Chart for Automated Factory Technology

Source: Motorola, used by permission.

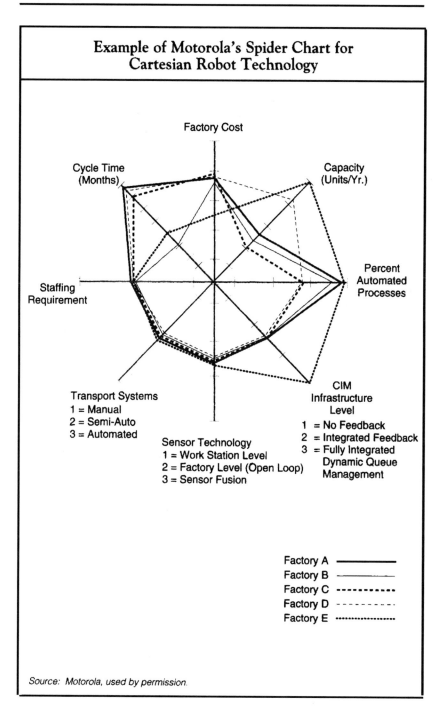

Example of Motorola's Spider Chart for Cartesian Robot Technology

Factory Cost

Cycle Time (Months)

Capacity (Units/Yr.)

Percent Automated Processes

Staffing Requirement

Transport Systems
1 = Manual
2 = Semi-Auto
3 = Automated

CIM Infrastructure Level
1 = No Feedback
2 = Integrated Feedback
3 = Fully Integrated Dynamic Queue Management

Sensor Technology
1 = Work Station Level
2 = Factory Level (Open Loop)
3 = Sensor Fusion

Factory A ——————
Factory B ——————
Factory C ············
Factory D ─ ─ ─ ─ ─
Factory E ··················

Source: Motorola, used by permission.

The spider charts indicate what is currently available in the market, and support an analysis of what the best performance envelope might be in a specific time frame. PPG has found it can do better than the market by seeking part and equipment designs that support better integration for higher performances, then asking suppliers of high-leverage items to pursue developments that will push the frontier beyond the projected technology envelope. How far PPG reaches for new performances is determined by cost constraints.

With spider charts in hand, a specific strategy—including objectives, tactics, and milestones—is set for each PPG product/market opportunity. These strategies include relevant technology road maps, pictorial charts that identify future products, a description of needed technologies and their completion dates, and current resource commitments required for the developments. In essence, the road maps indicate critical development paths that must be followed to succeed.[2]

Technology road maps fall into three categories. One is for established, available technologies. A second is for developing technologies that are not available for use because of cost or performance reasons. A third is for critical technologies yet to be developed. The second and third kinds of road maps are the basic planning documents for Motorola's internal efforts and for joint developments with suppliers.[3]

Launching Supplier Developments. The Paging Products Group requires all suppliers to stretch continuously with their technologies. To guide this effort, the group describes its needs at two levels. At one level, PPG gives suppliers a general description about what a future factory will look like, avoiding any discussion of core competencies. More specific performances, sometimes including quantitative matters, are discussed with selected equipment suppliers on a need-to-know basis.

Suppliers that PPG wants to stretch beyond their normal pace receive spider charts indicating desired performance target for their equipment. For example, Sunil Lakhani and his team benchmarked the placement accuracy of robot controller manufacturers, then showed Seiko the spider chart illustrating what others could do. Next, the team indicated the performance criteria expected from Seiko. This information sharing, says Lakhani, necessarily stops well short of disclosing proprietary information other firms have shared with PPG. Instead, discussions focus on the kinds of performances sought and the timing. There is no mention of how others might achieve their results.

Planning time horizons with suppliers are typically two to three years, depending on development lead times. Planning proceeds through phases, beginning with conceptual discussions at the time that Motorola internal concepts are crystallizing. PPG works with the supplier to develop an implementation plan, which may include acceptance testing. To ensure critical teamwork through the course of a development, the same people remain involved on both sides from initial concept to final specification.

PPG occasionally pursues parallel early developments with rival suppliers and selects one for final design. While this practice can get expensive, it is followed if the development risk for either source is high. There may also be applications for both types of devices. When this happens both suppliers are informed, and PPG shares costs as necessary. There have been times when joint internal and external developments were pursued simultaneously.

Pressed by ever-shrinking product cycles, Motorola has had to fit inherently long development times into shortening time frames. In particular, final development of some capital equipment is sensitive to pager features, which are unknown when equipment development begins. In such cases, relevant aspects of the equipment specifications are kept open until the product features are known. At the heart of this process is a constant dialogue with the equipment supplier.

Suppliers sometimes resist requests to stretch for PPG because they think this would threaten their independence. Suppliers may have their own plans that cause them to avoid dedicating resources to a particular customer's unique needs. For example, PPG wanted robot vision with certain attributes, which robotics suppliers did not see as important. PPG had to convince them that others would also want the attributes it was seeking. Increasingly, though, suppliers see development opportunities Motorola brings them as occasions for gaining competitive advantage in their own markets.

Helping with Development. Within the boundaries of protecting its product plans and core interests, PPG makes an ongoing substantial effort to transfer relevant know-how to key suppliers to help them keep moving ahead. Examples include technology transfer on plastic design tools and rapid tooling processes.

By carefully selecting suppliers, involving them in early design, and providing needed help, PPG avoids most equipment failures and escapes the problem of missed development targets. Each development effort has explicit targets agreed to up front. If these are not met, efforts are increased and, if necessary, the agreement is rewritten or a recovery plan is developed to retrofit.

To make certain it gets what it needs on time and within specifications, PPG sometimes devotes its own resources to initiate or complete a development, possibly even dedicating a few people or providing funds or equipment to help the supplier. There is no expectation of payback (such as lower pricing from the supplier) on that investment. Says Sunil Lakhani, "The real payback comes from better service and a faithful supplier. You can't buy that." Adds Len de Barros, Lakhani's predecessor: "If they slip, we had better be there to help them. If they fall, we suffer tremendous problems in cycle time."

PPG also lets selected suppliers use its facility as a "beta site" for testing preliminary versions of their equipment. This allows the group to check all relevant features on items being made for it. PPG also sometimes serves as a beta site on new equipment it may not use, a practice that helps it keep up with advances.

The practices described in this section are summarized in the tables shown on the following pages.

More Powerful Competitive Strategies

Each alliance with a supplier may advance the customer's competitive position by improving its costs, quality, design, and timing. Both separately and as a group, supply partners may also affect *how* the customer competes, due to their knowledge of the customer's business.

Recently, for instance, Clinton Silver, vice chairman and managing director of Marks & Spencer, met with the CEOs of six children's wear suppliers. M&S was not doing as well in that area as it desired. The meeting was not to criticize them, however, but to explore what to do together. Without sharing any proprietary information, the clothing firms said that M&S had gone too far into "character merchandizing"—that is, selling garments that display well-known cartoon characters—and had neglected classic children's wear. The CEOs also said the M&S structure, which grouped all children's wear in one buying department, did not give enough emphasis to small and emerging product lines. M&S accepted these ideas and acted on them; the result was a substantial increase in volume and market share.

Cooperating in Design and Development		
	Factor	**Design or Development Practice**
Customer	Supplier directly involved in market	*Yes:* Cooperate on all aspects of final good *No:* Cooperate on relevant aspects
	Competitive edge	*Price:* Stress cost drivers in design, with selective emphasis on other attributes *Value:* Emphasize features, style, etc.
Customer's product, system, service	Highly complex	*Best:* Use analytic model of total final product or system to optimize, define stretch targets *Next best:* Optimize subsystem or function
Suppliers	Direct suppliers are key innovators	Cooperate in design Continuing dialogue about new opportunities
	Other firms are key innovators	Monitor wider supply community Reach upstream for design participation
Supplier's product, system, service	Fast change	Constantly monitor innovation sources
	High development risks	Give needed development help Introduce item gradually
	High leverage on customer value	Involve early in design process

Another way that supply alliances can improve a customer's strategic position is by making this more difficult for others to duplicate. Compared with when a company limits its creation of unique value to its own resources, an alliance with a supplier raises the market entry barrier. Working with many suppliers can make a barrier all but impassable. For its food product lines, Marks & Spencer is constantly seeking opportunities with significant technology leverage on quality and value that would be hard for rivals to clone. For instance, fresh egg pasta is

Reaching Together for Advanced Technology	
Activity	Specifics
Marketing research, competitive analysis	Define customer satisfaction frontiers
Technology forecasting, benchmarking	Define technological frontiers and possibilities
Combine marketing and technology analysis	Pinpoint value-creation opportunities Create technology road maps: what performances are needed by when
Communicate	Share road maps with partners, with ample lead time for their planning
Develop	Cooperate, assist, share risks as necessary
Protect each firm's proprietary position	Nondisclosure to others; plan for separate or joint inventions (see Chapter 4)

more delicate and requires unique cooking and handling compared with the kind other retailers sell, which is made with dry eggs.

In developing its food products with suppliers, M&S combines its substantial knowledge of consumer taste and food technology with their complementary expertise in food products, markets, technology, and manufacturing. To ensure the highest possible quality—and make duplication even more difficult—M&S and its suppliers develop product specifications for each unique food that describe all relevant processes used to achieve the required product standard. This includes every raw material, from the farm to processing and packing, as well as all factory processes for making the product, and chemical and microbiological standards.

For the Most Benefits, Take a Wider View

Most cooperative efforts focus on specific objectives, such as ways to improve product performance through better design or technology. Occasionally, though, sharing a wider view of an alliance may surface opportunities that would otherwise be overlooked. Once each quarter, for instance, Molex and Philips Consumer Electronics Company hold joint improvement meetings at which both firms brainstorm about how to help each other be more effective.

The meetings, which have a broad focus, involve people from PCEC purchasing, materials, operations, and information systems, and their counterparts from Molex. They have led to better PCEC scheduling (for easier interpretation by Molex), less PCEC paperwork, better mutual understandings that eliminated premium shipments, and improvements in other areas. The success of these meetings has caused Molex to meet quarterly with its other customers for the same purpose.

6

COOPERATING FOR BETTER TIMING AND COSTS

If they slip, we had better be there to help them. If they fail, we suffer tremendous problems in cycle time.

Len de Barros, corporate vice president and general manager, advanced messaging systems division of the Paging Products Group, Motorola, on helping suppliers when they have problems

Motorola's implementation of Schedule Sharing was startling. In all other cases, the customer tells us when and how much to ship. With Schedule Sharing, we do that analysis—to our and their mutual advantage.

Jerry Deutsch, Molex liaison with Motorola for manufacturing and information systems

In nearly every industry, rising competition and rapid technological advance have shortened the available time between initial concept and volume production, as well as the times to respond to customer requests and changed demand. These trends create an advantage for the fastest companies. "Any idiot can reduce a price by 10 percent to become more competitive," says Percy Barnevik, chairman of Swiss-based Asea Brown Boveri. "But if you can offer an electric power transmission cable under the Baltic one year earlier than your competition, that is of tremendous value to the customer, and your competitor can't touch you."[1]

Concurrent with the time imperative, cost management has never been as important as it is today. Because a firm's suppliers manage a large share of its costs, any rational cost reduction strategy should include supply alliances.

Joining to Compete with Time

The time needed for an activity depends on practices within and between customer and supplier firms. For instance, companies that use multifunctional teams and perform separate activities in parallel are faster than those that operate in sequence. But while such efforts are necessary, the best timing comes when partners understand how their separate cycle times interact and cooperate to reduce those together.

Although many factors influence timing, several elements are common to many firms. High quality, for instance, avoids many delays and missed opportunities. Other common factors include a small, stable supply base; early design cooperation; getting to target designs early; using standard parts; knowing suppliers' capacity limits; better operating flexibility; and direct communications.

START WITH A RELIABLE SUPPLY BASE

Working with suppliers that have already undergone a rigorous selection process and with which one has built clear understandings and trusting relationships is a virtually universal source of reduced cycle times. PCEC, for example, has found that moving to full volume production with a new supplier takes much longer than in an established supply relationship, because the process requires a shared learning curve. Similarly, with a committed supply base, firms can share systems like electronic data interchange (EDI) and benefit from the mutual learnings and adjustments that get the most value from these arrangements. Having fewer suppliers also reduces the time required for acceptance testing before volume production and increases each supplier's commitment to a relationship.

Motorola has found that a dedicated supply base also reduces cycle times through faster part qualification cycles, because this task can be delegated to suppliers with proven quality systems reliability. In Hewlett-Packard's alliance for temporary office staff with Reed Personnel Services, the change to a single agency from dozens reduced delays in filling positions. One reason was that the increased volume gave Reed an opportunity to assign more skilled and dedicated staffers to H-P's needs. Further, because working with one agency improved communications and increased understandings, Reed was able to fill vacancies faster.

COOPERATE EARLY IN DESIGN

Cooperation in design, like concurrent engineering within a firm, shortens development cycle time by avoiding the need for sequential design iterations. At Motorola's Paging Products Group, this practice has made it possible to get a new product to market three to six months earlier than before. This is significant, because product cycles are often twenty-four months, can be as brief as six to nine months, and are getting ever shorter.

Bob Becknell, a PPG vice president, says that before the group began supply alliances, weak communications and the inherent inflexibility of the old ways caused design errors or defective parts 75 to 80 percent of the time. Typically, the process of sending out specifications, checking suppliers' designs and prototypes, and finding and correcting errors took additional design cycles to resolve problems. With early design cooperation, the percentage of errors or defects has dropped to single digits.

Chrysler used to take five years to develop a new car from concept to volume production, three of which were required for design. The automaker has shortened the design cycle to eighteen months, a 50 percent reduction. It has achieved this by delegating piece-part design to suppliers, with early supplier participation and with multi-functional integration in its platform teams. These changes, as well as doing the design, engineering, and manufacturing cycles in parallel rather than sequentially, cut Chrysler's concept-to-volume time to fewer than three years. The company's current objective is to come out with new cars two years after the initial concept date.

At PCEC, Gordon Couch, a component applications engineer, says, "The more we do together in design, the better the design and the less time needed to complete it." He estimates that design cooperation with suppliers lowers the product development cycle by 25 percent. In the old way, the parts did not always fit, and iterations between the firms were necessary. "If one designs a new product with advanced features without knowing what a supplier can make, the chances are high that one will have to start over again," Couch adds. "Redesign time spent on both sides can be enormous."

Do It Right the First Time

Early cooperation in design makes it possible to reduce cycle times even more if the target—such as the desired cost—is achieved at the outset. The alternative is a sequence of design cycles that slow things down.

Use Standard Parts

One reason for using standard parts, as discussed earlier, is to benefit from the scale economies of their wider use. Another is to cut manufacturing cycle time by avoiding several tasks that can add to the time burden, including part set-ups in stockrooms or on production lines, design and engineering approvals, prototype acquisitions, part qualifications, and production problem solving.

Know Supplier Capacity and Give Needed Help

Bottlenecks at suppliers, whether in their design or operating capacity or other areas, can inhibit fast responses to volume growth or new demands. This problem can apply particularly to the best suppliers, which are often at the edge of getting more business than they can handle.

For these reasons, Motorola maintains supplier capacity charts, updated yearly, that describe the capacity and useful life of equipment used in critical processes by each firm. The charts help determine the supplier's current capabilities and describe its expansion plans. Reported by Motorola product and part number, the data are given to development engineers to help them understand suppliers' ability to respond to its needs now and in the future.

From experience, Motorola has learned that capacity data must come directly from the supplier's factory. Salespeople tend to say their firm has capacity when it does not, which leads to problems when the firm starts shipping parts. To prepare for a large increase in business, Motorola also sends teams of engineers, purchasing personnel, and others to visit key suppliers to be sure the latter are ready and to provide needed help in critical areas.

UNDERSTAND SUPPLIERS' SKILLS

By knowing what its suppliers can do and having close working relationships with them, a firm can become more responsive to its own customers' particular needs and enhance its credibility with them.

For example, PPG customers often seek distinct plastic pager housings to differentiate their products from those of rivals. One may want a unique control layout, a second a flat housing, a third a rippled housing, a fourth a large label, yet another a small label, and so on. Not everything is doable with current tooling. PPG can respond to customer inquiries almost instantly, however, because it knows the limitations of tooling used by firms like Advanced Dial, an important supplier of pager plastics. In the past, answering a customer inquiry may have involved a major engineering effort. Today it is done by an individual engineer for the supplier, on a moment's notice.

DESIGN FOR BETTER OPERATING FLEXIBILITY

Any customer or supplier activity is likely to affect their combined flexibility. Factors that can advance this ability include the development of better processes, equipment, and logistics. As is often the case, a creative look at traditionally separate activities may uncover new and better ways of working.

Take Marks & Spencer. When the company began buying sofas, the industry typically offered two design options, with delivery in twelve weeks. M&S knew that consumers wanted a much wider choice of fabrics and faster delivery. To reach that objective, it worked with Christie Tyler, a supplier, to develop a production method that uses pre-sewn loose covers for a standard frame instead of a fixed sofa cover. This technique made it possible for consumers to pick whatever cover they liked, trimming delivery to four weeks.

At Motorola's Paging Products Group, manufacturing analysts pinpointed specific parameters on particular pieces of automation equipment as having high leverage on order response cycle times. This understanding led to new developments with suppliers that cut the time for moving from one product model to another down to lot sizes of one unit.

USE DIRECT COMMUNICATIONS

Direct links between relevant customer and supplier activities helps speed shared tasks. As an example, making order changes by first writing them on paper and then sending them is not as fast as using electronic document interchange. In situations where EDI is not applicable, oral communication is followed by documentation to avoid placing the supplier at risk. In an alliance between Baxter International and St. Luke's Hospital in Houston, Texas, the operating rooms suggested that Baxter become part of St. Luke's voice mail system. As a result, anyone in an operating room can reach the company directly and get an immediate response.[2]

CO-LOCATE FOR BETTER UNDERSTANDINGS

Locating people who are part of the customer–supplier value chain at the same facility adds to direct communications; helps build understandings that avoid problems regarding fit, functionality, manufacturability, and in other areas; and resolves issues quickly. At PCEC, for parts such as custom chips that significantly affect TV set performance, the chip supplier's designer may be on site for weeks, months, or even a year because of the need for ongoing, intense design interactions. Similarly, engineers from about 200 suppliers relocate Chrysler's Technology Design Center during those months when design activities are most critical.

In the Hewlett-Packard alliance with Reed, the firms have been cooperating to cut response times in filling vacancies. To do that, they are working on ways to have more accurate reporting in requests for temporary staff. One aspect of this is a continuing effort to refine the job descriptions H-P gives to Reed. Another has been to locate a Reed employee in H-P's personnel department, which gives Reed better data at an earlier time. To complement the formal evaluation process, the Reed person regularly visits line managers to get informal feedback on its performance. Having someone on site also helps Reed better understand the H-P culture, which makes it possible to judge candidates better and faster in terms of a good match.

In Plantation, Florida, Motorola promotes direct links between its shop-floor manufacturing people and their counterparts from key suppliers. In one case, a sales engineer from a circuit board supplier is on site two or three days a week, to help spot and resolve issues quickly. The result: a tenfold reduction in the time needed to find and solve problems, compared with the old way of first communicating production problems to management, which then contacted the supplier's managers, who finally spoke with their own manufacturing staff. In other discussions, plant people from Motorola and suppliers teach each other about how circuit boards are made and used on the line.

One time, for instance, Motorola factory workers did not understand why solder flow was not more even on a new circuit board. When the supplier representative on the shop floor observed the trouble people were having, he got his factory to make some simple changes in how the board was made to end the problems. The representative also invited two production operators to his firm's plant, demonstrated and explained the process in more detail, and showed them how to spot difficulties more accurately. The experience vastly reduced the time needed to find problems. It also created a team atmosphere between employees in both plants that paved the way for future cooperation.

WORK WITH FACILITIES IN THE SAME LOCALE

While co-locating a few people can facilitate cooperation in design and other tasks, it is inadequate when entire organizations must quickly respond in unison. Marks & Spencer, for instance, favors domestic firms to supply its U.K. stores; about 80 percent of its clothing is made in Britain.

Even though there is great price pressure to go abroad, particularly to the Far East, most manufacturers there use large factories to get full advantage of low labor costs. The resulting inflexibility is not consistent with Marks & Spencer's needs. Further, it is impossible for M&S personnel in the United Kingdom to know their counterparts abroad as well as those closer to home. When it places a contract with a U.K. supplier, both firms expect to cooperate in a flexible relationship, changing production volume and mix quickly in response to market demand. Today, the best British knitwear firms move from raw material to a complete product, delivered to M&S stores, within six to ten days. For the same reasons, as M&S expands abroad, it is building similar relationships with suppliers in each geographic area.

When Marks & Spencer does buy in the Far East for its British stores, the decision balances cost, which may be lower, with flexibility. Regardless of the manufacturer's location, M&S applies the same rigorous quality standards. M&S does not expect Far East suppliers to respond as rapidly as its U.K. firms; distance militates against that. In addition to cost, however, foreign suppliers can have natural advantages. For example, silk comes from China, and the Chinese have developed a strong culture in manufacturing silk items.

Like Marks & Spencer, Motorola also requires quick reaction and close cooperation with its suppliers to meet local needs. This has increased the value for Motorola of working with suppliers whose facilities are near its plants around the world.

BUILD EMPOWERED INTERFIRM TEAMS

Two-company teams can achieve cost and cycle time reductions far better than both companies working toward the same objective separately. Craftsman's president, Bruce Bendoff, notes that his firm has worked that way with Motorola's Cellular Infrastructure Group to quickly develop a design and convert that to a physical prototype. They began by creating a plan of action, starting at the predesign concept stage, which integrated relevant processes in both firms. Next, a concurrent engineering team from the firms worked together at both sites, from start to finish. This teamwork, plus computer-aided design transfers and automated machines, cut the time to completion from eight weeks to one. More recently, Craftsman has brought its own relevant suppliers—such as metal finishers—into the process at the earliest point for even better timing.

The several ways that customers and suppliers can cooperate to shorten times and increase responsiveness are summarized in the table on the following page. Another practice used by Motorola and its suppliers has them placing bar codes on their shipped parts. This reduces cycle time in receiving, which can be an important factor in manufacturing cycle time. Logistics is often another key factor in timing. Consider, for example, that delays in customer shipments may be due to mis-timed deliveries from suppliers.

Sources of Joint Time Reduction	
Cycle Time	**Action**
General	Require high quality
	Have a small, dedicated supply base
	Use direct communications
	Co-locate people who must cooperate
	Work with facilities in same locale
	Use empowered interfirm teams
	Resolve issues at point of contact
	Reduce or eliminate paperwork
From concept to volume	Early cooperation in design
	Rapid prototyping
	Computer-aided design
	Use standard parts
	First design reaches desired target
	Supplier design, capacity available
	Help supplier with ramp-up
Responsiveness	Operating flexibility
	Understand supplier skills
	Fast ordering, logistics

Inventory Management that Beats Just-in-Time

Customer and supplier inventories can be important factors in cost and cycle time management. Clearly, the more stock either firm carries, the higher total costs both face. By contrast, having too little stock may halt operations. Further, the analysis required to keep a customer's desired inventory levels can be costly, and it causes a delay in the cus-tomer–supplier response time. These problems are magnified as the customer's requirements grow more uncertain—a phenomenon that is becoming characteristic of many markets.

When a company faces erratic short-term demand fluctuations for its products, carrying enough inventory to accommodate those swings adds costs. So does the need to calculate and readjust inventory levels to keep them at a minimum while avoiding stockouts. In an alliance, the partners' ability to rely on each other, share sensitive information, and resolve any issues quickly makes it possible for them achieve better total costs with fewer problems than traditional inventory management methods, including the popular "just-in-time" (JIT) technique.

The first step in a joint inventory management system is for the customer to share its demand forecasts with suppliers for as much as a year or more in advance, to guide their volume and capacity planning. Near-term demand, as for the next week or month, is also shared to facilitate close-in adjustments.

Accurate customer forecasts are a key determinant of cost, because they help minimize inventories. Two constraints on those forecasts are uncertainty in demand in the customer's own market, and limits on what can be shared with suppliers. For example, if a retailer plans to feature a supplier's products in its advertising, it is not likely to share that information with suppliers of competing goods.

In traditional practice, the customer tells each supplier when to restock its inventories, and by how much. The most common restocking methods blend what are known as "push" and "pull" systems. With a push system, the supplier ships according to the customer's forecasts. This works well if forecasts and actual demand are closely aligned. However, if demand grows slower than forecasts, inventory builds; if it grows faster, there is a risk of stockouts. While the problem of demand uncertainty can be partially avoided with better and more frequently updated forecasts, inherent short-term uncertainties limit the value of that option.

In a pull system, the customer orders goods from the supplier as replacements for those that have been used. Because pull reflects actual use, it tends to keep work-in-process inventory lower than the push method does. As with push, better forecasting helps keep the pull approach aligned with actual need. Pull does not give the supplier any planning flexibility to deal with inherent volume uncertainty, however, which can cause overstocking or stockouts, which are avoided by carrying more inventory.

With either push or pull, or any combination of those methods, orders for specific quantities to be delivered on certain dates are sent periodically to each supplier. With JIT ordering, the customer asks its suppliers to make deliveries shortly—sometimes within a day or less—of when they are needed.

THE PROBLEM OF UNPREDICTABILITY

When demand is highly predictable, suppliers can plan their capacity use for best efficiency. JIT has the added advantage of very low or even zero customer inventory, provided the supplier's goods do not require incoming inspection. If demand is uncertain, rather than carry extra inventory, which adds costs, the customer could reorder whenever its stocks get below preset minimums. But that method gives the supplier unpredictable order patterns and causes it to hold more inventory to meet its customer's needs. The problem is magnified by JIT, because the customer has no buffer stocks. The supplier must be ready to handle any fluctuations on a moment's notice, which adds more cost.

Further, as demand gets more unpredictable, suppliers must adjust to less certain and more exacting order and delivery patterns. The scramble to respond sends waves through a supplier's stock control systems, production schedules, order processing, invoicing, sales, and field support operations. Under these conditions, JIT has caused stockouts at suppliers and at their suppliers, leading to line stoppages along the value chain. The supplier's challenge is even greater—and its costs are higher—if it is receiving unpredictable orders from several customers, or from more than one plant of a single customer.

Another problem with uncertain order quantities is that, to avoid stockouts or overstocking, the customer must analyze its inventory level regularly and send order changes to the supplier to keep up with actual variations in demand. Then, the supplier must do more analysis to fit those unpredictable changes into its own schedule. Not only is all of this extra work labor-intensive and hard to do accurately, but it inhibits the supplier from using its plant most efficiently.

One response to demand uncertainty is for the supplier to make its production cycle time as short as possible, a practice that reduces the finished goods inventory it must carry. Since this also cuts work-in-process inventory and thereby lowers costs, it should always be done. This may not adequately accommodate short-term uncertainty, however, and capacity limits at the supplier may still force it either to build extra inventory or to use overtime or other costly practices to accommodate unpredictable order swings. A second response is for inventory to be carried by whichever firm has the most flexibility in adjusting its size and nature. Unless logistics is a problem, usually this is the supplier. While this is generally good practice, it can only accommodate very small demand swings.

ACHIEVING LOWEST COST AND BEST SERVICE

The most complete way to minimize inventory-related costs is to consider all relevant cost sources—including the customer's incoming inventory, the supplier's finished goods inventory and its operating efficiency, both firms' costs of analyzing needed adjustments, and the cost of lost revenue from service disruptions—as parts of one system. If transportation costs are significant, those must be included as well.

In some markets and under some conditions, occasional stockouts or incomplete orders are accepted because the alternatives are less attractive. If customer service cannot be compromised, though, this becomes a constraint on cost reduction. When there is inherent demand uncertainty, a cost minimization strategy must include some flexibility in the total system. Two essential element of that strategy are having the best possible forecasts and shortest internal cycle times. The joint inventory management process is illustrated by two examples: Motorola's Schedule Sharing system, and the current practice used by some retailers with their suppliers.

Motorola's Solution. Motorola, which must respond to erratic short-term demand swings for its products, stay on a steep cost reduction curve, and avoid interrupting deliveries to its customers, solved the cost and flexibility problem by developing an inventory management system it named Schedule Sharing. (For details on how Schedule Sharing works, see the endnotes to this chapter.)[3]

With Schedule Sharing, suppliers are asked to keep Motorola's inventory within stated maximum and minimum limits. That gives each firm the freedom to mesh Motorola's needs with its own plant situation—to allocate resources and level load, for example, if that offers an advantage. Suppliers no longer have to respond to precise order quantities that may not fit well into their current operating plan and, given Motorola's demand uncertainty, may not accurately reflect its requirements. Now, rather than Motorola doing the analysis leading to order quantities, the analysis and delivery decisions are made by the supplier in a far easier manner than is possible with specific orders.

This approach significantly lowers costs compared to when Motorola placed the orders for several reasons:

- The inventory analysts are no longer needed. The number of purchasing positions has been cut by about 30 percent where Schedule Sharing has been implemented.
- Suppliers need fewer people to analyze Motorola's data and adjust their plans.

- With less bureaucracy, the number of inventory turns has doubled compared to when Motorola sent orders to its suppliers.
- Fewer people are needed to expedite orders when something goes wrong.
- Suppliers operate more efficiently.
- Firms that supply a variety of similar parts can more cost effectively meet Motorola's requirements.
- Each supplier that serves more than one Motorola facility can better allocate its resources across those facilities.

Schedule Sharing also cuts delivery cycle time compared to when Motorola placed the orders because, with the old way, the inventory analysis had to be done before the data went to suppliers.

To create the advantage for multiple facilities, each supplier regularly gets the inventory requirements from all Motorola locations it serves. This allows the supplier to set priorities across those facilities, according to the inventory status within the minimum/maximum window at each site. The ability to set priorities, in turn, gives the supplier better economies in terms of its plant use and inventory requirements. It also takes the edge away from buyers that once could persuade suppliers to give their plants top priority without regard to needs at other locations. With Schedule Sharing, the supplier can ship based on objective criteria alone.

In Motorola's Land Mobile Products Sector (LMPS), an early user of Schedule Sharing, better material deliveries have netted operating efficiencies equivalent to forty people who formerly revised delivery schedules, expedited late deliveries, and performed day-to-day part-specific inventory management. Bill Hanks, manager of supplier quality programs at LMPS, notes that for its markets, the task of making frequent changes had become virtually impossible. "There is no way we could afford enough resources to order specific quantities to react to the dynamics of our customer markets," he says. Of course, Schedule Sharing will not respond to wild demand gyrations, but neither will any system other than carrying high inventories.

From a supplier's perspective, Jerry Deutsch, who is the Molex liaison between his firm's manufacturing and information systems departments, says that "Motorola's implementation of Schedule Sharing was startling. It made us the planner to support their inventory management system. In all other cases, the customer tells us when and how much to ship. With Schedule Sharing, we do that analysis—to our and their mutual advantage."

Deutsch adds that Schedule Sharing has greatly improved his firm's equipment and material availability, and substantially reduced overtime. Now, Molex can see when its production schedule has to be initiated to keep Motorola's inventories within its minimum/maximum window, an ability that helps Molex level its production load. Molex does not have to carry inventory in anticipation of an order, as long as its manufacturing cycle time is within practical limits.

"Schedule Sharing," says Deutsch, "takes MRP [material requirements planning] one step farther and passes the customer's inventory replenishment planning to the supplier. Now, we can see the minimum and maximum inventory levels Motorola wants to maintain, their projected build schedule, and their current inventory position. So long as the min and max levels do not change, we can go as long as two weeks to meet Motorola's requirements without their going out of stock or into a high inventory condition. Because we actually see their inventory status, we can plan our work center capacities, and we have the visibility to initiate any necessary corrective actions."

The Retail Solution. To achieve lowest cost and best service, a typical retailer and its suppliers must consider inventory carrying costs; the amount of product that can be held on store shelves; and delivery costs, which reflect both efficiencies and delivery frequency. With those factors plus an understanding of normal week-to-week demand fluctuations, an inventory-turns target is set that achieves the lowest possible total system cost while avoiding stockouts and overstocking.

Suppliers are held responsible for meeting the turns target, and are given sales projections and on-line access to the retailer's data base for that purpose. Some flexibility is built into the turns target to account for forecasting uncertainties caused by holidays.

Without alliances, a retailer and its suppliers may share electronic data links, but are limited in their ability to discuss and optimize their performance as parts of an integrated system. With alliances, the gains can be dramatic.

In one case, a retailer and manufacturer achieved such major gains in inventory turns that a new warehouse would have been needed without the improvements. In another alliance, cooperation on setting and meeting a better turns target greatly reduced variations in ordering and delivery. It also allowed the supplier to schedule delivery appointments with its customer, thereby reducing the truckers' downtime.

That step alone took almost 50 percent off of the average unloading time and made it possible to reduce the number of trucking firms by a factor of five. Each of the remaining firms better understood the partners' needs and yielded far better rates.

More generally, alliances between retailers and their suppliers have cut the total cost of goods at the retailer's loading dock by 25 percent or more, compared to inflation-adjusted costs before the alliances. For consumers, cost reductions due to these alliances have ranged from 15 to 20 percent. These figures are distinct from cost-cutting efforts pursued separately within each firm.

Cutting Costs Together

As with cycle time, the cost of an activity not only depends on many factors within and between customer and supplier firms but also varies with each situation. Also like the situation with cycle time, an effective cost reduction program entails collecting and analyzing data about relevant separate and joint processes to identify and reduce chief cost drivers.

At most manufacturing firms, as well as in retail businesses, purchased materials are the largest component of product costs, having an influence several times that of internal direct costs. Further, the cost of less than perfect quality and delivery are key elements of total material cost, which is often the largest part of manufacturing or operating cost. Similarly, in the services—where labor can be an important component of cost—quality and timing are also key factors in total cost.

To better understand how customers and suppliers can cut costs together, it is helpful to classify the techniques into three areas: those where the customer generally takes the initiative, those where the supplier usually has the initiative, and those that are shared by both firms.

CUSTOMER INITIATIVE

Major cost drivers under the customer's control typically include reducing the supply base; stabilizing long-term relationships; using focused competition; improving logistics and inventory management; and providing technical assistance, especially to smaller firms.

Supply Base Reduction. Having fewer suppliers raises scale economies and spreads supplier overheads over a larger volume, both of which are one-time savings. It also substantially lessens the need for the many ongoing costs associated with selecting, developing, and maintaining suppliers—including initial evaluations, quality audits, technical assistance, purchasing activities, and more.

A reduced supply base may also have economies of scope. For companies that supply a number of varieties of the same kind of part, various aspects of design and manufacturing will be common to all of the parts. So cutting the number of suppliers of those parts gives the remaining ones opportunities to reduce costs by sharing designs and production resources. Of course, shipping costs are also lower when similar parts can be made in the same plant.

For Motorola and PCEC, the one-time savings from supply base reduction were about 10 percent of total purchased material costs, compared with the traditional process of getting three quotes from the marketplace. In the Hewlett-Packard alliance with Reed Personnel, lowering the number of recruitment suppliers allowed H-P to redeploy two human resources people and at least one person in receivables.

Long-Term Relationships. Unlike arm's-length supply links, where joint value creation is close to nil, customer–supplier alliances benefit from durable relationships—a point that underscores the importance of supplier selection. Such relationships encourage new and better ideas from suppliers regarding improved designs and processes, yield more product functionality per material dollar, cut overheads, permit shared learning curves, avoid the high costs of frequent supplier turnover, and support longer production runs.

Motorola is constantly discussing its needs and interests with suppliers and learning more about their abilities. This is hard to do with a new supplier. It requires a basis of trust and understanding regarding needs and commitments that can come only from nurtured relationships. Further, maintaining supplier relations helps guarantee the same vocabulary on both sides and enables people to understand each other's cultures, thereby easing cooperation.

The security of a lasting relationship, as well as a substantial amount of business, gives suppliers an interest in their customer's well-being. Kelly Howell, the independent sales representative, says Molex has often suggested that PCEC change its design to eliminate a Molex part when doing so is in the best long-term interests of both firms. At Chrysler, which has led in the use of supply alliances among U.S. automakers, one castings supplier recommended replacing its own intake manifolds with plastic ones, saving Chrysler three dollars a car. That suggestion cost the firm the business, because it does not make plastic parts. But it was rewarded with new orders for other components.[4]

Comments Barry Morris, the Marks & Spencer director for men's clothing: "Our suppliers' knowledge that we will be in business together for the long term gives us better interfaces with them and reduces costs by lowering organizational overheads and encourages planning and investment." Regarding overheads, consider that to generate the same volume from the marketplace that Xerox gets from its alliance with Kinko's Copy Centers, 150 additional sales representatives would be needed.

Alliances create value over time through ongoing efforts to improve mutual knowledge about how to raise quality, lower costs, cut cycle time, and increase customer satisfaction. When suppliers are changed, that shared learning bridge is broken and must be rebuilt. For instance, Motorola has learned that subtle changes a new supplier makes in a part can damage interactions in the product it goes into; final product performance then suffers, regardless of how much testing is done. Supplier continuity, on the other hand, has meant shared learning curves that for the past decade or more have helped improve materials costs by 10 percent annually in some of Motorola's businesses.

More durable relationships also support longer-term investments, which tend to be more efficient. The CEO of one electronics industry supplier tells of his firm receiving a three-month order from a customer, when one year would have been more cost effective. Being uncertain of future business, he bought cheaper equipment for this order that was also slower and less productive than other equipment, which would have increased productivity for the customer by 30 percent.

In general, the costs of changing supply partners may include any of the factors listed in the table shown.

Focused Competition. Another powerful cost reduction tool is focused competition—not because it motivates suppliers to offer their best price, which is not necessarily the case, but because it forces them to concentrate on better cost management. Motorola has found, for example, that less competition leads to smaller cost reductions. And, as noted in Chapter 3, focused competition is a key factor behind Motorola's getting twice the annual cost reductions from essentially the same supply base that serves PCEC.

Costs of Changing Supply Partners	
Higher overheads	More purchasing staff to manage supplier turnover
	Initial quality audits, plus organization, financial evaluations
	Setting up logistics, EDI, point-of-sale, bar coding systems
	Bringing new supplier into customer rating system
	Quality testing, accelerated life testing on all newly sourced items
	Establishing new part numbers, stock locations
Smaller, less efficient investments	Anticipating change, suppliers-minimize investments unique to customer
	Higher unit costs due to small volume start with new suppliers
Lost learning curves	Lost shared understandings, trust, experience
	Less effective integration of supplied items into customer's product

Improved Forecasts, Logistics, and On-Line Communications.
Logistics systems that include reliable long- and short-term forecasts and that give suppliers flexibility to best allocate their own resources can also lower costs significantly; recall that Motorola doubled its inventory turns with Schedule Sharing. The use of Schedule Sharing, says PPG's Neil MacIvor, saves "a whole army of people" who would have to do the data collection and analysis manually.

Motorola is linked to its suppliers with EDI, which not only dramatically reduces paperwork and speeds response times but also is a conduit for automatically sharing forecasts, inventory levels, quality reports, and other data. Requiring suppliers to bar code all shipped goods is used to facilitate pay-from-receipt. Both practices cut cycle times and require fewer resources in receiving.

Commonality in Design. For companies with similar products, it is often possible to reduce costs by using parts that are common to more than one product or, alternatively, to begin with a standard product design and make variations to accommodate different needs of different models. PPG uses the first approach; M&S and Chrysler the second. The best approach depends on whether a local design with some standard parts has better combined cost and value than a central design with some local variation.

Multi-Unit Consistency. One source of cost reduction for a firm with multiple business units or buying groups is to develop standard purchasing practices. The alternative is higher costs because orders to the same firm from various units involve different paperwork, procedures, specifications, and part numbers.

Before Motorola began using global specifications, the firm in one case had twenty-three part numbers for the same part around the world. Multiple part numbers are a cost driver in data processing, material handling, purchasing, and accounts payable.

Level Loading. It was noted earlier that helping suppliers level load their plants can lower their costs. Similar effects are possible with their design and engineering staffs. In the past, Ford allocated design responsibility between internal designers and suppliers in a way that gave its internal staff a steady work flow. Doing this meant that any fluctuations in demand for designers were carried by the suppliers, a practice that caused havoc with them and raised their costs. By more clearly defining design responsibility and using better planning, Ford now secures design continuity for its suppliers. For the same reasons, Motorola wants some tooling made by its plastics suppliers and some made for them. A supplier that makes all of its own tooling may have problems level loading its tooling output because of changes in demand, and such difficulties can raise tooling costs.

Volume Purchases. One way multi-unit customers can reduce their costs is by negotiating volume purchase agreements with suppliers. A related practice is for a customer to have similar agreements with second-, third-, or lower-tier suppliers to help its higher-tier suppliers get better prices than they might on their own. Motorola asks its piece-part suppliers to give its assemblers the same price it gets from them. The company also deals directly with suppliers of major materials such as plastics, negotiating a global price in those instances.

Technical Assistance. Generally, it is impossible to expect every supplier that meets a firm's selection criteria to have the resource depth needed to stay near the cutting edge of quality and productivity. This is why many larger customers find it worthwhile to help smaller supply partners in areas like process characterization, plant layout, and materials selection.

Motorola's Materials Quality Engineering (MQE) function was created to solve technical material problems discovered in its own factories. Now, based on experience that includes data from quality audits, MQE focuses on problem prevention in product design and at the supplier, as well as root-cause analysis. When MQE engineers visit suppliers, they learn what the firms' processes are capable of doing and help improve performance. At times, what MQE personnel learn from suppliers leads to changes in Motorola designs. Because MQE has markedly influenced cost and quality improvement, most Motorola factories now have an MQE department. Motorola also provides technical assistance through development engineering plant visits, manufacturing process characterizations, and training at Motorola University.

Financial and Accounting Strategies and Other Methods. Without alliances, companies sometimes pay for suppliers' tooling to ensure capacity is available when needed, and to be able to move the tooling to another firm in the event of problems with a supplier. Those issues are reduced in alliances, but it can still make sense to pay for tooling. Chrysler and Ford, for example, enjoy lower costs of capital than many of their suppliers. As a consequence, the automakers pay for suppliers' tooling used to make their components and benefit from the lower costs that result.[5]

To keep track of cost management, accounting methods that accurately reflect actual improvements should be used. For example, the traditional way of tracking inventory costs uses the lower of either cost or market value. All purchases are tracked relative to a formula cost, which is based on the cost at the end of an accounting period; future buys are compared to that cost. Such methods, however, do not identify real cost improvements from suppliers. To do that, Motorola compares the prices for the current and previous years. This method is termed *actual-to-actual analysis*.

Activity-based costing (ABC) is another useful way to manage costs, because the process gives the user a better grasp of cost drivers. Chrysler encourages its suppliers to use ABC for this reason and effectively manages the cost information provided. The automaker also derives separate target costs for piece parts and the investments needed to make them. This separation makes it easier to understand the variable costs of a part, which is made difficult by periodic volume swings in the auto industry. Further, says Steve Zimmer, director of supplier development at Chrysler, if equipment were included in part costs, one could lose track of when that is fully amortized, and depreciation charges might still be included in part prices after the equipment was fully written off.

Finally, growing demands for quality have spawned expensive and disruptive multiple quality audits at suppliers. One company that supplies the auto industry and others is subject to more than twenty full-scale audits a year. To reduce this burden, Chrysler, Ford, and General Motors are jointly developing a third-party system of quality audits for suppliers that is expected to be in place by 1997. The third parties will be established organizations that already audit and certify companies under the aegis of the International Standards Organization. Each customer expects to continue managing its own audits at the piece-part level to meet its unique needs. Other industries are becoming involved in the same third-party process.

SUPPLIER INITIATIVE

An alliance brings a supplier closer to its customer than any other arrangement. This closeness gives the supplier better knowledge of the customer's situation and, with trust and the security of a stable relationship, opens the door for the supplier to suggest how the customer can improve its ways. To illustrate, Tom Nord of Jos. T. Ryerson & Son, a unit of Inland Steel Industries, recently suggested to Honeywell, which is a customer, that it switch to a different grade of aluminum that was available for weekly deliveries. Because the aluminum Honeywell was buying had to be ordered every six months and stockpiled, Nord knew that changing to a different grade would lower his customer's total costs.[6]

In one retail alliance, the supplier helped its customer develop an in-store demonstration program that the retailer could manage with its own employees—a method that saved costs compared to having outsiders handle the demonstrations.

Of course, every supplier is also a customer. To achieve best costs, quality, and cycle time—both for its own benefit and to support its customers' advancing expectations—a firm must form alliances with its own suppliers. In alliances, as noted earlier, suppliers may also initiate sessions with customers to brainstorm ways to create more value together, as PCEC has done.

SHARED PRACTICES

Ron Schubel of Molex, who is a strong champion of alliances, says the largest overall cost savings come from a mutual belief—and consequent actions based on it—that continuous cost and quality improvement are important to both firms. Further, both Motorola and its suppliers report that savings from joint efforts such as cooperation in design and to improve quality and productivity are significant, and can be comparable to those resulting from activities wholly within either firm. Marks & Spencer's Guy McCracken also says that most cost reductions in his firm's experience have come from mutual efforts.

Shared understandings are the basis for joint improvements. When companies work separately and exchange little information, one firm may reduce a cost in a way that raises costs for the other. If a customer changes its plating process to lower its direct costs, for instance, this may cause quality problems and raise the defect rate for parts made by the supplier. By the same token, sharing future plans also helps drive down costs. For example, the Paging Products Group's regular sharing of its product technology road maps has led to supplier suggestions about new materials and processes that worked better and cost less than what PPG had planned to use.

Such understandings should be pursued across every interface between customer and supplier. This practice can be seen at Molex, where people have regular discussions with Philips Consumer Electronics Company shop-floor employees as well as with plant managers and their teams, product engineers, and top managers regarding their work with Molex products. In each case relevant data from PCEC factories, warranty experience, and more are shared to find ways to do better together. Such sharing cuts costs significantly. To illustrate, Philips had a scheduling system that required thousands of purchase orders. Drawing on its own experience, Molex suggested a new method to alleviate the paperwork burden. When implemented the method reduced information processing time, lowered errors, and trimmed overhead costs. The amount of premium transport work went to zero.

Quality, of course, also has a critical effect on cost because of the high costs of inspection, repair, rejects, field failures, and more. This is one reason why Chrysler, Motorola, and Marks & Spencer seem so obsessed with quality in everything they do. For instance, in 1984 Motorola inspected virtually every item of production material received from suppliers. By

Alliance Cost Reduction Sources	
Customer initiative	Partner choice
	Supply base reduction
	Continuing with same suppliers
	Better quality
	Volume, including corporatewide scale
	Include lower tier suppliers in volume purchase agreements
	Focused competition
	Long production runs and level loading
	Common design/specification for different items
	Consistent practices across buying units
	Better design, early supplier design participation
	Improved materials, processes, productivity
	Accurate forecasts/reliable order patterns
	Manage both firms' inventory, and logistics, as one system
	Short operating cycle times
	Lower tolerances for noncritical item
	Paperwork reduced or eliminated through EDI
	Bar coding, pay-on-receipt
	Technical assistance
	Pay for suppliers' tooling if cost of capital is lower
	Separate fixed and variable costs
	Activity-based costing
Supplier initiative	Partner choice
	Shorter cycle times
	Timely shipments, correct volumes
	Accurate invoicing
	Better quality, productivity
	Lower costs at own suppliers
	Propose alternative parts, tooling, practices to customer
	Activity-based costing
Shared activities	Joint quality and productivity gains
	Avoided delays
	Shared understanding at all levels
	Know effects of firms' separate costs
	Identify nondesign cost drivers
	Joint planning
	Joint cost-cutting/value-adding workshops

1994 virtually all material receipts went directly to manufacturing without having to be inspected by Motorola. In the Land Mobile Products Sector, direct savings included expenses related to more than one hundred employees who used to perform incoming inspection, as well as many others who used to detect and fix material problems in production operations.

Early design cooperation is another key to lower costs. One time, when PCEC was pursuing a 75 percent reduction in the number of product models, its suppliers observed that they would have used a different approach and achieved better results if they could have made their inputs earlier. PCEC's own engineers concurred with that observation. In essence, supplier understandings of their tooling and other cost drivers, if included in the reduction effort, would have led to lower costs than what PCEC achieved alone. More generally, in a recent $600 million annual purchase, joint design and value analysis with suppliers produced about 35 percent of PCEC's total cost reduction.

Shortened cycle times also reduce costs. Consider that if a company has a one-week factory cycle and a quality problem is found late in the cycle, then it has one week's worth of products to fix. By contrast, with a one-day cycle time there is just one day of production to fix. This is more than a one-time cost reduction. Due to the resulting increased flexibility, short cycle times also avoid costs associated with making changes in response to demand fluctuations. Molex used to do a large amount of costly expediting to meet Motorola's cycle time requirements. Now, following internal changes, the amount of expediting is low because Molex processes are getting closer to the customer's target cycle times.

The cost-reducing practices discussed in this section are summarized in the table shown.

7

SUPPLY BASE
MANAGEMENT

*If a supplier has a problem and we can't fix it, that is a
failure for us as well.*

Tom Stallkamp, vice president for procurement and supply and
general manager for large car operations, Chrysler

*The real payback comes from better service and a faithful
supplier; you can't buy that.*

Sunil Lakhani, director of advanced manufacturing technology,
Motorola's Paging Products Group, on helping suppliers when they
have problems

Individually, each supply alliance adds value for the customer. Given that most firms spend about half their revenues with suppliers, however, having alliances across the entire supply base is a powerful competitive resource. To get the most value from these alliances, they must be managed as a collective whole.

The practices articulated here apply to individual alliances as well as an entire supply base. They can generally be implemented by any firm, regardless of size or strength. Of course, increased value comes from investing more resources in better measurement systems, technical support, and other activities. Still, many firms underinvest in these areas relative to the substantial benefits they offer. One reason for underinvesting is a short-term attitude; as with quality, the major benefits of supply base development are gained over the longer term. Another reason is that many firms do not yet recognize the link between such investments and their own bottom line.

Taking Motorola's experience as a guide, its supplier-related programs are achieving cost reductions that are twice what others get with similar purchases through arm's-length transactions. And except for technical assistance, Motorola's programs cost a fraction of 1 percent of the value of the purchased material that is involved. For comparison, consider that Philips Consumer Electronics Company has not used focused competition because of internal resource constraints. These have kept Philips from investing in better quality audits and benchmarking—both of which are necessary to develop needed metrics—and supplier training. One PCEC executive notes this absence has caused adversarial relationships with suppliers, among other problems.

It would be a mistake to conclude from a discussion of how a customer can strengthen its suppliers that customers are somehow inherently smarter. Clearly this cannot be, since every firm is both a customer and a supplier. Indeed, the idea that customers can learn a great deal from their suppliers is one rationale for alliances. Because alliances are supposed to create more value for the customer's market, however, that firm must take the lead in setting and holding suppliers to stretch goals. Only the customer is positioned to understand the health of its supply base and to affect this for its own best interest. The process begins with objective performance measures.

Objectives-Based Performance Measures

Effective supplier management requires a set of impartial measures—often called metrics—that are used as elements of rating systems to assess progress toward objectives, set priorities, spot issues, indicate corrective actions, allocate business among suppliers, select new suppliers, and further develop the supply base. Consistently applied, such metrics are valuable for customer and supplier alike. They also make relationships more predictable, which is needed for mutual trust.

Molex, for instance, competes for Motorola business with six or seven rivals in its commodity group. When it loses to one of them, says

Ron Schubel, Motorola's use of unbiased metrics to govern the entire process guarantees that the defeat will be seen as fair and aboveboard.

MONITOR BOTH SIDES

Because alliances link customer and supplier processes, the customer needs to use the same metrics to assess its own contribution to joint activities. Consider that Motorola uses virtually the same audit for both its internal activities and those of its suppliers. Relevant supply metrics are also built into the performance evaluations of Motorola personnel, who are held accountable for supplier performance. Going farther, a customer's activities may directly affect supplier conduct; a useful set of metrics should reflect such behavior.

To illustrate, when Motorola adopted shorter development cycle time as a new corporate goal, early design cooperation with suppliers was acknowledged as a major contributor to reaching that goal. Even so, not everyone was on board. Some of the firm's development engineers did not see the benefits of supplier design; were so pressed by schedules that they thought it was faster to design a part themselves; and—as in many firms—had a not-invented-here attitude. Some suppliers also lacked the necessary design capabilities.

In response, a subcommittee of Motorola's supply management council developed early participation metrics to be used by suppliers and Motorola's engineering community and reflected in their job evaluations. All Motorola groups and sectors were encouraged to use the metrics or face poor internal assessments. The metrics show when the supplier got involved, its contribution to design, and the results of those efforts. Each engineering group is now measured on its ability to work with suppliers early in the design cycle. Best practice is defined as when the supplier does the entire design, based on a Motorola need. The lowest score is given when Motorola does the design without supplier involvement. In addition, suppliers are monitored to assess the degree to which early participation in the design cycle affected their prototype and production part cycle times.

Clearly, customer–supplier alliances depend on commitments and effective practices on both sides of the relationship. For those reasons, as much as Motorola wants to have the best suppliers, it also wants to be *their* best customer. To understand how it can reach this goal, the firm annually surveys its preferred suppliers, asking them to compare it on several measures, on a plant-by-plant basis, with their other customers.

METRICS FOR SUPPLY ALLIANCES

An effective set of metrics derives from the customer's objectives for its alliances and is based on marketing, benchmarking, and other data that define desired performances. The copper materials firm Outokumpu, for instance, wants to reduce impurities from its scrap suppliers, so measures and tracks impurity levels in the scrap it buys.

What Is Measured, and How Often. The sophistication of a measurement process should correspond to the customer's dependence on its suppliers and the complexity of their interactions. All important desired results and key contributing factors should be regularly observed. The frequency of measurement and reporting to each supplier depends on the cost of collecting and analyzing data, compared with the cost of problems caused by monitoring too infrequently.

At Marks & Spencer, formal metrics cover each supplier's design creativity, quality, value, production reliability, investments in technology, EDI and point-of-sale (POS) systems, and ability to meet delivery targets. M&S measures some parameters qualitatively; among them is creativity, which is based on an internal consensus of those at M&S who work with the supplier. Others are gauged quantitatively. Complaints and a supplier's delivery record are tracked weekly. Quality is assessed through quality audits and by monitoring the number of faulty goods consumers return. In addition, M&S looks at every new line it launches and makes weekly sales reports to the supplier.

The company also pays attention to each supplier interface. Factors considered include flexibility, responsiveness, and professionalism in relationships. Carole O'Beirne, the senior selector, calls this the "stickiest issue area." People do not always get along well with each other: There may be discourtesies, or someone may violate trust. Relationships per se are regularly discussed with suppliers. Another area M&S monitors is a supplier's technical performance. Metrics for that include the time required to help a firm, as well as technical contributions it is prepared to make (such as in new machinery and fabrics). All these considerations are combined with each firm's past and anticipated future volume with M&S to forecast its volume growth compared with other suppliers.

Its deep interest in long-term relationships has led Marks & Spencer to survey its supply base periodically to spot future management and financial issues, and to keep abreast of supplier health. Among the topics are profitability and management continuity, as well as what percentage of an M&S product range is made where. The latter issue receives attention to ensure that far-off sources do not become too prominent, thereby compromising lead and response times.

Faced with acute competitive pressure on costs, quality, and cycle time, Motorola uses metrics to monitor all key supplier results and the factors that influence these. For instance, piece-part quality is measured in factory fallout (defects found on the production line), customer returns, and outgoing quality from the supplier. The cost of quality is also reported. To do this, the cost of defect prevention (including training, quality tools, and improvement teams) is compared with the costs of assessment (including inspection and testing), and the costs of failure (including repairs, returns, and shipping costs). Similarly, total customer cycle time—the period from order receipt to shipment—is measured, along with cycle times for design, procurement, manufacturing, unique long lead items not carried in inventory, and delinquencies.

Because quality is a major factor in cost and cycle time, as well as a direct source of customer value, Motorola goes beyond monitoring current performances to spot and help fix suppliers' defective quality processes. This is done with its comprehensive quality audits, which identify areas needing more attention, whether these are in management systems, manufacturing, engineering, administration, purchasing, or other activities. The same audit is also used to assess suppliers' cycle time abilities and other skills that contribute to Motorola's desired performances.

Suppliers are asked to draw up improvement plans based on the quality audits. They are then monitored and encouraged to complete the plans on a timely basis. Since the manual that details audit procedures is readily available, suppliers can review them at any time to determine where they need to improve.

Because the audits are costly and time-consuming, Motorola originally did them every two years. Through benchmarking with Chrysler, it found the audits unnecessary for top suppliers. Consequently the company changed its approach and now plans audits based on each supplier's initial scores. Further, Motorola has asked its best performers to substitute self-assessments and send it the findings. Quality is still monitored in Motorola plants from parts problems on the production line.

To complement the audits, Motorola asks suppliers for monthly reports on their in-house quality and cycle time trends. These reports help identify problems quickly, keep the company updated on supply base progress in critical areas, and support planning generally.

Unlike Marks & Spencer, where most suppliers to its U.K. stores work directly with its London headquarters, Motorola and its suppliers' operations are found worldwide, with many local links. To monitor key performances, Motorola has a global defect-tracking system. Every Monday morning, the system gives each supplier, along with its Schedule Sharing file, a quality report on defect rates for the prior week based on data from around the world. (For more on Schedule Sharing, see Chapter 5.) The information is provided by part number; whether the defect was found in receiving, work in process, or finished goods; and whether it was administrative, cosmetic, mechanical, or electrical. Suppliers also get a monthly report card on quality, stockouts, and inventory turns. Measures are reported at two levels: by customer and supplier facility, and in the aggregate.

Motorola's Paging Products Group makes supply-related performance results, the worldwide forward procurement list (composed of preferred suppliers), and other relevant information available on a global network server computer. All PPG supply managers and engineers thus have ready access to the latest data from anywhere in the world. Among the other supplier activities Motorola measures are service, design participation, current and five-year capacity plans, and five-year technology road maps. Formerly, Motorola experienced unexpected volume constraints at suppliers that prevented it from completing all customer orders.

Like Marks & Spencer, Motorola actively monitors the health of relationships at each supplier interface. Both firms also monitor volume trends with each supplier. One reason for doing this is to maintain balance in allocating business among suppliers. Another is to identify firms that may be having longer-term problems, and to initiate solutions as early as possible. A third reason specific to Motorola is that if a preferred supplier's volume trend for all Motorola locations is declining, there is an objective rationale for dropping the firm. Typically, this happens when Motorola's need for the firm's technology is declining, and it has not been feasible for the supplier to change to a new technology.

Having some balance in the business awarded to different suppliers serves three purposes: to help motivate each supplier to make its best efforts, to achieve low costs through better economies, and to avoid overdependence on any one firm. At Motorola, for example, one packaging firm had most of the business; finding another source was difficult. Eventually others were located, and Motorola discovered that the first supplier was not doing well in some areas. PPG's Neil MacIvor says this experience showed the importance of constantly challenging a supply base, and being particularly sensitive when one firm has a dominant share of business.

The various metrics used to monitor trends, spot issues, and guide supplier performance are summarized in the table below.

Ongoing Metrics Development. To stay useful, alliances must continue producing unique value for the markets they serve. Since markets

Metrics for Supplier Alliances	
What Is Measured	**Examples**
Desired results	Quality, timing, cost, design, weight, safety, volume, functions, other value sources
Key components of results	Quality data from supplier and customer, various cycle times, key cost drivers, design creativity and participation, technology factors, EDI and POS capabilities, capacity, ramp-up, plant location
Firm's interface	Relationships, service, responsiveness
Organization and management	Supplier financial strength, management continuity, organization processes and systems, functional skills, relationships with own suppliers
Future plans	Capacity needs, technology road maps, expected performance and process improvements
Volume compared with others	Trends in each firm's position in the supply base

keep advancing, one's expectation for alliances—and the corresponding metrics—must progress as well.

For example, Marks & Spencer and Motorola have stretch targets for their suppliers in quality and other areas, and both firms regularly introduce new objectives and practices to maintain their competitive edges. Further, value frontiers are shifting toward harder-to-measure areas like service and behavioral qualities (for example, a firm's effectiveness on an early design team). With a reduced supply base composed of high-performing firms, there is also a tendency toward parity in key areas. These factors make consensus judgments, which are often used in the absence of quantitative measures, less effective. For these reasons, both companies continue to improve their measurement systems.

Motorola's Paging Products Group illustrates. To select preferred suppliers, it recently installed a more comprehensive and quantitative set of criteria for selecting preferred suppliers, backed up by hard data. The new system helps build trust with suppliers by providing clearer guidance about how a firm qualifies as a preferred supplier. Before, this question could be answered only qualitatively. The system is also a broad measure for the overall status of the supply base, which can be used to refine the definition of the base and plan for its future development. Parameters in the new broad rating system are weighted according to their judged importance. Those unique to particular commodities are considered separately.

DEFICIENT MEASUREMENT SYSTEMS

Without objective metrics, alliance building is inhibited. In the advertising business, for example, effective ads can clearly advance a company's market position.[1] But the inability of advertising agencies to gauge the contributions of their creative work objectively has stymied their movement from traditional commercial relationships into alliances with their customers.

When adequate measurement systems cannot be created, it may still be possible to have useful partial measures. For instance, the Kodak–IBM alliance includes many complex activities that are unique to the relationship. Further, from a supplier's perspective, alliance performance depends on a customer's level of sophistication, and this requires different kinds of training and of software for each customer.

Both factors have made it difficult to benchmark total cost against comparable alternatives, which has been an issue in the Kodak–IBM alliance.

As a partial substitute, Kodak business units are asked to weigh the cost of contemplated new activities with IBM against commercial alternatives. Both firms recognize that such comparisons—of isolated outside alternatives with integrated elements of the alliance—are not fully analogous, but a better approach has not yet been conceived.[2] To gauge services in their alliance, the firms compare current performances (based on surveys done by an independent consultant) with past service levels. Again, this is not as satisfactory as having an outside benchmark, but it is better than not having any metrics.

CLASSIFYING SUPPLIERS

In a dynamic market where every company is reaching for better performances, a supply base is in constant flux as each firm strives to outdo others. Therefore it is useful to know which members of a supply base have proven themselves over time and thus deserve more attention.

Marks & Spencer informally recognizes two kinds of suppliers: those they have grown up with, and those that have more recently come in with a specific product. The established suppliers are producing goods at high volume on a regular basis. Their understanding of M&S requirements is clear, and their ethos is very much linked to that of M&S. Reflecting the firms' long history together, Carole O'Beirne observes, "They are as much locked into our way of thinking as we are." These firms are more willing to take risks for M&S because there is more trust in the relationships. Should there be cutbacks, M&S would remain most loyal to this group. Even so, there is no room for complacency. All must keep pushing for more excellence. This group of suppliers is relatively static; there have been no recent entrants.

While the most intense links are with high-volume firms, relationships are also close with some lower-volume suppliers, depending on how their business relates to the consumer. For example, Littlestone and Goodwin, a handbag manufacturer, makes products that are highly valued by M&S customers. Although this small firm is a low-volume supplier, the relationship is critical to the ladies' handbag department.

Compared with Marks & Spencer, Motorola has a larger, more globally distributed supply base. The company also specifies more performance dimensions, and many suppliers serve several Motorola units, often at different locations. Accordingly, Motorola has developed a more formal and globally consistent system for classifying suppliers. One category, preferred suppliers, includes those firms that best meet specified criteria. They can get new Motorola business; other firms cannot. (Motorola expects eventually to have all its business with preferred suppliers.) Firms not in this category, holdovers from the pre-alliance days, still serve because they have unique designs, processes, or technology. These are being weeded out as Motorola continues to trim its supply base.

To be a preferred supplier, a firm must have served Motorola satisfactorily for at least one year. Furthermore, its total performance—reflecting its metrics on quality, delivery, capacity, quality audits, commitment to continuous improvement, early design participation, technology road maps, cost improvement, and service—must be above a defined level. Each parameter is weighted according to what Motorola sees as its relative importance. Other requirements include systems availability, such as EDI and bar coding and the compatibility of those systems with Motorola's, a commitment to apply for the Malcolm Baldrige quality award, and a firm's projected five-year trend in business with Motorola. Additional considerations are a firm's financial stability, whether its staff has taken specified training courses, data transfer ability, plant locations, participation in total customer satisfaction team competitions, and environmental performance in areas like recycling and the elimination of chlorofluorocarbons in manufacturing.

SUPPLIER RATINGS

To sustain focused competition and keep a supply base at advancing cost and value frontiers, there must be a consistent, objective way to measure each firm's overall current performance. The metrics used for this are a subset of the customer's full system of measures described earlier. Clearly, supplier ratings should reflect the customer's priorities.

At Marks & Spencer, each supplier is measured on specified performances in quality, delivery, consistency, adherence to agreed programs, management support, and product innovation. These parameters are weighted by the competitive priorities of each M&S department. Quality, as has been noted, is always a first-order requirement; no firm can be an M&S supplier without meeting its high quality standards. Because M&S competes on value, price is often the second consideration, followed by volume capabilities and timing. Supplier performance is judged on a consensus basis in each buying group and agreed upon with senior management.

Chrysler's rating system adds weighted supplier performances in four categories: quality, cost management, delivery, and technology. (Quality counts for 40 percent of the total; each of the others, 20 percent.) Each category has several subcategories. For example, cost management includes the number of improvement suggestions made by a supplier, the percentage of those that are implemented, and cost reductions as a percentage of the total buy from that firm. It also encompasses how well a supplier is managing its own supply costs and how effective it is in achieving the automaker's variable cost and investment objectives in its work with Chrysler teams.

The technology category includes the testing of a supplier's parts and its program management skills. Among these skills are the ability to run the whole program in terms of timing and integration, the effectiveness of interfaces, the firm's management of its own suppliers, its ability to keep tooling and prototype programs on track, and generally reducing the risks inherent in a new product.

Compared with those of Chrysler and M&S, Motorola's rating of parts suppliers' current performance places more emphasis on cost, reflecting steeply declining price curves for its own products. Except in the case of a few commodity groups, Motorola's piece-part suppliers are often less important sources of new technology than are internal developments and equipment suppliers. The firm combines its metrics reflecting quality and inventory turns—major cost drivers controlled by suppliers—with a metric for stockouts. Stockouts are included because Motorola wants to meet its own customer delivery commitments, and suppliers are expected to maintain a lean inventory without endangering these commitments.

Each firm's rating is then multiplied by its proposed pricing; the result is a composite indicator of supplier cost. Motorola recently began using the same formula around the world to permit consistent global comparisons of suppliers within a commodity group. The company's monthly report to each supplier shows its rating, and how it compares to others (with identities masked) in the same commodity group.

Consistent with its renown as a world leader in quality, Motorola requires exceptional quality performance from its suppliers and measures them accordingly. One criterion is passing stringent quality audits. Another is its Six Sigma quality goal (described earlier), which Motorola employees and suppliers alike take very seriously. A third is the supplier's ratings. For multi-location suppliers, a quality problem at any one plant will harm the firm's rating, regardless of Motorola's volume at that plant. Motorola wants the same high quality at all volume levels.

For convenience, supplier ratings for partnership status and current performance are summarized in the table below.

When Suppliers Have Problems

Focused competition, constantly advancing metrics, and tactics that earn suppliers' commitments help keep them from becoming complacent about the need for ongoing improvement (see Chapter 3). Still, every firm has occasional troubles. In alliances, the high cost of replacing established supply relationships with new ones suggests that the most effective approach is to mend the problem.

Out of a concern for its own well-being, Marks & Spencer wants a healthy balance among suppliers for multiple sourcing and seeks to maintain the vitality of all of them. Comments Barry Morris: "Most clothing suppliers have been with us for many years. They have good

Ratings for Supply Alliances		
Category	**Application**	**Metrics Used**
Partnership status	Partner selection, awarding new business, termination	All operating and organizational factors that gauge a firm's current performance and its ability to meet the customer's long-term needs
Current performance rating	Assigning volume, finding and fixing problems	Key performances such as quality, cost, delivery regularly reported to monitor continuous improvement

years and bad years—in terms of quality and delivery problems, inadequate development, products that don't sell. But running through it all, we understand we are in it together. Our relationships are like marriages. Only if a supplier fails to perform over a continuous time do we part company. Those are the exceptions that prove the rule. We want long-term relations; they give us the benefits of mutual understanding and quality based on constancy of production. Our suppliers' knowledge that we will be in business together for the long term gives us better interfaces with them and reduces costs by lowering organizational overheads and encourages planning and investment."

Further, Morris says, if one firm's share suddenly drops, Marks & Spencer has to question itself as well as the supplier. M&S may have given the firm poor guidance, communications or technical help may have been inadequate, or early warning signs may not have been spotted.

Chrysler's Tom Stallkamp, vice president, procurement and supply, and general manager of the company's large car operations, shares Morris's philosophy. If a supplier's plant is not doing well on quality, he says, and the problem is not fixed, Chrysler will move its business out of that plant. However, Stallkamp observes, "If a supplier has a problem and we can't fix it, that is a failure for us as well."

Understanding each supplier's situation at any time, through effective metrics and constant communications, makes it possible to know how best to manage a relationship. At Motorola, if a supplier's rating drops below a certain level, the first reaction is to discuss the issue with the firm to identify the issue and determine how well it is understood. The ensuing exchange surfaces root causes, which may be in the supplier's service, capacity, or other areas, or in something Motorola did not do right such as a poor design, or allocating too much volume.

If the problem originated with the supplier, the firm may not get new work from any part of Motorola until the situation is rectified. Motorola may provide training or help overcome a capacity problem. If the issue is not resolved by a specific date, the company is dropped as a preferred supplier and Motorola actively looks for a replacement. Since all suppliers receive monthly performance ratings, there is no surprise if one's status is changed.

Motorola's Tom Slaninka observes that to keep and strengthen the best suppliers requires empathy with their situation. A new plant, a fire, work force turnover, or some other temporary condition may cause his firm to be more flexible or to look for issues that suggest deeper management problems. Slaninka cites the example of a printed circuit board supplier that experienced frequent employee turnover. Concerned that this might indicate more serious difficulties, Motorola discovered that the firm was having financial problems and was squeezing its employees' salaries. When such problems surface, Motorola determines whether it should end the relationship, make a loan to the firm, or give it other assistance. If the firm's management understands Motorola's priorities but has lowered its commitment to them, termination may be necessary. Most often, the problem can be fixed.

Marks & Spencer also steps in to help suppliers with difficulties. Says vice chairman and managing director Clinton Silver: "There is no quick exit for suppliers with problems. If a firm's offering for a season is not acceptable, or if there is another problem, it is our mutual duty to help them get it right. This does not mean there are no fluctuations in a supplier's volume. At times, M&S will shift overcapacity from another supplier, with its blessing, to a supplier having a low volume problem."

If a supplier's products are not selling well, M&S may spur its development efforts to bring the volume back up. More generally, when M&S adjusts a supplier's volume downward, this is discussed with the firm and done to avoid damaging the firm's margins—unless M&S is getting exasperated. Still, M&S sometimes has had to drop long-term suppliers that could not keep up with its needs. While this does happen, it is rare. There is no formal process for abandoning a supplier, but the topic does involve senior management.

Introducing New Suppliers

There are two reasons for considering new suppliers. One is to stimulate the current supply base. The second is to meet product, capacity, technology, or other needs that current suppliers cannot readily satisfy.

REACHING FOR NEW FRONTIERS

Until the mid-1980s, Marks & Spencer was regarded as middle-of-the-road in terms of fashion. Now, it offers fashionable (what it calls "fashion right") goods that are priced to fit consumer budgets. This new emphasis was prompted when other High Street retail chains took the stylistic lead and succeeded. In response, M&S stepped up its emphasis on design, both internally and with its suppliers.

Many suppliers shifted to producing more fashionable styles quickly, because they were aware that doing so was increasingly important in their markets. Since the M&S ethos is not to drop suppliers, it helped those that were having difficulty with the transition.

Meanwhile, Marks & Spencer added some new suppliers, including German and Italian knitwear and tailoring manufacturers, which already were producing the kinds of merchandise it wanted. One was Steilmann, a highly regarded German firm that makes fashionable women's dresses and blouses, as well as women's and men's suits. Once M&S proved it could sell these, its existing suppliers said they could make them, too. M&S gave them technical assistance and identified the appropriate manufacturing equipment and processes. When they lacked internal design skills, M&S gave suppliers prototype garments and helped them develop the relevant abilities. In meetings with supplier executives, M&S constantly reinforced the need to invest in design.

As the retailer's traditional suppliers improved their designs, Steilmann lost the lead position. For the British market, M&S favors local suppliers for flexibility and quick response. Nonetheless, Steilmann remains an attractive supplier on the Continent for M&S retail business there.

FILLING GAPS

A customer's first obligation is to its current proven suppliers. And this includes keeping them posted on desirable future technology and capacity requirements. At times, however, existing suppliers cannot meet all of a firm's future needs.

Occasionally, for example, Philips Consumer Electronics Company must leapfrog its supply base to take advantage of new technology generations. One such case is work with Texas Instruments: The only product it supplies to PCEC is a deformable mirror device that is intended to replace picture tubes in projection TV sets. PCEC could not have gotten this leading edge technology from its picture tube suppliers.

Similarly, computer chips are a critical component for PCEC. Because chip technology keeps moving ahead, PCEC cannot stay with one supplier but must first understand what each can offer before choosing a source. It does this by reviewing proprietary information about future designs, which chip firms share with it. To avoid taking undue technological risks with a new and unproven chip, PCEC uses it only in low-volume, high-end products until the technology is confirmed.

Strengthening the Supply Base

Several factors—including focused competition, more volume, and opportunities to improve—nourish a base of well-chosen suppliers. To further strengthen that base and move it toward ever higher levels of quality and performance, a company must monitor its health as a collective whole, plan for its future, identify priority actions, provide assistance as needed, be sensitive to the needs of smaller suppliers, and protect its interests. Often, addressing the needs of those firms that supply one's suppliers creates even more value.

Monitoring and Planning

Every week, Marks & Spencer talks informally with each supplier about its performance, current issues, and future plans. If the retailer is not getting what it wants, M&S discusses this with the supplier, involving several management levels. Once a season (every six months), each M&S team that interfaces with a supplier must reach consensus on overall assessments. It then meets with the supplier's senior managers to review where both parties stand, discuss desired improvements, and receive feedback on any issues. Because performance information flows constantly between M&S and its suppliers, there are no surprises in the discussions.

To guide its supply base development and management, the Paging Products Group at Motorola collects data from its quality audits, performance ratings, part qualification tests, and other sources to identify best practices among its suppliers. That helps PPG know how far to press suppliers on the road to continuous improvement, and it facilitates the spread of best practice so long as no firm's proprietary information is shared.

Using the same data sources, PPG also maintains an overall supplier-capability road map that displays plans for supplier training, development, Schedule Sharing, and other activities. This road map reflects the current status of the supply base and projects capabilities needed in the future.

There are also commodity-specific road maps, such as those for line spacing on printed circuit boards and the thinness of plastics, which are updated annually. These road maps show what and when something is needed. PPG also asks suppliers what capabilities they will have by specified dates. When they are ahead of Motorola, that information is used to adjust its strategic planning. As an example, by sharing road maps with suppliers PPG learned about a carbon ink process that worked better and cost less than its planned use of gold on circuit boards.

Also like Marks & Spencer, Motorola anticipates the future through business reviews conducted twice yearly with each preferred supplier. These in-depth reviews are similar to Motorola's internal quarterly management and operating reviews. They examine suppliers' monthly quality and cycle time data and any correction action plans. To be accepted, plans must have due dates and names on them. Expensive and time-consuming, these reviews help explain why Motorola wants to keep reducing the size of its supplier base. For the last agenda item, Motorola always asks suppliers how it can be a better customer.

Review locations alternate between the supplier's and Motorola's facilities. When they are at the supplier, Motorola people visit the firm's management and tour its plant for a firsthand look at what is going on. When reviews are at Motorola, its sourcing and engineering people get exposed to what the supplier is doing. This practice helps sell Motorola engineers on working more with the supplier, particularly in the early design stages.

PROVIDING TECHNICAL ASSISTANCE

Motorola and Marks & Spencer both view their supply partners as worthy of investments to advance their strengths. By English law, M&S cannot help its suppliers financially; like Motorola, though, it can and does help them in other ways.

For Motorola suppliers, technical assistance comes in the form of periodic quality audits and other on-site visits, which may include analyzing their practices and suggesting changes to improve costs, cycle time, and quality. Motorola also encourages its suppliers to seek expert help in areas where it is not strong, and encourages them to share information with each other. Courses at Motorola University, a fully accredited institution, provide some of the academic and more formal parts of the education process. These are available to any customer or supplier, or to any other firm. Specific courses are recommended to individual suppliers, depending on results from quality audits.

Motorola has a Materials Quality Engineering function that originally was set up to solve technical material problems in its factories. Now, based on an analysis of how it can contribute the most value, MQE focuses on problem prevention in design and in suppliers' processes. Much of the work involves finding root-cause solutions to obstacles that cause expensive and ineffective tests and inspections.

MQE and development engineers help suppliers plan new factories and are often at the latter's locations, advising them in areas such as material flows, layout, equipment, process streamlining, technology development, and moving to new technologies. Some suppliers have dramatically increased their throughput and profits from this assistance. Neil MacIvor, PPG's director of strategic sourcing, Americas, says MQE work with suppliers has dramatically affected his firm's cost and quality improvement. At times, what is learned from suppliers leads to changes in Motorola designs. Most Motorola factories have an MQE function, or the equivalent with another name.

Comments PPG vice president Bob Becknell: "The technical assistance we give a supplier is free of charge. We travel, prepare material, spend time, do analysis and system reviews, all at our own expense. On occasions when we know the job is very big, we might suggest they hire a permanent employee or get consulting help. We usually try to convince them that they can recover the cost of an additional employee. We then work closely with that person in a 'train the trainer' mode. We impart as much knowledge and information to the individual as possible so he or she can work on a day-to-day basis within the supplier's organization."

On anything deemed highly important, Motorola helps a supplier with its R&D. For example, Hewlett-Packard and Motorola often work together to design test equipment. Motorola helps H-P define future needs, and H-P provides new state-of-the-art equipment in time to meet Motorola's technical demands.

Motorola gives needed assistance to any source of critical parts, whether it is a preferred supplier or not. By contrast, since every item Marks & Spencer buys is offered to its customers, M&S gives technical help to each supplier that needs it.

Like Motorola, Marks & Spencer's top-priority concern is the quality of goods across its entire product range. At M&S, quality standards are higher than at other High Street chains. To sustain these standards, over the years an enormous technical input has been provided to help suppliers improve their quality. This has ranged from complete plants down to specific machinery. M&S also helps its suppliers in garment construction and fit, fabric and raw material specifications, and dying and finishing of raw materials and finished goods. In clothing and home furnishings, M&S employs eighty professional technologists; they are on-site with suppliers as often as two to three days a week.

Starting in the early 1990s, all M&S suppliers that still used the old final-inspection method to ensure quality began moving to the more powerful root-cause approach. Some needed a lot of help (which M&S offered) to make the change; others lacked the required culture and found the transition difficult. M&S made it quite clear that the changes it sought were for the quality of its goods and for customer satisfaction. This message forced changes in suppliers' styles, and sometimes in their management. Further, rising pressures on costs forced the suppliers to look at root causes and move away from final inspection.

MAINTAINING BALANCE

As noted earlier, a healthy supply base sustains focused competition, with no firm being in a position to dominate. One way to keep that balance is to consider each supplier's current share when awarding new business. Another is to give more assistance to lagging firms.

Marks & Spencer, for its high-value unique foods, seeks to avoid large volume swings among its suppliers. Part of its skill in development planning is to spur all suppliers involved in a product range, so as to avoid having only one firm launch new lines. To promote creativity, M&S encourages suppliers to visit high-quality restaurants, work with innovative consultants, and travel to places known for introducing new recipes and foods.

HELPING SMALLER SUPPLIERS

Because they tend to be more innovative, smaller suppliers can be important members of a supply base. Often, this benefit is accompanied by a disproportionate need for more technical assistance. Both Motorola and Marks & Spencer provide the extra help, because they appreciate the value of working with these firms.

Motorola's Paging Products Group plant at Boynton Beach, Florida, has about 120 production suppliers, roughly half of which are small local firms that make parts and other items not otherwise available. These suppliers typically have less experience and technical depth and thus need more assistance than PPG's other suppliers, which are mostly global companies.

M&S also spends a disproportionate amount of time bringing small suppliers up to speed. Its goal with them is to help the relationships grow to nurture new product lines. Senior selector Carole O'Beirne says small firms, in addition to being a key source of new opportunities, can be more flexible than large ones. It can be hard, she says, to get high-volume manufacturers to bring in a new line quickly, if that is necessary.

Small firms may also be swept aside by the volume demands of large customers. Marks & Spencer avoids this by keeping them in the picture. To illustrate, when a small supplier introduces a line that does well, it may get an exclusive for the first season. M&S also discusses its volume needs with that supplier and gives the firm every opportunity to meet future demand before talking to others. Depending on what the firm can do, M&S may give volume beyond its capacity to a large supplier for the following seasons. Still, the small firm would continue to make as much as it could; M&S will be fair and allocate some volume to it.

WORKING WITH SUPPLIERS' SUPPLIERS

The rationale for a company to have alliances across its supply base is that, with about half of its revenues going to those firms, they have a major impact on its performance. By the same logic, *their* suppliers also significantly influence its performance. Such firms, usually called second-tier suppliers, may also be important innovation sources. It is in the customer's interest to heed their conduct.

Motorola has agreements with its direct suppliers, especially for critical parts, that it must approve second-tier suppliers. It also evaluates those supply relationships as part of its quality audit process, and it trains direct suppliers in how to audit their own suppliers. Ideally, Motorola would like all its suppliers to do the audits as well as it does. But since its process is one of the most rigorous in the world, even if they do only half as well this is regarded as progress for the time being.

Motorola also wants its direct suppliers to have the equivalent of its MQE function so they can help their own suppliers as needed.

Given the importance of smaller suppliers, their inherent resource limits, and rising quality expectations in every market, these firms probably will not have the audit or technical assistance skills to meet the demands implied above. One way to keep them from constraining customer performance is for the firms to change to second-tier status, supplying the customer through larger direct sources that can be expected to have the needed skills. Another option is for customers to keep direct ties to smaller suppliers and to work with second-tier suppliers as necessary.

On first consideration, the merits of moving smaller suppliers under the aegis of better-endowed direct suppliers seem clear. Invariably, a second-tier base is much bigger than a direct base. If a typical firm has, say, twenty direct suppliers, and each of those is also typical, then there are 400 second-tier suppliers. That can be a heavy burden for audits and assistance. Adding suppliers to the base of other suppliers, however, only increases *their* load. Further, there is great value in maintaining close ties to all suppliers that significantly affect one's performance. For example, a large innovative contribution to garments sold by Marks & Spencer comes from fiber, fabric, equipment, and other firms that are at least once removed from the garment manufacturers. Getting the most value from such firms requires joint creativity and close understandings between the customer and all innovators, and these necessitate direct links among all of them.

Another reason to keep the customer in the loop is that it may be best positioned to promote superior performance across all suppliers having common traits. To illustrate, Motorola has about ten direct suppliers that, in turn, have about thirty plating suppliers whose performance was uneven at one time. Due to its central role, Motorola was able to develop profiles of the platers, help its ten direct suppliers determine which firms were most qualified to meet its needs, and suggest improvements for better quality, delivery, and cost.

With a variety of possible ties between a firm and its direct, second-tier, and more remote suppliers, there is no one best way to connect them—just as there is no single best way for members of a team to work together. As with a team, the most effective links are determined by each task to be done, guided by the customer's objective of optimizing value and cost.

All second-tier suppliers are approved by Marks & Spencer and by

Motorola (when the latter purchases assemblies). For first-tier suppliers, the M&S and Motorola quality functions tie in directly to their quality functions on an ongoing basis. In general, M&S assigns the responsibility for maintaining quality, cost, and cycle time supervision of second-tier firms to its direct suppliers, subject to M&S review. M&S does quality audits of them if the direct suppliers cannot. Since M&S does tremendous volume with second-tier fabric suppliers, it wants good relations with them as well, and maintains these independent of its relations with the direct manufacturers.

The multiple interfirm links implied by this experience are consistent with how effective teams work. Like teams, the links are feasible only when all members are committed to the same objective, trust each other, can react flexibly to needs and opportunities, and share a root-cause attitude toward problem solving. In other words, they require an alliance environment. Some guidelines that flow from this logic are summarized in the table shown.

PROTECTING SUPPLIERS INTERESTS

Suppliers of all sizes may be vulnerable to adverse currents in customer organizations. To maintain their commitments, some customer group should be assigned the task of caring for suppliers' well-being. At Motorola, this is done by the commodity management function.

Guidelines for Customer–Supplier Links		
Company	**Audits and Assistance**	**Innovation**
Customer	Responsible for major direct suppliers. Responsible for small and second-tier firms when direct suppliers are unable or dependence is high	Direct links between all contributing firms
Direct suppliers	With adequate resource depth, accountable for own suppliers, subject to customer review	Direct links between all contributing firms
Small and second-tier firms	Assign to customer or direct supplier according to whichever has relevant process knowledge, proximity advantages, and importance to customer.	Direct links between all contributing firms

One time, for example, a U.S. plastics supplier was being cut off sooner than expected by the Paging Products Group plant in the Far East. The plant was aggressively lowering costs and going to a less expensive local source, a switch that was also expected to ease communications and logistics. Out of concern, the U.S. supplier called Neil MacIvor at PPG's Florida plant. MacIvor raised the issue with his counterpart in the Far East, who agreed to postpone the changeover to avoid hurting the U.S. plastics firm.

The delay cost PPG considerable money, "but our relationships with our suppliers are worth more to us than that," says MacIvor, "and this firm was important to Motorola in plastics, which are a key commodity." The Far East plant stayed on its cost reduction plan by focusing on other activities. Moreover, as the local plastics supplier was moving into line, it had a tooling problem, and the U.S. firm was asked to keep supplying parts beyond the planned cutoff date. It did that, out of gratitude, until the Far East supplier could meet production demands.

CHANGES IN SUPPLIER OWNERSHIP

The power of a supply base flows from close links and commitments between customer and suppliers at all functions and levels—technical, operations, quality, management, and philosophical. In fact, the heart of an alliance is in the shared values and understandings that keep firms dedicated to the same course. This bond can be broken by ownership changes, as Marks & Spencer has experienced.

While it prefers long-term durable relationships, M&S is not immune to takeovers of suppliers by others having philosophies that conflict with its own. Should that occur, M&S would shift volume away from them. Says Barry Morris, "Our programs are not transportable" to firms with contrasting styles.

M&S occasionally favors the purchase of small suppliers by larger ones for better efficiency. Experience, however, has taught it that facilitating such deals is unwise. In the late 1980s, Paisley Hyer bought a number of M&S suppliers. M&S saw this as a good move because it consolidated the suppliers under a single management, but Paisley soon became insolvent. The experience taught M&S that it could not foresee the consequences of ownership changes. Consequently, any interest it may have had in making or brokering deals among its suppliers is now gone.

Still, Marks & Spencer does ask to be informed before deals are done, because a purchase could damage the high-trust, relationship-intense links with suppliers. Both potential buyers and M&S suppliers appreciate this. Since M&S is an important customer, it often gets informal queries early in the deal-making process. Clinton Silver notes that in his entire career, he indicated disfavor with specific deals only three times.

Keep Focusing the Supply Base

Because Motorola's supply base still includes some nonpreferred firms, the company is very strict about awarding new business to preferred suppliers. At the Paging Products Group, individual divisions are measured against this criterion, and all division sourcing organizations have agreed to a goal of doing a specific percentage of their business with those firms. The percentage is increased by consensus each year, leading to an eventual goal of 100 percent.

Increased volume for preferred suppliers comes from moving business to them when it is within their core competencies. Motorola also provides technical assistance to selected suppliers to help them advance to preferred status. Firms drop out for various reasons. Some cannot keep up with Motorola's advancing metrics or with desired technological changes, while others fall short of the company's ongoing effort to standardize parts across products and business units to achieve better costs, quality, and cycle time.

Motorola is constantly moving toward more volume and scale with each firm, and sharpening its definition of best-in-class as it knows the world. Although the company is sometimes at a supplier's mercy, it works out of these situations by developing other sources. Motorola encourages the best to broaden their product lines and to become involved in new programs. As they succeed, Motorola rewards them with more business, further downsizing its supply base.

8

MANAGING CONTINUOUS IMPROVEMENT

We all sing from the same hymn sheet: long-term relations based on trust, openness, and integrity. It is totally unacceptable to do anything that would hurt our suppliers—such as squeezing them in the short term to help our profits. Suppliers making the greatest contribution of quality and value to our customers benefit from an increased level of business.

Guy McCracken, joint managing director, Marks & Spencer

Guided by the customer's stretch goals and supporting metrics, and prompted by focused competition, every firm in an alliance supply base is expected to stay on a path of continuous improvement. The best way to manage this depends on whether the customer uses single or dual sourcing, and on the need to maintain balance among suppliers. Other considerations include economics, the supplier's performance for all of a customer's buying units, whether a supplier produces a unique design, and the amount of integration with the customer.

Sole sourcing should be used only in special situations (see Chapter 3). Even then, because sole sourcing is not consistent with focused competition, it does not provide the same opportunity for continuous improvement as having two or more suppliers in a commodity group or product range.

Sourcing Strategies for Supplier Management

The experiences of Marks & Spencer, Motorola, and Chrysler illustrate how sourcing practices are used in different situations to support supply base balance and continuous improvement.

MARKS & SPENCER

In its clothing business, suppliers' capacity limits often cause M&S to use dual or multiple sources for any one garment. To sustain focused competition, the volume allocated to each supplier by a department's selectors is determined in part by the firm's performance ratings at the department. Other factors include how a supplier is performing for all of M&S, as well as a need to keep some balance in the supply base, higher-level scale economies, and the economics of each firm.

With M&S, volume allocations may reflect business directives from upper management to ensure the highest degree of overall performance. For instance, if a supplier is doing well in menswear but having problems in ladies' wear, M&S may delay any volume growth until the difficulties are resolved. Also, says menswear director Barry Morris, M&S needs its suppliers to compete on product development and cost reduction. If a manufacturer becomes dominant, he adds, it may not drive as hard toward those goals; it may even become an adverse influence. Relationships might also get so comfortable that people's judgments are affected. For these reasons, M&S manages competition among its suppliers to keep their performances advancing, and will not let any firm dominate.

Allocations to individual firms vary from season to season. At times, says Morris, some firms seem to be getting more than their fair share of the M&S business due simply to their superior performance. By rejecting pressures to reduce their volume, M&S forces everyone else to keep on the path of continuous improvement.

If one supplier gets constantly lower volume, M&S visits it, identifies the causes, and encourages it to refocus. M&S does not want a supplier's position to erode, especially if the reason is a short-term problem in the context of an excellent track record. By contrast, persistent problems may not be fixable, in which case the firm will be dropped. When a supplier starts to slip, warning bells go off, and M&S

spends time with the firm to help it wherever performance is falling, be that design, quality, or delivery.

MOTOROLA

As Motorola gets closer to having an optimal-sized base of preferred suppliers, its attention shifts from supply base downsizing to managing preferred suppliers as a group. Efforts focus on advancing best practice in quality, cycle time, and other critical areas while working to bring the weakest firms up to speed. Motorola typically uses single sourcing because most suppliers have sufficient capacity to meet its needs on that basis. Like M&S, Motorola seeks to avoid overdependence on any one firm and wants to maintain competition within each commodity group. Business is not awarded only to the highest-scoring firm. Instead, allocation is guided by suppliers' ratings, each firm's capacity levels, and opportunities for cost improvement. Motorola typically has three or more suppliers in each commodity group, both to sustain focused competition and because most suppliers do not have all of the technologies needed to meet its needs.

CHRYSLER

The automaker's chief priority in allocating business to its first-tier suppliers is each firm's development and manufacturing capacity. Chrysler has learned from experience that shifting significant volume among suppliers often causes quality problems and harms investment planning. Such changes also raise engineering costs because they make it difficult to plan staffing levels. Consequently, the company wants suppliers to have steady and predictable volume to avoid the pains and higher costs of large volume cycles.

Chrysler's next allocation consideration reflects the economics of its operations. Because of its need for substantial integration with each supplier, the company single sources by car model or platform (the starting point for designing different models with similar attributes), and by plant. The choice depends on costs, including opportunities for using common parts. Some plants build more than one product, and some just one, while other products are made at two or more plants. Sourcing is split by car model when the relevant components are quite different on each model. It may also be split by plant location if costs, including shipping and scale economies, warrant this. These sourcing strategies are reviewed once a year.

For balance and focused competition, the automaker has at least two and sometimes three suppliers in each commodity group. Most often, a supplier is single sourced for a whole platform. As an example of sourcing at the plant level, the company has two paint suppliers (PPG Industries and BASF), with one or the other being a single source at each Chrysler plant.

As a third priority, business is allocated to suppliers according to each firm's rating based on Chrysler's metrics.[1] All suppliers are expected to keep improving in defined areas such as cost, quality, delivery, and technology. Since the company needs a high degree of integration with its suppliers on current and future generations of their components, it prefers to avoid shifting business among them based on ratings alone. A company can lose business, however, if its ratings fall significantly compared with others. For example, a supplier of wheels slipped on quality, losing half of the minivan business to another source.[2] There is no permanent loss of business unless a supplier fails to fix a problem.

Should a supplier lose business for performance reasons, any current design efforts are continued if a disruption would be too painful for Chrysler. But no additional business is awarded. Any loss of business could be for the whole firm or one of its plants. If the issue is at the plant level, a supplier usually fixes that quickly itself. A problem that occurs at multiple locations, though, implies a more pervasive management difficulty in the company.

Strategies for Integration and Unique Design

In the single-source relationships it has with suppliers of standard parts, Motorola uses focused competition and the other factors noted earlier to award new business, usually on an annual basis. That causes some shifting of business among the firms.

Regarding cost improvement, for standard catalog parts, the highest-rated preferred supplier may be asked for a bid, or Motorola may seek competitive bids from several preferred suppliers. The approach used depends on how critical price is in the final product, as well as whether Motorola has already achieved the lowest price through volume purchases with a corporate contract—for which a competitive environment is maintained among preferred suppliers.

By contrast to the practice with standard parts, if a customer asks a supplier to design and make a unique item, that firm will want to protect its investments in design and any unique tooling it may need. This is usually done with a life-of-part agreement, in which the supplier is assured the business as long as it continues to meet the customer's advancing performance targets and as long as the part is needed. Expected cost reductions due to productivity and other gains are reflected in an agreed price curve.

Motorola is moving toward using life-of-part agreements, but it is first working to get a better grasp on predicting cost reductions. In the interim, a supplier can expect to have the business for the part's life, unless it does not meet volume requirements or has a serious quality or other problem. At the end of a custom part's life, Motorola may seek design competition among its preferred suppliers for a new generation of parts if those will be custom designed. Each supplier's track record will influence its opportunity to win the new business.

For a few parts, such as certain semiconductors and liquid crystal displays, there is substantial design cooperation on future generations, and changing to other suppliers would be too disruptive. In those cases, while Motorola keeps the right to award business to others, performance problems are used mostly to initiate corrective actions rather than move the business. Constant improvement pressures are maintained because every supplier knows how its rating compares with others in its commodity group, and that it risks being displaced if this rating drops significantly below those of others.

These two factors—the need for integration and unique design— further determine the choice of sourcing strategies and practices to maintain continuous improvement.

WHEN INTEGRATION IS NEEDED

For its manufacturing equipment, technological change is far more rapid than for most of the parts Motorola's Paging Products Group buys. Typically, as many as three or four suppliers of any kind of equipment leapfrog each other every year in specific performances. Even so, PPG would not change suppliers just because one is ahead of the others on a given parameter at the moment. One reason is that it is difficult to move from one firm's factory support services to another's.

A second reason is that for unique equipment designed for PPG, the process of adjusting the various parameters and related services builds deep shared understandings about trade-offs and how to get closer to PPG's desired performance envelope in areas where that matters most. What Motorola looks for in such suppliers is a long-term commitment to continued change, to keep close to the frontiers that are important to its objectives.

Suppliers of equipment to PPG are promised single-source arrangements if their developments succeed. However, this is not an endless agreement. PPG shares its stretch objectives with equipment firms, as described in Chapter 5, and they are expected to stay at the leading edge. A firm will be asked to stretch further if PPG needs this and if it makes business sense for the supplier. Only in drastic situations will PPG change suppliers. In one case, pick-and-place assembly machines, a second supplier was brought in because the first could not meet PPG's delivery requirements. The first firm lost the business for that machine; its timing was far off of agreed dates. Staying with that firm would have meant a serious loss of new production capacity for PPG.

Motorola will go to a new supplier if that firm can do far better than its current arrangement. But given the cost and threat to cycle time that shifting suppliers entails, the current supplier gets ample opportunity to improve its performance. For instance, PPG's Len de Barros notes that if Seiko, which supplies robot systems, had a problem with its robot motors, PPG might link Seiko with a motor manufacturer having the relevant skills.

WITH UNIQUE DESIGNS

For standard goods available from more than one supplier in a commodity group, if integration is not needed, the easiest way for a customer to ensure continued advances is to share its stretch goals with those firms and periodically ask them for bids. Suppliers' ratings and the other factors discussed above are then used to award new business.

With low-volume purchases of standard or custom items, such as equipment bought by PPG, most improvement efforts focus on future generations once an item is shipped to the customer. The situation is necessarily different at high volumes, where ongoing progress with quality, cost, or in other areas can make a substantial difference between early and later shipments of the same items.

As noted before, life-of-part agreements are used with custom goods to protect the supplier's interests. One problem with those understandings is that predicting future costs to establish price curves can be difficult. Motorola's Neil MacIvor points out that while many firms have life-of-part contracts, a weak grasp of the underlying factors leads to imbalanced benefits. MacIvor illustrates his point by noting that if a customer and supplier do not know how cost drivers will evolve for a particular part, a price or productivity curve they use may increasingly deviate from reality over time. Such deviation may allow a supplier to make unfair margins while depriving its customer of lowest cost, or may damage the supplier by squeezing it too hard.

For these reasons, Motorola now enters an agreement for a newly designed part for the first year, but not for the life of the part. Although it is expected that the supplier will continue after the first year, Motorola wants to be able to seek improved cost opportunities. For example, experience may indicate ways to redesign the part, the original price may have been well off target, or the process technology may change. Any such events would require a renegotiation.

To supplement this target-setting strategy, Motorola is using data from quality audits and other sources to characterize generic supplier processes and develop a generic cost model for each industry. For example, some printed circuit boards are processed in gold tanks; through an understanding of the characteristics of that process, output quality can be reliably predicted. Such knowledge also helps Motorola get savings by highlighting problems in the process, knowing what to avoid, and deciding the best performance envelope.[3]

In the future, when it has a better grasp of cost projections, Motorola may award business for the life of custom parts, with the first year being used to establish a base price—given that there are many design changes and process improvements during that period. After the firms have worked on the part together for a year, Motorola will identify what the projected price should be on a learning curve basis that reflects the cost characteristic of each commodity.

For Motorola, most purchased goods are standard items. For instance, about 30 percent of the piece-parts the Paging Products Group buys are custom designed, and that number is declining as PPG increases its use of common parts. By contrast, more than 90 percent of all Chrysler purchases are custom designed for the automaker, a figure that is typical of this industry. Further, Chrysler's need for substantial design cooperation on future products favors continuity with each supplier. With virtually its entire supply base integrated into its design work, frequent shifts among suppliers would be expensive and highly disruptive. Chrysler has consequently taken steps to avoid this problem by building improvement incentives into its relationships.

At Chrysler, suppliers of custom-designed parts get life-of-part agreements, but without any price curves. Instead, all commodity suppliers are asked to meet the same price reduction target over the next year. The target, which has recently ranged from 3 to 5 percent, is set annually by Chrysler based on its experience and forecasts. Within this context, each supplier suggests changes it could make to save costs. Any accepted savings are shared by Chrysler and the supplier, usually on a 50–50 basis, with the actual percentage reduction being decided by the supplier. This sharing is done regardless of whether the supplier meets Chrysler's price reduction target.

Obviously suppliers benefit from the suggestions, because they share the savings. Moreover, consistent with auto industry practice, they cannot make significant changes without Chrysler's approval. Companies that propose many useful changes also strengthen their relationships with Chrysler. Further, because the automaker keeps them aware of benchmark data from its work, suppliers know they have to keep improving to retain the business. If a supplier were to underreport the proposed savings on a suggestion to keep more for itself, Chrysler would find out. Such behavior would damage the firm's relationship with the automaker. Submitted ideas go directly to the Chrysler buyers and engineers who have to implement them; those people are quite knowledgeable about the relevant cost drivers. The program requires no auditing of suppliers.

This activity is part of Chrysler's Supplier Cost Reduction Effort (SCORE), which asks suppliers to cut mutual costs without reducing their profit margins. Another part of SCORE credits suppliers for suggestions that improve on Chrysler's stretch objectives for variable cost, quality, technology, weight, functional performance, timing, and investment. The remarkable benefits Chrysler has gained from SCORE were noted in Chapter 3. (The endnotes to this chapter describe Chrysler's program in more detail.)[4]

It is difficult to compare the savings of Chrysler's method with productivity or cost curve agreements in life-of-part contracts. Chrysler says its approach has achieved better cost reductions than those of other auto firms, either with variations of its method or with the more traditional agreements. These results may, however, be attributed to other factors such as relationships between Chrysler and its suppliers that encourage more sharing, or possibly different starting points.

Steve Zimmer, Chrysler's director of supplier development, says the company adopted a strategy of sharing cost savings to build trust with its suppliers. Now that trust is growing, he says Chrysler expects to become more disciplined in cost cutting. One possible approach—an extension of its current practice—would be to use a cost or productivity curve, and share only cost savings that exceed the predetermined reductions. Another possibility is to benchmark suppliers within each commodity group against each other according to the number of suggestions made, the savings realized, or both. In principle, these practices could be adapted by firms outside of the auto industry; apparently, this has not yet been tried.

With a need for high design integration, Chrysler maintains continuity by having suppliers of unique parts continue from one generation to the next. If suppliers were to compete on the basis of design, this continuity might be disrupted. Nonetheless, competition might be worth considering if the gains from changing suppliers exceeded the costs. (This is how Motorola decides on supplier competition.) Commenting on Chrysler's desire for continuity, Zimmer says that unlike products in some other industries, no single piece of technology will jeopardize a car line. Additionally, a supplier that is measured on continued technical advances is likely to stay near the relevant frontiers. At Ford, by contrast, director of strategic planning and process improvement Charlie Ross says his company frequently asks suppliers for design proposals for electronic components. Ross notes that Ford wants to keep up with rapidly changing technology in this area, and design competition seems to be the best way to do that. Besides, shorter product cycles in electronics make it easier to integrate new developments into Ford's design cycle.

Clearly, the approach used by Chrysler disrupts supply relations less than Ford's, and thus may contribute to stronger relationships for Chrysler. Which method produces better cars is hard to tell. Both companies are open to proposals from suppliers that do not currently have the business for a part. This practice is a valuable way to bring in significant innovations, and wins more business for a supplier if its proposal is accepted. As an example, Chrysler used to have fuel doors made of welded stamped metal parts until a plastics firm suggested a three-piece assembly of plastic parts for the same purpose that weighs and costs less.

The basic techniques discussed here that are used to keep suppliers on a path of continuous improvement are described in the table shown. Recall that these methods must be used in conjunction with the other sourcing strategies described earlier.

CHOOSING SUPPLIERS FOR UNIQUE DESIGNS

Under the conditions noted above, choosing suppliers to develop unique designs may offer more value than staying with the current firm. To qualify for this role, a company should meet the criteria for being a full-fledged partner. Once the design is complete, a supplier then will be able to meet the customer's operating needs and be positioned to continue making improvements over the longer term. Further, shrinking cycle times create the need to build effective interfirm design teams quickly. This is difficult unless relationships between firms

Continuous Improvement Practices for Working with Suppliers		
	Standard Item	**Custom Design**
High integration	Continue with same supplier for future generations	Continue with same supplier for future generations
	Consider suppliers' proposals for step-change improvements	Use life-of-part arrangement if volume warrants
		Consider suppliers' proposals for step-change improvements, and/or use design competition in fast-changing areas
Low integration	Seek periodic bids from commodity group members	Use life-of-part arrangement if volume warrants
		Use design competition for next generation

and those involved in design are already close. Given time constraints, design participation should involve only trusted partners. This is why whenever possible, only preferred suppliers are asked to join Motorola in early design.

To help identify suppliers for early design before a program starts, PPG annually benchmarks its preferred supply base to earmark capabilities that are relevant to its needs. But surveys cannot pinpoint everything suppliers can do. Nor can they anticipate design needs that have not yet surfaced when the surveys are done. For these reasons, PPG product designers may have needs they are not sure preferred suppliers can meet. PPG therefore often seeks ideas from two or three suppliers about what innovations each can offer.

As long as this behavior is understood and participating suppliers win a fair share of the business, they regard it as acceptable practice. Molex's Ron Schubel says that his firm, like other suppliers, must devote its most creative engineering and tooling people to these contests. Further, they are among Molex's scarcest resources; a substantial percentage of its growth stems from their developing new product lines. Schubel does not think Molex needs a 100 percent win rate with a customer to be successful, but the rate must be high enough to justify using these resources.

Across Motorola, the preferred supplier for a previous custom-designed part is in the running for a new part but does not automatically get the job. Each firm's design strength is known from its track record. This leads to a short list of design candidates. Next, Motorola discusses the possible design with each one individually, asking for design concepts and ballpark price estimates. A firm is chosen based on this information. If engineering does not believe the price is good enough, Motorola may solicit quotes from other preferred suppliers.

For each design opportunity, Motorola uses selection criteria covering technology competence, cost, quality record, and quality systems. Although another criterion is ease of working with a supplier on a new development, Motorola has not yet developed a metric for that.

Using Premiums and Penalties

Traditional incentive contracts award or penalize a supplier—typically with higher or lower fees—according to whether its performance is above or below agreed targets. In alliances, rating systems also contain awards and penalties, because these are used to help allocate business according to each supplier's relative performance. But that is where any similarity ends. At Motorola, for example, performance problems revealed by rating systems are regarded as a first step toward finding and fixing root causes, not as a way to punish suppliers. Further, as one PPG purchasing executive notes, "many times we are contributing to the supplier's problems." These kinds of penalties encourage suppliers to raise issues; if Motorola caused the problem, the penalty is revoked.

Similarly, listen to Guy McCracken of Marks & Spencer: "M&S does not believe in fines for unsatisfactory supplier performance. Over time, those suppliers with the best track record will develop more business with M&S. We are not a soft touch here, but fines don't create the kind of atmosphere we need with our suppliers; it would be an abuse of our relationship. To impose fines, we would also have to judge whether an event was one-off, or beyond a supplier's control, or due to bad planning on our part. If a mistake were very serious and cost us a lot of money, then we would have a serious discussion and assess the situation. And, of course, if a supplier sends us poor quality items, the goods are destroyed, with the supplier paying the cost."

9

BUILDING TRUST AND HIGH PERFORMANCE

An alliance is really just two groups of people. You can analyze it to death, but in the end it is people dealing with people. Solid relationships will always produce more than the analysis indicates.

Willard C. Kennedy, senior vice president and general manager for digital videocommunication systems, Philips Consumer Electronics Company

An alliance is not a mutual admiration society. Frank and I talk about the pitfalls ahead of us all the time. We must be aware of them before they happen and deal with them before they occur. And we must manage the expectations of both firms' managements.

Vaughn Hovey, Kodak director of information processing services, on his firm's outsourcing alliance with IBM

In a commercial relationship all relevant tasks are done separately within each firm, and expected performance is fully described in a legal agreement. In an alliance, partners' activities are joined across the interface, and contracts cannot embrace the broad range of tasks and issues involved. Here best performance requires developing shared management processes that serve a mutual objective and a high degree of trust that each firm will work as expected. These relationships thrive on close and regular personal contact at all levels of the business.

Make Connections at All Levels

With constant improvement being the essence of alliances and many joint activities, partner firms must regularly share ideas and adjust to each other as they keep reaching for more value. This sharing demands an ongoing discussion at policy and operating levels about all aspects of a relationship, including people, practices, strategy, and organization in each firm.

TOP MANAGEMENT LINKS

Once a year, Chrysler's top management meets with the CEO of each of its largest-volume suppliers to discuss their business together. Attending these meetings are the automaker's chairman and CEO Bob Eaton; COO Bob Lutz; Tom Stallkamp, vice president of procurement and supply; and often Francois Castaing, vice president of vehicle engineering, plus selected others. Additional quarterly meetings are held with the highest automotive executive from each supplier. Agendas for both visits include a brief review of the supplier's quality and how the business is going. Most of the discussion is on future plans and investments. Stallkamp says this can be a major issue with conglomerates, because during good years for the auto industry they may invest their profits from that in other business areas.

Senior management discussions build needed understandings there, keep customer and supplier firms aligned, help resolve difficult issues, and promote an open and constructive dialogue at all management levels. Because of its outside perspective, each firm has useful views of its partner in these areas. In the most productive relationships, all such topics are open for discussion.

During the early 1990s, for instance, top executives from several suppliers joined about seventy Motorola engineering and manufacturing people in a private meeting in Phoenix, Arizona, to discuss product co-development between their firms. At one point, a supplier described an organization structure used by another firm that seemed to have advantages over how Motorola was organized. When a Motorola executive

responded that his company would not use that structure, another supplier pointedly and colorfully criticized his position. Gary Tooker,
Motorola's president, reacted by saying, "Now I am sure we have the
right suppliers with us," emphasizing the value he placed on critical supplier feedback. At other firms, such sharp public criticism could damage
or even end a relationship.

Similarly, while Chris Haskins of Northern Foods says M&S is "the
hardest customer I have and can be the most demanding," he adds that
"if I am concerned about something, I go in and tell them; if I did that
at another retailer, I would get kicked into the street. Because we know
each other so well, we can accept serious confrontations." In the same
spirit of open, constructive dialogue, M&S managers have given Haskins feedback on his personnel and organization.

From his side of the relationship, Guy McCracken, who heads the
foods business at M&S, adds that "if Chris Haskins strongly disagreed,
we would listen, because he knows our business so well. We have not
forced an unwanted policy on any supplier I have been involved with."
M&S suppliers generally speak to the retailer in a direct and frank
fashion, without fearing they will offend someone. "It is not always
palatable for our executives to hear what a supplier says," observes
Clinton Silver, "but when they are right about something—and they
often are—we do it."

On an annual basis, about eight M&S executives have formal
"around the table" meetings with an equal number of their peers from
each of the company's top twenty suppliers to look at progress and
opportunities across the complete spectrum of business. Other suppliers
are engaged in similar discussions or visits at least once a year, but these
are less formal, involve fewer people, and take less time. Management
links and shared understandings are further strengthened through ongoing visits to suppliers' manufacturing plants and design units.

In addition, each group executive, along with the executive's senior
management team, has regular contact with the chairman or CEO of
every major supplier, meeting or talking on the telephone every few
weeks. As part of these discussions, the executives examine facets of
the business that are underperforming and look for root causes. Individual people are not discussed at this level unless there is a serious
issue that could damage the relationship. The purpose of these meetings, says Guy McCracken, is to set priorities in order to hit major targets, create an overall environment in which policies can deliver

desired resources and results, and sustain trust and empathy with suppliers so as to keep earning their drive in the same direction.

Such high-level discussions have led to useful changes in both Marks & Spencer and its suppliers. Denis Desmond, for example, describes his firm's alliance with M&S as candid, open, and mutually constructive. Just as M&S makes suggestions about his business, he raises issues with the company about their people and organization when he believes they can do better. "We can always talk about things," he says. "One healthy aspect of our relationship is that they are extremely demanding. And we can challenge them." Desmond meets formally with the M&S chairman every six months and with the vice chairman, who has lead responsibility for supplier relationships, four times a year.

Although it sells exclusively to M&S, Desmond & Sons makes independent decisions regarding the relationship. There have been times, says Denis Desmond, when his firm chose not to accept M&S suggestions, just as there have been times when M&S wanted to do something that Desmond & Sons convinced it not to do.

Broadly speaking, top-level meetings should focus on all matters that influence the firms' separate and joint performances. For example, the failure of one M&S supplier to deliver due to poor controls led to a meeting between Barry Morris, who heads men's clothing for the retailer, and the supplier firm's CEO. They reviewed the short- and long-term issues resulting from the event, and what could be done to fix the situation. As another example, because of its need for close relationships with suppliers, M&S is naturally concerned about any changes in their management. For that reason, top M&S executives have frank discussions with suppliers' board chairmen when continuity seems threatened. Says Clinton Silver, "We would feel free to say to senior board members of a supplier that their management is not right, and we would expect them to be frank about our weaknesses."

In addition to those high-level visits, M&S and its suppliers maintain an ongoing dialogue with top executives in each major product area that focuses in more detail on the particular sector. Barry Morris and his management peers spend about a third of their time in discussions with suppliers. Issues covered include the supplier's performance, quality, delivery, specific products, product development, and events such as rapid changes in turnover with M&S. Due to its own dependency on long-term relationships, M&S has a natural concern for its suppliers' well-being, and so Morris and his colleagues regularly inquire about suppliers' management and financial health. The intent is to identify potential problems and, when necessary, help resolve them before they become serious. They also review any issues in the relationship that have risen from lower levels, although such concerns are rare.

Another discussion topic is high-level strategic matters. For example, in 1992 Marks & Spencer was not happy with its sales and product values in men's suits. To strengthen its position in that market, it worked with suppliers to get prices down, arguing that they would be rewarded with higher volume—which they were.

At Motorola, as noted earlier, the transition to supply alliances from traditional relationships was led by Bob Galvin when he was chairman; leadership of the effort eventually evolved to middle management. Then, in the early 1990s, growing demands on the company's alliances prompted efforts to build stronger links at senior levels. Early on, Hector Ruiz, vice president and general manager of the Paging Products Group, initiated regular visits to PPG's major suppliers around the world. Accompanying Ruiz were his director of quality, the manager of materials quality engineering, and a purchasing manager. Such visits are now a regular part of PPG supplier relationships.

The visits, conducted with each supplier's top executive responsible for the Motorola account, include sharing PPG business plans, along with discussions of quality, capacity, and technology issues. While these topics are covered during lower-level contacts, the meetings raise them to the highest relevant level at the supplier, reinforcing PPG-related activities there as well as strengthening the supplier's role at PPG.

One result has been a better understanding of the paging industry among higher management in supply firms. This knowledge also existed at lower levels, but it had not completely reached top executives. Another benefit included learning from suppliers about more opportunities to work together; PPG was not fully using them as a resource, especially in early design. Agreements to improve operating links—for example, by reducing sales contacts and increasing joint technology reviews—have also come from these visits.

The view from middle management levels suggests the value of these high-level contacts. John Ihle, the engineering manager responsible for product design, says PPG gets better commitment when suppliers' top people are involved.

DIRECT LINKS AT OPERATING LEVELS

While policy-level discussions provide critical support and help sustain alignment, strong operating links contribute directly to increased value creation. At Marks & Spencer, the principal day-to-day issues involving suppliers concern reactions to the marketplace—assessing how value is perceived by the consumer and adjusting the product mix, as well as colors and style—to increase that value and improve M&S' responsiveness to the market. If M&S is not getting what it wants from a supplier, it will discuss the matter with that firm at several management levels.

Companies that supply both Marks & Spencer and its rivals say that no other retailer can come near the close relationships they have with M&S, which creates a remarkable ability to respond quickly to changes in demand. This flexibility, they say, depends on trusting relationships and the knowledge that M&S will always be fair.

To support fast-response operations, suppliers relate to all levels of M&S management, a practice that gives each firm a clear understanding of the entire process. At intermediate levels, such as the M&S menswear division, discussions cover trends and broad product ranges as well as key products. On the supply side, such as at Desmond & Sons, every employee in sales and design and all factory managers have a point of contact with M&S. "It is important to have the right relationships at all levels," says Denis Desmond, adding that "it is absolutely essential to say to them what is wrong when something happens." When necessary, people from each firm comment to their counterparts about management and organization issues.

Both above and below the division level, other employees within M&S have regular links with their counterparts at supply firms. Carole O'Beirne, who is two levels below the division directors, and her merchandise-manager counterpart regularly discuss each supplier's performance through both weekly informal discussions and more formal meetings. Topics include quality and quantity levels for each style, as well as how work for the next season is shaping up compared with that of other manufacturers in the same product group.

At Chrysler, where more than 90 percent of all parts on a new platform—from which variations are made for different models—are designed uniquely for that platform, as many as 600 employees from some 200 supplier firms are resident on design teams at the company's Technology Center. As full-fledged team members, they have offices at the center and participate in the conceptualization, design, and development of every new car and truck project. The criteria for a firm's early design participation are the amount of engineering delegated to the supplier and the need for coordination of that firm's advanced engineering with Chrysler's.

The principle of direct ties between firms applies to every value-creating activity; such ties are the fastest and best way to build understandings where they are needed. Often overlooked, to each firm's disadvantage, are direct links between shop-floor workers.

Recognizing the benefits of such links, Bruce Bendoff of Craftsman Custom Metal Fabricators and Patty Barten, an operations director in Motorola's Cellular Infrastructure Group (CIG), organized reciprocal visits of plant employees between their firms. In the first visit, seven production workers and supervisors from the third shift of CIG were given a plant tour by their counterparts—assemblers, machine operators, and a supervisor—from the same shift at Craftsman. "Third shift people are the forgotten ones," says Bendoff; by focusing on them, the firms highlighted the importance of the connection they were making. During that visit, CIG people saw how the Craftsman part was made "and helped us appreciate the pain we cause each other," said one employee.

At a later date, Craftsman plant employees visited CIG during one of its monthly employee meetings, a move that helped build rapport. In the meeting, CIG described its expected business with Craftsman, giving the workers more comfort in terms of their future paychecks. Later, CIG shop-floor employees took their Craftsman counterparts out to the production line, where they saw their parts and rivals' parts being assembled into finished units. The Craftsman people were fascinated to see how the parts they made were actually used. Both sides then discussed issues and problems associated with assembling the parts and began forming shared opinions about how to solve the problems they had found. Since then, some proposed solutions—such as making changes to improve how parts fit together—have been adopted.

These experiences, says Bruce Bendoff, enlightened and energized people on both sides and opened windows to more possibilities. He describes the process as "empowering the interface," adding that it "helps our whole organization get better than the competition." Now there is direct shop-floor to shop-floor discussions of such issues, and about ways to jointly improve their operations. People just pick up the phone and call their counterparts when they have a problem to resolve.

Like that of other Motorola suppliers, Craftsman's relationship with CIG includes many such contacts. At all organization levels, people in quality, engineering, and management talk to their counterparts in the other firm. On a daily basis, Craftsman has employees at the CIG facility serving some aspect of its needs. Craftsman quality and manufacturing people are on the factory floor, production control people are talking to the CIG person who handles shared supply production (that is, more than one supplier for the same part), and service engineering staffers are working with CIG purchasing.

To monitor the overall relationship, Bendoff developed a chart that targets all areas where his firm and CIG should be building a closer relationship. Priorities reflect the cost-effectiveness of such efforts. Virtually all operating issues get resolved at immediate contact points without elevation, which can become a cancer in a large organization as more people get involved and an issue spreads across functions.

Use Teamwork in Multifirm Alliances

When more than two firms are involved in the same value-creation activity, direct relationships among all of them as members of a multi-firm team are the best way to work. To illustrate, Marks & Spencer often involves firms that supply fibers, as well as fabric manufacturers and garment makers, in its quest for higher-value clothing. Getting the dynamics right between all these firms is critical and can be difficult.

In the past, M&S met with one firm at a time to work on improvements. This practice caused misunderstandings. For example, if Marks & Spencer thought a problem had been caused by the fabric supplier, the retailer met with that firm alone. If, after this discussion, M&S concluded the real issue was with the garment maker, it met with that supplier. Sometimes it turned out that the real problem was a shift in Marks & Spencer's own priorities. From such experiences, M&S learned the best way to identify the root cause of problems was to meet with all involved suppliers at the same time and discuss issues openly and honestly.

Constant Communications Avoid Trouble

Most companies have clear reporting patterns to keep people informed on routine activities. In alliances, where so much is nonroutine and the risks from misunderstandings can be high, an extra investment in communications helps ward off problems. As a general rule, each firm should take the initiative to keep its partner informed on all matters and to surface issues as soon as they are evident.

Listen to PPG vice president Bob Becknell, who was at the center of Motorola's transition to supply alliances: "Many firms believe they can talk to a supplier about process issues once or twice a month. In practice, you have to discuss these things daily, if not more. The importance of ongoing communications should not be understated. We tend to put off minor issues, but then small problems grow into big ones. To reinforce trust and enhance mutual understanding, frequent visits and an open discussion are very important. Face-to-face is better than telephone, and frequent telephone contact should be the minimum baseline. Some firms try to reduce the number of interactions with their suppliers by communicating only in infrequent large packages. But those are more difficult to absorb and miss many emerging issues."

To illustrate the result of poor communications, the CEO of a supplier to the chemical industry (here called SupCo) describes a painful experience that he does not intend to repeat. Recently, a buyer at a major customer told SupCo that it had won the business it had sought, and he instructed it to purchase the needed equipment. At the last minute, however, the customer gave the business to another firm. That left SupCo in a bad position: Wanting to help the customer reduce cycle time, it had quickly made the investment, hired personnel, and was already making some of the product.

In exploring what had gone wrong, SupCo's CEO learned that the customer had weak internal communications, and others there had not supported the purchase from his firm. A related problem was that a new SupCo sales executive, who was handling the account, was not scanning for issues in the relationship. Neither was the CEO, who maintained contacts there himself. In fact, although the customer had been unhappy with SupCo's service support, it had failed to tell the firm. The customer also had perceived a weakness in SupCo's technology base. While the defect had been fixed, the customer had not been told. Compounding the problem, the customer believed it was SupCo's responsibility to spot issues in the relationship, whereas SupCo's CEO had thought the customer would let him know if there were problems. SupCo was aware that a rival supplier had been approached, but due to weak communications the CEO thought it was only for a "sanity check" on prices. When that firm won the order, SupCo suffered a substantial loss.

Experience conforms that face-to-face meetings often have a clear advantage over the telephone. Even at Motorola, a world leader in telecommunications products, people prefer direct contacts. John Ihle, the PPG product design manager, says that although Motorola has budget for videoconferencing, it has not been as effective as face-to-face meetings. Ihle explains that travel to meetings does not require more time than videoconferencing. When people use video, he notes, they tend to have more misunderstandings, which can take considerable time to correct. Ihle believes this is especially true with cross-cultural teams. But even with domestic suppliers more work is done face-to-face—a format which creates more confidence that real understandings have been reached.[1]

Because Chrysler believes face-to-face cooperation has clear advantages, particularly for nonroutine work, the automaker has borne the expense of officing hundreds of supplier engineers at its design center. Steve Zimmer, the company's director of supplier development, says that having the suppliers on site has yielded substantial advantages at the concept stage of design because it facilitates problem solving and helps ensure that people really understand each other. Cooperation at the same location, he says, also builds team spirit and creativity, affords more "soak time" when people are working through difficult issues, and provides more opportunity for informal meetings. Chrysler also uses electronically shared data files and teleconferencing to coordinate with its suppliers for more routine activities when people are not co-located.

Seek Root-Cause Solutions

Like the pursuit of true quality, interfirm relationships are most effective when people focus their energies on identifying and resolving underlying problems rather than on looking for someone to blame. Solutions found with the first approach lead to improved costs and performances; the second way polarizes relationships and causes poorer results.

At Marks & Spencer, Carole O'Beirne says she and her colleagues pick up and respond to all issues immediately. The next step, she says, is always more dialogue to develop a clear understanding, followed by action to resolve the issue. The ethos among M&S and its suppliers, she says, is to look for root causes and not to be concerned with "who shot whom."

People, of course, make mistakes. When that happens, the best path to follow is to raise the issue and constructively look for how it might be avoided in the future.

One time, for example, a Motorola commodity manager was trying to line up three of her firm's divisions to develop a common standard for a purchase from Molex. "We were turning Molex upside down to respond to Motorola's need," says Ron Schubel. "Suddenly, the order went to another firm. We talked to the commodity manager and said Motorola had not done as good a job as possible in communicating its needs and position." That led to discussions with Tom Slaninka, the sector sourcing manager, who asked Schubel to share his experience at a supplier advisory board meeting, which includes participation by Motorola management. Slaninka saw a broader issue and wanted it broadcast.

In the ensuing discussion, people learned that neither Motorola nor Molex had asked enough questions to build real understandings. This new awareness caused a new effort to clarify the rules of engagement. In commenting on the experience, Schubel says many customers would not have handled things this way. "This kind of action does not get us more business," he says. "But it helps create an environment where you can get more business on the merits. We are all winners when we can openly share our good and bad experiences with each other and then change the way we work to do even better than before."

Have Clear Rules of Engagement

Inside most companies, key procedures are described in a set of policy documents that help communicate how things get done. Practices not recorded are implicitly understood and reinforced by each firm's culture.

Between two firms, there is less opportunity for shared informal understandings—and thus more reason to articulate desired procedures. Doing so reduces the risks of favoritism or misperception and, if things proceed as described, helps build trust. The need to publish procedures is even greater when a firm has alliances across its supply base. In such cases, documentation provides a high degree of consistency with all suppliers that is difficult to achieve with informal understandings alone.

For these reasons, Motorola records, regularly updates, and routinely shares with its suppliers descriptions of all important activities involved in its alliances. This documentation includes metrics for supplier status, performance tracking, and volume allocation; procedures for schedule sharing and other joint activities; and appeals processes to be used when issues cannot be resolved where they arise. Another important task is to clearly define the boundaries of an alliance: what tasks are included, and those that are not. This was not done during the first years of Motorola's early design relationships with its suppliers, causing many of them to lose business they believed they had won and reducing trust.

Marks & Spencer relies more on informal understandings that have been reinforced over the years. This is because M&S has fewer suppliers, a much longer history with them, and most are headquartered nearby.

Maintain a Fair Balance

With alliances, as with all business relationships, there is a natural tendency for events to favor one company or the other. To keep commitments and trust, each firm must work to shift the balance when that happens. The same principle applies in negotiations for future activities, as discussed earlier.

Chris Haskins of Northern Foods points out that Marks & Spencer tries to keep a fair balance between its benefits and those of its suppliers. He says that if a product sector is working well for M&S and not for his firm, or vice versa, the issues are identified and discussed, and both firms try to help each other adjust as necessary. This task may involve an investment of more resources on either side to create more value. Haskins says Northern Foods' relationship with other retailers is very different; if the price is not right, they go their separate ways.

When imbalances arise, M&S management acts as a facilitator to help resolve the problem. In ladies' footwear, for example, there had been considerable pressure on the department involved to improve its performance, but it had not done as well as desired. When a supplier developed a new product, the department negotiated so hard on price that the supplier was losing money. While the buyers knew the situation was unhealthy, they had been unable to solve the problem. The supplier made its unhappiness known to M&S management, who agreed the situation was untenable. They helped develop a course of action that included changing the price and making the product more appealing through value engineering. (Of course, there are also situations where the buying group and supplier disagree; these can take more effort to resolve.)

In the data processing alliance between Kodak and IBM, when labor costs exceeded the agreed amount, the contract specified that IBM should cover those costs alone. But Kodak had contributed to the increase, and agreed to share the costs. Motorola uses a similar practice of standing behind its projections when it is wrong: Within an agreed lead time, it makes the purchase if it told a supplier to produce more than it used, or if the supplier bought needed raw material in advance. Of course, trust works two ways. Says one Motorola sourcing executive: "There have been many times when the supplier could have stuck us with material, but they had other customers they could sell it to. This has never been an issue."

Make Fair Demands

Chrysler, Motorola, and Marks & Spencer expect excellence from their suppliers, and today's top performance is never good enough for tomorrow. Still, those expectations carry a lot of credibility, because both firms make the same demands on themselves.

For example, while Motorola expects stiff annual price cuts by its suppliers, the anticipated cuts are not as great as the cost reductions it gains on its own through quality advances, new processes, better designs, and more. Further, because Motorola is pushing the same frontiers in quality and other areas that it expects its suppliers to be working on, there is a strong shared sense of everyone being in the same boat together. This facilitates problem solving and helps build trust. Says Bill Hanks, who is in Land Mobile Products sourcing: "We ask nothing of them that we do not expect of ourselves."

As another example, the quality audit Motorola uses with its suppliers takes a considerable amount of their time, and at first the suppliers resisted because they thought it not worth the effort. "Nobody is going to do anything with that except file it," said a top executive of one firm. But Motorola staffers pointed out that their company used a more stringent version of the same process for its own organization, and that the results had been highly cost effective. "What we try to do is keep driving into our supply base the programs we have found that bring Motorola its success," says Ron Vocalino, a regional sourcing manager based in Schaumburg, Illinois.

Build a Spirit of Community

Within and between organizations, as in other fields, the whole may be greater than the sum of its parts. Effective teams, for example, can be more powerful than people working in isolation on the same task. Motorola has applied this fact to its supply alliances in several ways. Results include an increased awareness of top management's commitment to the alliances, more acceptance at operating levels, and better supplier understandings of Motorola's objectives and context. Another benefit is stronger links between suppliers—which enhance joint creativity, benchmarking, and other shared activities, and a reinforcement of the values that make these alliances effective.

Every eighteen months, all preferred suppliers meet at a two-day conference to hear talks, participate in workshops on metrics development and other practices, and show their latest wares to a wide cross-section of Motorola people. At the opening plenary session, talks by top corporate executives (typically including Motorola's president and sector CEOs) describe the firm's dedication to its alliances. Also discussed are its outlook for suppliers; at one meeting they were reminded of the competitive pressures on Motorola, its continued drive for Six Sigma quality, and its intent to continue reducing the supply base. During the same opening session, a top customer executive gives a speech that includes candid comments on how Motorola is doing and where it needs improvement, emphasizing those performances influenced by Motorola suppliers. Some recent talks were given by Federal Express and by the U.S. Army, which described its experience with Motorola radios in Operation Desert Storm.

The supply conferences are an opportunity to be exposed to the customer and other suppliers, all demonstrating their best practices. Says one supplier CEO: "I usually come back from a supply conference feeling that Motorola and its suppliers are pushing the state of the art, and that it is good to be part of that. It leads us to ask how well we are doing, and can we do even better. It has also helped us appreciate that we are a better supplier than customer to our own suppliers."

Once each year, most Motorola groups and sectors hold a full-day "strategic alliance" meeting with the CEOs or presidents of their top thirty suppliers. Agendas include briefings on future plans, expectations about supplier performance, new initiatives (such as changes in Schedule Sharing), and the status of important work (like early design participation). Also included are responses to significant supplier complaints. For example, if negotiations have not gone well, Motorola investigates, takes corrective actions, and tells suppliers what has been done.

Suppliers also attend meetings at lower levels. Once each month, for example, Motorola's Cellular Products Division invites a small number of preferred suppliers to business forecast meetings that include sales, receiving, engineering, purchasing, manufacturing, and other employees from all three shifts, numbering several hundred people in all. These meetings create a team spirit among everyone in the organization and its suppliers. Says one supplier CEO who has attended: "By sharing the same information, we become more a part of the business. Meetings are run to build a team, and they succeed."

Agendas cover reviews by division management of progress against plan, plus data on quality, cycle time, and any problems, including those internal to Motorola and how they are being fixed. Motorola shares sensitive information about internal quality and its market performance, forecasts about the next quarter and year (such as sales and new business), and customer satisfaction (including independent polls on trends comparing Motorola with its competitors).

Typical of this candor are the remarks of Rick Chandler, general manager of the Cellular Products Division. Noting that everyone was there "for our mutual benefit and to satisfy our customer," he underscored the importance of being best in the customer's eyes by understanding the customer's business and striving to support it.

Introduce New Programs Together

Most people and organizations are more willing to introduce a new activity if they have a chance to participate in its development and shape it to fit their needs. That rule certainly applies to alliances, where acceptance is the first step in implementation.

The best way to begin new programs depends on the structure of a supply base and how it relates to the customer's market. At Motorola, where a product reflects the contributions of all suppliers, many of which are small firms, there is a deliberate effort to include their interests in early plans. By contrast, at Marks & Spencer, where each supplier's products sell directly in the market, new projects can be focused on those suppliers that are best positioned to implement them.

Motorola introduced bar coding by first presenting the idea to its supplier advisory board, where small firms responded that it was too expensive for them. Motorola then found a less costly method that could be used by large suppliers as well and saved money for everyone. Similarly, when electronic funds transfer (EFT) was launched, its implementation was negotiated with suppliers because it would have been costlier to craft a system tailored only for Motorola. Also, since suppliers could get their money sooner through EFT, Motorola wanted to share in these benefits.

At Marks & Spencer, new initiatives such as cycle time reduction are always managed as joint projects. They arise from discussions with suppliers, and implementation often begins with the largest firms. For example, since long-term commitments must be made for yarns and fabrics, a fast-response capability centers on dying and finishing those items. Garment suppliers large enough to have their own dying and finishing functions were thus first in reducing cycle time. The development of fast-response dying capabilities, for instance, was done by technologists from M&S and Coats Viyella learning together.

Coordinate Long-Term Alignment

In traditional market relationships, suppliers have relatively few clues about a customer's strategic direction and specific needs in that context. A firm's planning therefore reflects general market and technology trends and lacks a focus on any one customer. Without the benefits of close cooperation, a customer has little to lose by changing suppliers according to whichever firm best meets its needs at the moment.

With alliances, the greatest benefits come from continuous mutual improvement over the long term. That calls for ongoing alignment of firms' plans, priorities, and investments at all relevant policy and operating levels. Otherwise, if decisions on matters like capacity, technology development, or strategic direction are made separately, partners may evolve away from meeting each other's priority needs.

To gain effective alignment, all relevant plans for the longer term are shared, and changes are made as necessary. This should be done at all organizational levels having long investment or development lead times and for large investments that cannot be used for other purposes.

SHARING PLANS

One purpose of the senior management meetings Marks & Spencer holds with each supplier is to ensure that both firms are marching in the same direction. During these annual visits, business plans are shared, and people discuss product development and where their firms are going in the longer-term future. These discussions include the kinds of products they expect to have, where they hope to break new ground to keep differentiating the business from its competition, resources needed to get there, and substantial investments that will be required. The discussions also cover all relevant policy matters, financial issues, and potential acquisitions.

As in all other matters, each firm makes its own decisions independently. While M&S seeks to influence supplier capacity-addition decisions, it does not control them. It does, however, consult with suppliers to head off unneeded investment for capacity unique to its requirements, because unfilled capacity could end up hurting a supplier. If it agrees with a supplier's expansion plans, M&S will do its best to fill the plant.

Every two years at Philips Consumer Electronics Company, top managers meet with their counterparts from about forty suppliers that either leverage PCEC products or have substantial volume with it. One purpose of these meetings is to be sure the firms maintain policy-level alignment. To achieve this goal, business, product development, and capital investment plans are shared on both sides, and needed adjustments are made to stay on the same path. Other objectives include sustaining mutual understandings at high levels to reinforce trust and a shared vision, reviewing current programs, initiating the resolution of any problems in the relationships, and sending a signal to others in both firms that top management values the relationship.

PCEC participants in these meetings include the senior vice president and general manager of the color TV business, along with the vice presidents of operations, purchasing, logistics, quality, engineering, and sales, as well as a finance representative. PCEC commodity team members are present for the full meeting. Supplier attendees are comparable-level business unit executives.

During the first hour of these three-hour meetings, PCEC shares its five-year plan—including volume expectations, pricing forecasts on its products, and targeted performance enhancements. During the second hour, the supplier describes its main rivals and compares their strengths and weaknesses; it also reviews its own five-year plan. PCEC wants to see suppliers reaching for growth and wants to see how these firms plan to support PCEC's needs. The final hour is reserved for a review of other issues as needed.

Formal alignment should include every aspect of each firm that affects their joint performance. For example, at quarterly business reviews Motorola and its suppliers share technology road maps (such as for future line spacing on printed circuit boards) at the individual piece-part level. Other topics discussed are current experiments, new technologies, materials and equipment of possible mutual interest, and new processes being installed. All of this helps the firms keep abreast of each other's frontiers. Product road maps are not shared, because the information is too sensitive and is less relevant to suppliers' development planning.

Motorola also shares with each supplier its expectations of where that firm's rivals' specific technological performances are expected to be at future dates. That information is gathered from across Motorola's manufacturing, R&D, and advanced manufacturing technology groups, but does not come from any suppliers. Providing this data to suppliers in effect says, "This is where you will have to be to keep up with the competition and our expectations." The projected performances reflect product-specific Motorola plans.

For more complex systems such as factories, Motorola describes its needs at two levels. At the higher level, it tells equipment suppliers what a future factory will look like. This is a very general description and stays away from any discussion of core competencies. More specific performances, at times including quantitative data, are shared with selected suppliers on a need-to-know basis. For instance, PPG told Seiko a projected robot controller had to have multi-tasking vision input and output, which were not available in the market at the time. Suppliers are never told what product the factory will be making.

Integrating Alignment and Implementation

The most effective way to translate plans into action is for the planners to also be the implementers. This is how PCEC manages alignment with its suppliers. The firm also inserts opportunities for joint brainstorming into the process, to help surface the best ideas and information. That is done through its annual town meetings, as well as the new product and technology planning meetings discussed in Chapter 5.

The same designers who participate in the planning and brainstorming meetings also work together in the product design phase, so they come to the meeting with high trust and mutual understandings. PCEC has found that this continuity of people—which produces a seamless flow of thinking from advanced planning through design and interactive problem solving to final products being shipped—speeds the entire process. At some stages of the process, particularly final design iteration, it is essential to have total continuity in personnel. Before that, to spark fresh thinking, new people are occasionally brought in as necessary. As an essential part of these meetings, working relationships are monitored and relevant issues discussed by managers who recognize each other as having that role.

Flexibility Is Essential

Long-term alignment is possible only if partners are willing to be flexible and accommodate each other's changing needs. Because the customer must set the course for an alliance, the greater onus for flexibility is on the supplier.

The Kodak–IBM alliance is expected to be a long-term relationship, yet no one can see the future clearly. At the start, the firms created a pricing model based on assumptions about Kodak demand and the price of technology. Since then, the evolution of Kodak needs and major changes in technology—from mainframe data centers (the basis of the initial arrangement) to client-server systems—have caused the firms to adapt to new price scenarios.

Still, while there was only an informal agreement to negotiate later changes, the growth of a trusting relationship between the firms made such changes relatively easy to work through. Issues could be resolved without either firm erecting the protective barriers that often foil joint problem solving in commercial deals. In that regard, the basis for agreeing on new scenarios was what met Kodak's needs and earned IBM a fair return.

Says IBM's Frank Palm: "If I thought of myself only within the confines of our original contract I would try to convince myself and the customer that a mainframe was the best solution for every information systems need. Instead, I perceive my job as furnishing computing and networking solutions to Kodak worldwide, without being tied to any particular equipment."

It is noteworthy that IBM people above Palm did not have to be convinced to support changes in the Kodak agreement. The performance of Solution Center Rochester—the IBM unit responsible for the alliance—is measured by IBM on customer satisfaction and profitability, and IBM was confident that Palm was pursuing changes that would grow that performance.

Developing Trust Between Firms

Unlike commercial relationships, alliances involve too much complexity and uncertainty to use legally binding contracts. Only trust can provide that confidence, which is essential for alliance effectiveness.

Without trust, firms will not share sensitive information, discuss costs, participate in early design, make large investments unique to a relationship, tolerate each other's mistakes, or raise difficult issues. Such activities are critical to achieving the market-beating costs, quality, cycle times, and other performances that are the reason for alliances. Trust changes many things.

Consider the case of a consumer goods firm that was having financial difficulties and sought help from its suppliers. When a senior executive visited his counterpart at one key supplier, he described the increasingly intense price competition in his firm's marketplace, what the firm was doing to reduce costs, and progress being made with an important labor union. He also said the company needed its suppliers to cut their prices by 10 to 12 percent: "We really need some help from you," he noted. In response, the firm made some reductions. Says the supplier's senior executive: "I understood his situation, and due to the trust we have built over the years and our relationship as a priority supplier, we had to respond. I know they will remember what we did, and will find a way to show their gratitude."

This same executive says his answer is different with customers that demand price cuts where there is no trust. In those cases, he decides what to do on the basis of "what is best for us. We may move away from a long-term relationship if we believe we will not be treated fairly. Then, we look at each situation as a deal for the moment and avoid long-term investments that would benefit the customer and might not help us."

ELEMENTS OF TRUST

To have trust between customer and supplier, people must recognize that their companies need each other to realize a mutual objective that is important to both of them. These conditions, which define an alliance, reduce the chance that either one will act in a way that lessens the other's commitment. "We work in a healthy environment in which everyone is striving to give the consumer what he or she wants," comments Denis Desmond on his firm's relationship with Marks & Spencer. "When we get it wrong, which does happen, we have the ability to respond."

While alliance conditions are necessary for trust, they are not sufficient. People and companies do not always behave in ways that an abstract framework indicates they should. Also needed is a set of understandings and resulting actions that make the trust real. Some of these depend on partner choice, which includes finding desirable behavior, a reduced supply base, and steps a customer takes to earn suppliers' commitments. Others reflect negotiating style and the measures described above, such as joint leadership and clear rules of engagement.

Additional practices include avoiding surprises, which damage trust by making relationships less predictable, and continuing to work on deeper understandings. The more that partners appreciate each other's situation, the easier it is for them to make needed adjustments. Spotting issues for a partner—not raising one's own concerns, but rather alerting it to problems it might not have foreseen—also builds trust by saying, in effect, "we care about your success."

Many of these practices are appropriate for both customer and supplier. For instance, Ron Schubel of Molex says that while selling a custom part to a customer may add more to a supplier firm's margins than selling a standard one, if doing so is not best for the customer it can damage trust. Further, if a standard item is better, the customer will eventually find out and opt for that item.

Trust is not a condition that, once reached, is automatically maintained. Firms and their employees change, and new events regularly upset the status quo. People learn differently from negative experiences than they do from positive ones. Breaking trust—a negative experience—is like touching a hot stove. No one has to be reminded to be wary afterwards. By contrast, positive experiences—such as actions that build trust—must be constantly repeated before people accept this as the way things are. Steadily constructive behavior is thus essential for alliances.

To illustrate, Motorola's support of its supplier partnership practices has been dependable through thick and thin. Ron Schubel, who served for several years on the supplier advisory board, credits the firm with keeping up its end of the relationships regardless of its own business climate. "I cannot tell from how they manage their relationships as to when they are having a good year or a bad year," he says. Supply programs at many other firms tend to wax and wane with their business results, and with changes in management. Suppliers that serve them as well as Motorola say this causes lower trust, less commitment, and weaker results.

Significantly, alliances involve many people in each firm, which requires trust beyond just a few individuals. Further, people eventually change jobs, and when others who are new to an alliance get involved, to keep trust they must honor the same understandings and use the same practices as their predecessors. Trust in alliances therefore calls for substantial consistency throughout each firm.

BUILDING TRUST AT THE START

Trust is hardest to develop in the early stages of an alliance, particularly when past relationships were adversarial. One early step, then, must be to listen for and respond to perceived injustices.

Bruce Bendoff says that when his firm, Craftsman, first tried to improve relationships with its metal finishing suppliers, discussions were difficult. There was a lot of finger pointing about sources of problems, with comments such as "you didn't prepare the metal right. . . . You don't understand our needs."

Once people vented their feelings and Craftsman responded constructively, relationships became more wholesome. "When you understand their problems, you see how great the challenge is for them," says Bendoff. "Many of their people don't even speak English. We have to open the parameters to help them. We should not ask them for more than the design requires. Now, they point out when we are overspecifying a job. They have asked to get involved with us in early design at Motorola, and we are bringing them in where it is valuable to do so. Once we got past our adversity and recognized we were causing problems for each other, we began picking off the issues, searching together for root causes, and building better relationships."

A second early trust-building step is to produce results that are meaningful to both firms. For instance, Gordon Couch of Philips says that past adversity with Molex was initially reduced when the firms worked together to modify a connector. Since there had been problems with the part, the benefits of cooperating to solve them were clear to everyone; resistance was mainly psychological. The openness and sharing that came out of that "expanded the comfort zone," he says. "There has to be an early benefit from cooperation that is sufficiently large that it dominates the old ways and submerges them." In the case of the connector, the benefits were reduced manufacturing failures and improved design flexibility for easier manufacturing.

TRUST BETWEEN COMPETITORS

Cooperation with rivals is more challenging than that between past adversaries because, in this case, the conflict continues. Three conditions make trust possible here: Conflict is separated from cooperation, the benefits of cooperation clearly outweigh the risks; and time is allowed for people to build needed comfort.

At IBM, Frank Palm sought to bring Hewlett-Packard and Sun Microsystems into the alliance with Kodak because doing so was the best way to meet certain needs. Since those firms are IBM rivals, in the first meeting they asked how Palm could make sure that proprietary information shared with his group would not flow more widely in IBM. Part of his answer was that his group was given substantial autonomy to be responsive to Kodak needs. Palm also said that he was measured on customer satisfaction, which gave him an incentive to work with H-P and Sun.

Further, Palm's group, as an independent unit of ISSC (the IBM data processing services group), was expected by his firm to be neutral regarding products he supplied to Kodak and to help the customer choose whatever solution best fit its needs. He would select IBM products when all else was equal, because as an IBM unit he would get better support.

Yet another part of the answer was to show enough reward for H-P and Sun to warrant their taking the risk. But Palm acknowledges that building the trust needed for effective cooperation takes time, and the issue cannot be resolved just by having a written agreement. "I am still climbing that hill," he notes.

TRUST FOR HIGHLY SENSITIVE INFORMATION

Sometimes information that both firms need is too critical to be shared between them. In such cases a trusted third party—or, better yet, a combination of respected individuals from each firm—is a useful way to be informed.

For example, in the food business, companies need to be sure that the ingredients they buy from others are safe. Often, however, those ingredients are based on proprietary know-how that suppliers are unwilling to share. To cross that bridge, food companies designate a staff bacteriologist who, acting as a liaison with the supplier, examines the ingredients and how they are manufactured to determine their safety. Everyone understands that this information never goes beyond the bacteriologist.

Kodak and IBM had a similar issue in their relationship and resolved it the same way. In this alliance, it is often sufficient to discuss costs without getting into quantitative details. When more specific information must be shared, however, a pair of respected financial analysts from the two firms who have developed a trusting relationship share the needed information between them. The analyst from IBM sees Kodak information that no one else in IBM sees, and vice versa.

If the information did go beyond these two individuals, the result would be destructive to the whole relationship. Says IBM's Frank Palm: "I lose my ability to manage my business if my weaknesses get exposed. If that were breached, our alliance mental set would be damaged." In both cases the issue is not within the firms, but rather with data leaking to others.

This sharing creates realistic expectations about what is possible. For instance, if Kodak has caused the IBM unit supporting the alliance

Building Trust Between Partner Firms	
Condition or Action	**Details**
Mutual need, dominant shared objective	Contributes to shared confidence that firms can only get desired results by cooperating and adjusting as necessary.
Partner choice	Ensures that each firm has relevant resources and strategic direction, can perform as expected, has alliance style.
Reduced supply base	Creates better chance for shared understandings; lowers suppliers' risks of winning business.
Clear rules of engagement	Objective performance measures, appeals processes, clarity about shared processes, alliance boundaries all build confidence.
Meet commitments	Deliver promised results.
Help suppliers and avoid damage	To help earn suppliers' confidence in relationship: provide growth opportunities, technical assistance; respect independence; focus on cost drivers in price negotiations; strive for healthy supplier margins.
Make fair demands on suppliers	By making equally stringent demands on its own behavior as on suppliers, customer contributes to sense of fairness in relationships.
Meet customer's needs	Contribute to customer's confidence by selling what is best for its situation, even if that means a short-term loss.
Balance benefits, share risks	Allocate gains and losses fairly between firms; take necessary actions to correct imbalances.
Constructive relationships	Joint leadership by top management from each firm; communicate often at policy and operating levels; use multifirm teams when each contributes to the same activity; surface issues early; spot issues for each other; accept occasional mistakes, admit own errors; use root-cause problem solving; build a spirit of community; introduce new programs together; maintain continuity in relationships when people change assignments; avoid surprises; keep deepening mutual understandings.

Building Trust Between Partner Firms, *Cont'd*	
Condition or Action	**Details**
Maintain long-term alignment	To build confidence in shared future, share plans, and integrate planning and implementation at all relevant organizational levels; flexibility, especially by the supplier, is essential here.
Be dependable	In all aspects of relationship, day to day and over the long term.
Be consistent across the firm	Everyone involved in or supporting an alliance honors the same understandings and uses the same practices.

to hire more people than necessary, that can be verified. Similarly, if IBM has not progressed toward desired standards and Kodak understands why, it helps the firms work better together. Or, if Frank Palm knows Kodak's costs—which cannot be more widely shared—before taking on a new project, he will not miss a cost he should have considered. "When they go into a room and reach agreement, says Palm, "Vaughn Hovey and I will support them."

The trust-building practices described in this section are summarized in the table shown.

10

ORGANIZING THE INTERFACE

If you want to be a customer-driven company, you have to design the organization from the outside in, around individual customers rather than around your products.

Richard Slember, president, U.S. power plant businesses, Asea Brown Boveri[1]

Within a company, the formal management structure reinforces key activities, focuses resources, supports controls, and defines accountability. One facet of this structure for alliances is an arrangement that provides needed support on each side of the partner interface.

In some ways, what suppliers do to link with customers mirrors what customer firms do to connect with suppliers. For example, just as marketing provides a strategic complement to sales, alliances require a management role that gives a strategic context to buying. Other aspects of the interface are distinct on each side, reflecting the supplier's need to focus parts of its firm on each customer while the customer must be consistent with all suppliers. The merits of arrangements that place a supplier's people or facilities at the customer's location depend on the specific situation.

A Focused Organization for Each Customer

To create more value than is possible in market transactions, a firm must align its activities more closely with those of each customer.

Doing this may involve changes in style, structure, sales, marketing, and other areas that are unique to each customer alliance.

THE CUSTOMER INTERFACE

When a company sells its products through arm's-length relationships, it responds to some variations among customers. At times, a person is designated as having lead responsibility for an important customer. Often a firm may tailor certain activities for each major market segment. Such differentiation must go further in alliances, because value creation is distinct with every customer, involves more cooperation than arm's-length relationships, and may require a specific set of resources, practices, people, or controls at each customer interface.

A Unique Interface for Each Customer. Each interface must have whatever degree of independence is needed to meet the customer's requirements. Take Motorola, where each preferred supplier has "tuned" its organization to optimize its performance according to Motorola's quality, cost, delivery, early participation, and other desired performances. The suppliers' other customers have different priorities, and such variations require suppliers to have a distinct emphasis for each firm. Also consider that Marks & Spencer expects unique value from its suppliers, which requires close links at all organizational levels. For these reasons, all suppliers have dedicated teams for M&S at the operating level.

The long-term mutual learning and adjustment that typify alliances like these benefit from low turnover among people at the interface, which facilitates trust and teamwork. These relationships create shared habits that make each customer interface culturally distinct. Says Northern Foods chairman Chris Haskins: "Effective cooperation with M&S is to a significant extent a cultural process. One must be able to identify with their culture, know when to be firm and not to be firm, and know where the pitfalls are. I am certain they feel the same way about us."

At Northern Foods, the controls on divisions that serve M&S are tighter, and the interface is more flexible, than with Northern's other customers. Compared with companies in an arm's-length relationship, Northern and M&S need to know more about each other's business and to get more closely involved in strategic investments, product development, and product management. Northern's controls for its M&S business are tighter because the firms work at the cutting edge in foods, where safety risks are higher. Northern also collects more data on its activities with M&S than on those with other retailers, because the two firms need more sophisticated information for their joint planning.

Similarly, the Courtaulds Textiles organization that serves M&S is distinct from other parts of the textiles company in style, people, and know-how. This is because M&S is much more deeply involved in product performance characteristics than other retailers, and is far more concerned with suppliers' management competence and financial strength.

This same pattern of crafting an interface to meet each customer's needs is shown by Chrysler's experience with its suppliers. In the auto industry, product development is a highly complex activity. To facilitate that work, each first-tier assembly firm has a full-time program management organization that is responsible for planning, integrating, and managing all relevant tasks, functions, and relationships with the automaker and with lower-tier suppliers. Steve Zimmer, director of supplier development, says Chrysler has found from experience that better performances of its first-tier suppliers correlate with their having program management organizations dedicated to its needs. By contrast, first-tier firms that have one program organization for all auto companies do not work as well. For activities that are not part of product development (such as manufacturing) Chrysler links directly with each supplier's organization as necessary.

Consider also that Integrated Systems Solutions Corporation, the IBM services unit, has a distinct program management interface with each major alliance customer. For its alliance with McDonnell Douglas, the mission involves integrating a wide collection of hardware from other suppliers, and supporting people who use desktop equipment to do unique jobs. By contrast, the alliance with Kodak is primarily mainframe and data networking oriented, and focuses on serving business units. As a consequence, the ISSC interface organization at McDonnell Douglas is much more complex than the one at Kodak.

Differentiation from Company Norms. In addition to reflecting customer contrasts, the differentiation necessary for an alliance interface depends on how much the interface must deviate from a firm's normal practices. In the case of the Kodak–IBM alliance, the computer firm took several specific organizational steps to get close to the customer.

The first step was to create a new unit—the Systems Center Rochester (SCR), which was independent of other links between the firms, including IBM's marketing team that sells to Kodak. SCR was not to be another marketing channel into Kodak. It focused only on its customer's needs. This has included placing products from IBM rivals at Kodak when doing so was best for the customer. SCR also had to view Kodak from a long-term perspective, whereas IBM marketers were more concerned about near-term revenue. IBM also fully understood and supported the idea that some country marketing organizations were going to be clear losers as the company built a worldwide data processing solution for Kodak.

Historically, IBM controlled its services on a line item basis for each customer. But this practice created rigid interfaces, would have prevented SCR from fully meeting Kodak's needs, and reduced its flexibility to evolve with those needs. So to support the alliance, IBM chose to manage SCR only on its bottom line contribution.

One benefit of the more flexible interface was that decisions about buying computing capacity could be made within SCR, allowing it to invest in capacity ahead of demand in order to meet that demand. By contrast, the traditional view—that when money is tight, investments are reduced—would mean lost revenue and less responsiveness to Kodak needs, implying a lower commitment and weakening the relationship. Frank Palm, who headed SCR at the time, says some financial people in IBM opposed his buying a large mainframe. Palm says he would not have added capacity if he were managed on a line item basis.

Another advantage of IBM's customer-focused interface became evident when Kodak wanted to cut its 1993 computing bill. Had SCR been subject to line item controls, Palm says it would have been hard for people above SCR in the IBM organization to understand the Kodak situation well enough to guide the optimization of SCR's profit under the new scenario.

The customer-focused design also provided more freedom in hiring and span of control, both being line items traditionally subject to higher-level oversight. All of these changes gave SCR a degree of flexibility that was unusual for IBM at the time. Together, they were a key factor in the early and continued success of SCR.

People and Structure at the Interface. As noted in earlier chapters, people at each customer interface must function as a coherent team. In arm's-length relationships it has been acceptable, although not very effective, for individual functions such as sales or engineering to operate independent of each other with customers. This practice slows responses and, if anything goes wrong, each function may blame the other. The higher costs, delayed actions, and friction caused by such arrangements are more damaging with alliances, because they defeat the trust and shared understandings needed for success.

Clearly, the functions represented on a customer-facing team and the authority it is given depend on the work of each alliance. In some cases, teams may include two or three people who meet occasionally as needed. In other situations, as in the case of the Kodak–IBM alliance or of first-tier assembly suppliers for automakers, each company has a full-time program management organization to manage the task of integrating complex activities. Such organizations may be part of a matrix structure in their firms, or they may have the full authority needed to complete their work. For convenience, the traits of interface teams and program structures are summarized in the table below. In general, teams cost less than program offices, but the offices can be more effective at coordinating complex activities.

To ensure clear understandings, build trust, and avoid bureaucracy at the interface, interface structures should not get in the way of direct contacts between personnel who have the skills relevant to particular tasks. In the Molex–Motorola relationship, people in marketing, sales engineering, quality, and division upper management talk directly to

Comparing Interface Structures	
Structure	**Characteristics**
Team	Members report to separate functions and cooperate as needed to meet their firm's commitments to the customer
Program organization	Members all work in a separate organization, report to the same executive, are subject to distinct controls needed to support the interface, and have sufficient authority to coordinate all relevant activities within their firm to meet its commitments to the customer

the commodity manager and others at Motorola rather than going through Dan Prescott, the industrial marketing manager responsible for the Motorola account.

For example, in quality, the corporate director of quality at Molex gets monthly reports of his firm's quality rating with Motorola and works to improve that. In the process, he speaks with his counterparts at Motorola, with the contact depending on the scope of interest. On quality audits, he connects with the Motorola person responsible for corporate quality. On matters regarding individual Motorola divisions, he works with division employees.

In all cases, Molex people who work with Motorola keep each other informed and conduct themselves as members of a single interface team. It works the same way on the Motorola side of the interface.

SALES AND MARKETING IN ALLIANCES

In alliances, customer and supplier share a desire to keep doing business together. This bond reduces the need for conventional selling. Still, sales continues to have a role in many cases, although it differs from traditional practice. It is worth understanding the new role of sales, as well as how the marketing function operates in alliances.

In concert with an organization adapted to each customer, sales and marketing must focus more on individual customers than they do in arm's length transactions. While the line between sales and marketing varies from company to company, the general pattern is that sales works on day-to-day issues involving the customer. Marketing, by contrast, operates from a broader and more strategic perspective, focuses on organizational alignment, and ensures that new activities serve both firms' interests. Both functions are aimed at enhancing long-term relationships.

Sales as Customer Liaison. In alliances, salespeople are facilitators rather than pitchmen. They are experts on the customer's business who coordinate with their colleagues in marketing, engineering, design, and operations to make buying easy and better serve customer needs. In a way, this is an extension of the traditional account manager's role, except there is much less actual selling and more coordination with alliances.

One responsibility of salespeople is to maintain a dialogue about new opportunities and to help match the customer's advancing needs with the supplier's evolving abilities, a task that includes new product presentations and technology seminars. Other activities are finding standard parts that best fit the customer's needs, participating in price negotiations, and closing sales on standard items and custom designs.

Due to growing early design activities with customers, Molex has an increasing need for salespeople who can coordinate the day-to-day work and keep it on track. Design engineers cannot do this. They are not trained in getting the right information from the customer, evaluating it, and integrating that with Molex engineering, marketing, and manufacturing. Further, the customer engineer may not be located nearby: Molex engineers are based at its headquarters in Lisle, Illinois, while customer design people are all over the world. Some Molex customers have asked that its engineers be closer to their design sites, but that cannot be done in all cases.

Sales Tenure, Incentives, and Support. In a partnering environment, the company-specific knowledge needed by a supplier salesperson requires more time on a customer assignment, with less rotation than in traditional sales positions—where good direct salespeople frequently move on for promotion or larger territories. At least two or more years may be necessary to appreciate a customer's unique needs and ways in purchasing, engineering, and operations; adapt to its culture; know how to judge its priorities; and build trust with everyone involved.

Clearly, alliances also require sales incentives that emphasize the long term. For example, since selling on design and development may involve a lengthy cycle extending over more than one year, sales compensation must be salary plus commission. Further, a firm must be willing to support those actions of its salespeople that are taken in the interest of building closer long-term relationships.

Kelly Howell, the Molex sales representative on the Philips account, says he has never had a problem favoring a customer's initiative to design out a Molex part to help the customer save money. In fact, while he would not do anything to hurt Molex, he has often taken the same initiative when to do so is in the best long-term interests of both firms. Such practices build stronger customer commitments and more volume over the longer term. But Howell says they require the support of the company he represents, and some firms are more comfortable taking such positions than others. Further, compensation plans that only reward short-term behavior will not encourage salespeople to do this. Howell adds that his toughest rivals are other sales representatives who are also working on long-term relationships.

Profile of Salespeople. "It is getting to the point where I don't want technically shallow sales reps out there any more," says Bruce Bendoff of Craftsman Custom Metal Fabricators. "We are replacing them with sales engineers who can advocate and support early design with customers and describe what Craftsman has done for other firms. Now we are selling process skills, not just products."

More generally, the demands on selling in alliances—in early design, liaison between different functions, monitoring interfirm relationships, and matching technical needs and abilities—call for substantial technical know-how. Given these requirements and a shortage of salespeople with the relevant expertise, some firms are adding liaison engineers at the customer interface to supplement the traditional sales function.

Also needed are the skills to facilitate cooperation and a personal orientation toward building long-term mutually productive relationships. At Molex, which uses long-term incentives, Ron Schubel says that a person's approach to selling depends on his or her style; selling in alliances also requires the salesperson to find those areas where both firms' interests overlap.

The Sales Organization. In alliances, each sales organization reflects the customer's buying structure. For instance, for a decentralized customer, salespeople must link directly with buyers in each business group, while more centralization at the customer requires more coordination in sales. Since centralization above individual customer business units can reduce differentiation at each unit, however, the potential for an alliance may be compromised unless needed flexibility is built into each interface.

Marketing Responsibilities. Alliances depend on a healthy flow of information between appropriate groups in each firm about their business together. That may include performance reports from the customer on the supplier's quality, delivery, and other matters—and similar reports from the supplier to the customer—as well as efforts to share technology road maps and launch new programs such as bar code labeling. Typically marketing or general management oversees these activities, or at least is kept informed, because they involve a wide set of issues regarding the overall relationship.

A second marketing or general management task is to know the customer's business well enough to support independent judgments about investments that will be unique for that customer. For example, to be sure its investments make sense for Molex, the firm may second-guess Motorola's volume estimates. Dan Prescott says part of his job is to know Motorola's market as well as it does: "If we don't know our industry, we could get in real trouble."

Another responsibility of marketing is to control relationships from a business perspective. In alliances, the close, multifunctional contacts between partner firms create some chance that a local initiative may not be in both firms' best interests. Molex, for instance, prefers that engineering contacts with Motorola and other customer partners work through sales and marketing. That allows it to determine how much engineering time should be allocated to such work, and prevents engineering from pursuing developments that do not make business sense for Molex. To maintain controls, marketing works with engineering with follow-up by the division general manager, to whom both functions report, to determine what needs to be put into a program in terms of time and investment, based on the needs and scope of each opportunity.

Marketing Organization. To complement sales, the marketing structure in alliances typically works on broader strategic alignment with the customer. When volume warrants, a specific marketing position may be dedicated to each customer.

Molex has an industry marketing manager for each major account requiring unique activities. The person in that position helps Molex align with the customer's current and emerging needs, and is expected to build more volume. As the primary contact person with Motorola's commodity team that interfaces with Molex, Dan Prescott networks as necessary across his firm, leading an informal team from manufacturing, engineering, and purchasing that ties the various Molex functions together to serve Motorola. Besides his involvement in annual contract negotiations and special events such as the Total Customer Satisfaction team competition, he champions new Motorola programs within Molex. That 50 percent of Prescott's activity with Motorola is focused on interorganizational processes underscores the importance of cooperation across the interface.

Meeting Motorola's requirement for bar coding illustrates Prescott's role. For each of its forty-eight plants worldwide, Molex had to buy a special printer and train people to operate it. To get that done, Prescott first sold the concept to Molex upper management by showing them the significance of the opportunity. He then worked with corporate operations, which had to install the practices at each site.

Prescott and Janet Robinson, Motorola's commodity manager responsible for Molex, see each other as sharing the overall responsibility for their firms' alliance on a day-to-day basis. They have a very candid and direct relationship, notes Prescott: "I can be as open with her as I can with anyone in Molex, and she is always willing to listen. Of course, we may not always get the response we want. Even so, in all the time I have known her I have never felt there were any hidden agendas." Prescott and Robinson meet once or twice a year and talk by phone about every two weeks.

Molex measures the performance of its industrial marketing managers by sales against plan. Salespeople responsible for specific accounts are also measured against this objective. Other measures include profit objectives, progress on the Motorola-targeted business plan, and new programs for Motorola.

BALANCING FOCUS AND INTERNAL INTEGRATION

Some resources, such as sales, aspects of marketing, and specific facilities, are best dedicated to individual customers when volume and the opportunity for value creation justify that. Others are centrally organized to take advantage of scale and specialization.

For instance, while each Molex division has an industrial marketing manager, customer service for all alliances is in one organizational unit, called the sales correspondence group. This structure gives customer service more focus and leverages the full power of Molex systems like E-mail documentation and monitoring of customer metrics. The centralized arrangement also makes backup available for each person and facilitates supervision. All of that was harder to do when service was previously organized in small subgroups within each Molex division. The value of integration reflects the fact that customer service requirements across the divisions are not significantly differentiated, while the need for a sharper focus within customer service is high. Along with the Molex sales force, the sales correspondence group is the primary interface with the customer for expediting current business.

As it does for a few other customers with unique requirements, Molex customer service has a dedicated inside salesperson for Motorola who is responsible for managing all purchase orders, shipments, and backlogs for that customer. This person also handles new opportunities (including sales drawings, pricing, and contracts) and coordinates responses to the supplier ratings index.

Structuring to Be Consistent with Suppliers

In customer–supplier alliances, the customer has the lead in setting objectives and related metrics, judging performance, and maintaining long-term alignment. All these tasks require that a broader, more forward-looking dimension be added to buying, which is traditionally a short-term function concerned mainly with price. While suppliers must develop some focus for each customer, the customer side of the interface should appear the same to all suppliers, to ensure consistency with them.

Traditionally, purchasing in most companies has been so remote from the market that it might as well be on another planet. The gap makes it almost impossible for purchasing to work with suppliers on anything except cost. Even then, cost must be narrowly defined, because purchasing's view of the market is too thin for it to make useful contributions to quality, design, cycle time, and the other elements of market value.

At Motorola, however, purchasing people not only have a deep understanding of their business's objectives, markets, and competitive strategies but also appreciate how the firm's activities combine to affect its quality, costs, cycle time, and other value sources. Ask the Paging Products Group's strategic sourcing director Neil MacIvor what he knows about its markets, and he is fast to respond: "You can ask virtually anyone in sourcing about the business. We know where we are strong and where we are not; we know why we are selling and why not. We go over the numbers in daily business meetings. It is inherent in the nature of our jobs that we have to know this. We are constantly asking about new products and how they will fit into the product portfolio, and questioning marketing about forecasts." Question Tom Slaninka, who heads sourcing in the Land Mobile Products sector, about any aspect of its business such as customer deliveries, and he quickly reels off current data about customer expectations, request dates, lead times, and more.

This knowledge is the foundation of supplier metrics, ratings, audits, capacity planning, business reviews, technology road maps, negotiations, and other processes that keep Motorola and its suppliers stretching toward its desired results and aligned for the long term. For example, to facilitate cooperation on design, PPG designers and new product sourcing managers are measured against market objectives, including customer satisfaction targets that are specified for each new product. The same kinds of market understandings guide teamwork and consensus processes within and across business areas; all of these elements add value to supplier performance.

The strategic thinking, analysis, and coordination needed to support a supply base are best done by people who do not have to satisfy day-to-day needs on the shop floor or meet other immediate requirements. These people should report to general management or other positions that can support longer-term strategic work so that they are not dominated by daily matters. As with the supplier side of the interface, appropriate organizational arrangements depend on the costs and benefits of integration versus differentiation within and among buying units.

Although the strategic and day-to-day aspects of supplier relationships are distinct, both must be close enough to the interface with suppliers to meet the unique needs of each situation. At the same time, the strategic component should have a sufficiently broad organizational scope to capitalize on scale economies and other commonalities (such as those for standard parts and shared suppliers and technologies) among different business units or product lines.

SUPPLY ORGANIZATION AT MARKS & SPENCER

Among Marks & Spencer, Motorola, and Chrysler, M&S has the most decentralized purchasing structure. For the retailer, the strategic and tactical purchasing functions coexist within each department, which is the smallest organizational unit. Every M&S department has a distinct product range; suppliers are managed to produce the greatest possible value for that range. As a complement to this structure, managers in each organizational layer above the individual departments have a corresponding higher-level responsibility to ensure strategic coordination with suppliers across the broader product range. Above ladies' skirts, for example, the director of the ladies' tailoring division is concerned with skirts, suits, coats, and trousers. This arrangement helps ensure needed consistency within and among the several suppliers of a broader M&S product range.

Each M&S department—such as ladies' suits and skirts—interfaces directly with its suppliers. A department is made up of three disciplines, each of which requires close links to suppliers: selectors (who envision what the consumer wants and later choose specific goods), merchandisers (who plan how much is to be bought and from whom, create a price balance across the department's product range, lead price negotiations, and allocate and negotiate production flows for delivery to the stores), and technologists (who work with suppliers to ensure quality and cooperate on new developments).

Each department maintains both a short-term and a more strategic perspective on its product line, with people at lower management levels working on current matters and those at higher levels on broader, longer-term topics. The arrangement supports a focused understanding of each department's products and facilitates constant interactions with suppliers and among the disciplines.

In ladies' suits and skirts Carole O'Beirne, the senior selector, coordinates the overall appearance of products in her department. O'Beirne has a team of product range selectors reporting to her, with each one responsible for a section of the department. They work mostly on short-term items relating to the current season and the next. Typical tasks include selecting specific garments, maintaining quality (together with the technical team), developing products, and resolving issues of fit. The department also has a fabric technologist who works with suppliers to be sure fabrics perform as expected, and sources new fabrics based on new fibers, yarns, and weaving technology. A garment technologist is responsible for how an item is made and fits, and helps achieve the look selectors want. The same person may work on finding new manufacturing equipment and bringing this to suppliers' attention.

More senior people in each department add the strategic dimension, with senior selectors planning future materials and directions M&S would like its suppliers to pursue. They also participate in decisions about which firms will grow with M&S and which will decline in their share of the business. Since the views of O'Beirne and her merchandise manager counterpart are both vital in the supply process, they must agree on all strategic matters. They also regularly discuss each firm's performance with it, both to spot potential problems and to improve long-term performance. At the same time, the department's technologists are working to develop and source new fabrics, yarns, and processes based on new fibers and weaving technology with raw material and garment manufacturers.

SUPPLY ORGANIZATION AT MOTOROLA

At Motorola, the primary interface with suppliers is through separate sourcing organizations (or their equivalent, with other names) within each group or sector—the largest building blocks of the corporation. In contrast to Marks & Spencer, Motorola must ensure the availability and integration of hundreds or even thousands of parts for individual products, as well as be consistent across the 100 or more suppliers to the many divisions that make up each group or sector. As a manufacturer, Motorola also has more internal activities to which suppliers must be linked than is the case at M&S. All of these tasks are best managed by a distinct sourcing unit in each group or sector. Each of the divisions within a group or sector has its own purchasing function.

This separation between strategic and daily activities reflects strong strategic and technological similarities in purchases across divisions within a group or sector, many common suppliers at that level, and strong, unique divisional needs for the day-to-day tasks done by purchasing. Further, the greater complexities and higher costs inherent in sourcing for a manufacturer, compared with a retailer, would make it hard to justify having sourcing units at the lower level.

People in each sourcing unit understand the design, technology, manufacturing, marketing, and customer issues that are common to suppliers of parts for related products, such as pagers. This broad awareness helps the divisions meet their quality, cost, delivery, and cycle time objectives; keeps the suppliers on an exacting path of constant improvement; ensures consistency in Motorola's relationships with them; and facilitates alignment with the divisions' future needs. The same familiarity helps sourcing manage programs like early design participation, bar coding, and schedule sharing across all suppliers.

The sourcing departments have formal authority for supplier

selection, performance monitoring, development, capacity planning, technology alignment, cost reductions, and early design participation. Each sourcing unit's priorities are set according to what best serves the competitive needs of the Motorola group or sector to which it belongs.

The sourcing units began forming in the early 1980s and are in various stages of development toward the same general goal. Differences among them reflect how long each has functioned, as well as distinct competitive strategies and demands in the group or sector. The units were created by shifting resources from various materials and purchasing functions and funded by productivity increases without significant new costs. The budget in the Land Mobile Products sector, where sourcing began, is 0.3 percent of the cost of the purchased material involved. While budgets are approved at higher organizational levels, all costs are allocated to the divisions being served according to the estimated effort for each.

Each sourcing unit consists of several commodity managers, plus others who maintain metrics and manage special programs (like Schedule Sharing). A commodity manager has lead responsibility for a number of suppliers, and is the primary focus for supply issues regarding those firms for all divisions within the Motorola group or sector. He or she also champions further penetration of a supplier into Motorola if it is better than an incumbent on the metrics. A commodity manager is assigned one or more commodity groups composed of parts that are technically and functionally related. The location of those manager positions at facilities where the relevant purchases are most critical also helps win local buy-in for the commodity management process.

At the division level, buyers focus on such day-to-day tasks as coordinating new product introductions, scheduling, material planning, awarding business to chosen suppliers, invoicing, expediting, maintaining the purchase order database, and monitoring payments. Other tasks include handling daily supplier quality problems, assuring that all requirements are sent to suppliers, managing capacity issues within a one-year time frame, and resolving all other day-to-day issues.

Commodity Teams. Typically an engineer, the commodity manager heads a team composed of buyers, quality and materials people, and designers from the relevant divisions. Sometimes, outside customers, manufacturing, and finance are also represented. The team's mission is to manage the supply base and show a single Motorola face to suppliers. Some or all team members make supplier site visits. There are no approvals for team decisions at higher levels. The commodity manager is evaluated on how well a composite of the suppliers of each commodity performs against defined metrics, how much of the available Motorola business in that commodity is awarded to preferred suppliers, and team performance.

While the managers lead and direct sourcing activities, buyers and designers who implement the programs do not report to them. Part of the commodity managers' role is to get participating Motorola divisions to reach consensus on relevant supply decisions—such as suppliers to be added or dropped—to maintain the same base across all divisions. The process works because there are objective metrics and a clear buy-in across Motorola on quality and other purchasing objectives.

In the Paging Products Group, commodity managers lead teams for capacitors, semiconductors, plastics, batteries, hardware, printed circuit boards, motors, labels, manuals, resistors, coils, crystals, lamps, displays, and packaging. For critical parts, commodity managers are at the major design sites in Singapore and in Boynton Beach, Florida. All commodity managers are expected to visit critical suppliers at least once a year, regardless of their location, for benchmarking, quality audits, and sharing of technology road maps. They are also expected to find and visit new potential suppliers to ensure that the base continues to maintain its world-class status. PPG strategic sourcing regards development engineering, purchasing, and suppliers as its customers; they are regularly surveyed to monitor sourcing's performance and help ensure that it is not becoming a roadblock to progress.

Promoting Supplier Health. Each commodity manager contributes to, performs, or maintains all data, analysis, and decisions about supplier selection and management. The tasks involved include supplier classification; metrics development; quality audits; critical supplier processes; commodity cost profiles and design guidelines; performance feedback and follow-up; training and assistance; benchmarking; volume allocations; and statistics on quality, delivery, and inventory. Frequently the commodity manager draws on local division resources for on-site supplier training and quality and technical reviews.

Supply Base Champion. Sourcing is charged with maintaining and advancing a healthy supply base. It has the authority to stop a purchase from going to a nonpreferred firm. On one occasion, for example, a

Motorola engineer telephoned a nonpreferred supplier regarding an insertion problem with circuit boards. Ron Vocalino, a regional sourcing manager in Schaumburg, Illinois, heard about the call and stepped in, saying that the proper procedure was to seek a solution from the preferred supply base. He also went to the division sourcing manager, who asked the engineering manager not to continue with the nonpreferred supplier.

Vocalino next called a meeting with division engineering and sourcing and the relevant commodity manager. Together, they developed a plan to present the problem to the three preferred suppliers of circuit boards. He then called each supplier, explained the problem, and asked if it would be willing to meet with the other two with Motorola present. Even though a joint meeting could have been awkward since the suppliers were rivals, they agreed to meet with Motorola.

As the meeting got under way, Vocalino said he did not expect that the task they were to embark upon would compromise any of their business with Motorola. Thus assured, the firms began sharing ideas about how to address the problem, volunteering to allocate tasks among themselves and report back to Motorola. They also shared know-how about their respective operations and agreed to meet regularly until the problem was solved. Further, the suppliers made immediate suggestions regarding changes Motorola could (and later did) make in its materials and design to help alleviate the problem.

The entire experience sent a powerful message to the preferred supplier base: Motorola was looking out for them. It also reminded Motorola engineers about the value of working with preferred suppliers. There was also value for the suppliers, who took the lessons learned to their own wider markets.

Technology Coordination. Commodity managers are expected to know the future product technology needs of the divisions they serve, develop technology road maps reflecting those needs, and ensure that suppliers' road maps match their own. They also organize supplier technology seminars, identify technology voids early to help direct suppliers to Motorola's design needs, and alert internal design teams to take advantage of an emerging supplier technology capability.

New Product Liaison. In some parts of Motorola, sourcing engineers are assigned to facilitate the early design participation process by helping engineers and suppliers work together. At the Paging Products

Group, this design link has proven to be most effective when senior sourcing people are resident in the product development labs.

These new product sourcing (NPS) managers provide one-stop shopping for supplier selection for early design, coordinate prototype tooling and parts purchases, direct relevant metrics implementation, help engineering understand Motorola's materials systems (the procedures for getting parts qualified and on order), and make key contacts in supplier organizations. To serve the PPG design centers in Boynton Beach and Singapore, there are parallel NPS functions at each location. Each NPS manager may be responsible for more than one product at a time; priorities are set by the division being served.

Because the NPS manager and design engineer are expected to work as a team, the lead on various tasks goes to whoever has the greater leverage on results, with appropriate support from the other person. Strategic sourcing holds the NPS manager accountable for doing everything possible to drive costs down; engineering management looks at its own people the same way.

One role of the NPS manager is to push for standard parts across product lines to help lower costs. Being in the development labs helps these managers spot such chances early enough in the design cycle to make a difference. When opportunities are found, materials quality engineering (MQE) personnel—who have more technical depth—are brought in to locate substitute parts or materials that might better achieve the same objective. Each division decides independently whether to use a standard component to lower its costs or pursue a unique design for more value. Still, if staffers from materials quality engineering weigh in against it, the rationale for a unique part would have to be strong.

Lead Negotiator. The commodity manager generally takes the lead in supplier negotiations, with other team members participating. The manager not only helps keep the desired balance among price, delivery, and quality but overcomes a tendency for buyers to favor price alone. At times the buyer with the highest volume takes the lead, especially if he or she has more expertise in the specific part. To prepare the commodity manager assembles relevant data, including a target price, division volume requirements, and common specifications. Since each division has substantial autonomy to support its distinct strategies, its buyer signs the purchase order once price has been agreed upon.

Preferred suppliers are encouraged to question Motorola forecasts and develop logic that might indicate one is incorrect. They may decline to participate if they think the risk for them is too great. Commodity managers play a key role here in counterbalancing buyers who may be inclined to say, "We are Motorola, and you will have to do things our way."

Capacity Coordinator. Sourcing takes the lead in giving each supplier, via the Schedule Sharing system, one set of consolidated time-phased requirements across participating Motorola divisions. This information is broken down by each supplier plant and by each Motorola plant worldwide. This improved forecasting has raised service levels, reduced supplier headaches, saved Motorola overhead costs, and cut friction between Motorola divisions over supply allocations. It also gives suppliers one person to talk to about Schedule Sharing issues and enables Motorola to resolve its own capacity conflicts at suppliers. In the past, inadequate capacity planning sometimes caused volume constraints that prevented the company from completing all customer orders.

Competition among Motorola facilities for parts from a supplier with limited capacity is resolved according to which facility has more delinquent or potentially delinquent customer orders. This is an informal understanding, not a policy; an irate top customer may get highest priority.

Relationship Managers. Commodity managers take the lead in improving understandings with suppliers beyond day-to-day matters, helping resolve issues to avoid damaging relationships. When a supplier has an interpersonal issue or general business concern, such as a parts shortage, the commodity manager is the person with whom the topic is discussed. To illustrate, at one time Molex let delivery slide below acceptable limits. The commodity manager, who was immediately on top of the problem, said she expected both a short-term containment by Molex and a longer-term solution. She stayed on top of the process at Molex to be sure the long-term fix was put in place.

Another task is to help suppliers having interdivisional problems. If, for example, one division complains that it is receiving inferior service compared with another, the commodity manager steps in to determine the reason and explain (or try to fix) the problem. It may be that the division experiencing poor service is a small part of the supplier's business and thus cannot command the same service level as the heavier user.

Which Suppliers to Include. Originally, only those firms having the largest cost and strategic impact on Motorola products were included in the commodity management process. For the others, purchasing people in individual divisions were asked to manage the commodities, but they were typically busy and it did not get done. Sourcing helped with some tasks, but not as often as it did with the top firms. The resulting gap caused a short-term focus for the neglected suppliers that led to cost, quality, or delivery problems for strategic or small-volume customers (which could become large-volume opportunities). These experiences have led to a growing trend among sourcing units to include all suppliers in the full process.

Low Volume Is Different. For commodities, objective metrics and focused competition allow sourcing to compare different suppliers of a particular item. For low-volume items like complex custom-developed equipment with a high engineering content, however, there can be a big difference between goods from separate firms. In such cases, engineering management decides what is to be bought and from which supplier.

SUPPLY ORGANIZATION AT CHRYSLER

Chrysler's organization is the most centralized of the three companies, because its cars and trucks have far more in common than Marks & Spencer's food, clothing, and home furnishings or Motorola's pagers, chips, automotive products, computers, cellular phones, base stations, and other businesses. For Chrysler, this commonality creates more opportunities to share technologies and suppliers across the corporation, and more reason for a central structure.

Consistent with this homogeneity, all strategic and day-to-day purchasing activities report to the firm's corporate procurement and supply organization. This includes people responsible for all metrics, ratings, quality and technology assessments, supplier value engineering, scheduling and production controls for assembly plants, releasing requirements to suppliers, and supplier relationships.

Suppliers interface with the automaker as members of its platform teams. To achieve needed differentiation for each vehicle platform, team members from Chrysler work in a matrix organization. Each team is a full multifunctional group that includes people from engineering, manufacturing, finance, and purchasing and supply. As a team, they are accountable to the executive responsible for that platform. As with purchasing and supply, other team members report to the relevant corporate functional organizations (such as engineering). To help ensure effective matrix performance, team executives also serve as functional heads; Tom Stallkamp, for instance, wears two hats as vice president of purchasing and supply and as general manager of large car operations. Stallkamp and his peers report to Bob Lutz, Chrysler's president.

Each platform—for large cars, small cars, minivans, jeeps, trucks, and special vehicles—is the basis for designing closely related product models. Negotiations with suppliers are conducted by platform team members including a buyer, engineering and manufacturing people, value engineering and supplier quality specialists.

The Pros and Cons of Co-Location

One useful interface structure is to locate a supplier's designers, engineers, or others at a customer's facility (see Chapter 5). This practice can help build useful understandings and shorten the response time for people who must solve problems together. Similarly, building a supplier's plant or warehouse near the customer's site can increase responsiveness and lower shipping costs. Still, determining best location requires a consideration of all variables important to the customer, including scale, shipping and storage costs, the supplier's resource needs, and whether colocating engineers or other people (if needed) also requires that entire facilities be nearby.

Further, *nearby* is a vague term. For computer chips it can be Tokyo for an American customer, due to high value, low weight (and thus low shipping costs), and the ease of having chips flown in daily. Quite a few American and Japanese firms use this arrangement and, when necessary, locate the appropriate personnel in each other's facilities.

Consider that most of the 339 suppliers to General Motors' Saturn unit are, on average, 550 miles from its Spring Hill, Tennessee, plant; moreover, Saturn has almost no parts inventory. Thanks to skillful supply chain management and an alliance with Ryder System (the transportation services company that handles Saturn logistics), in four years the plant has had to stop production just once—for eighteen minutes—because the right part did not arrive on time.[2]

Customer and Supplier Advisory Boards

When a firm has alliances across a large supply base, there can be value in regularly meeting with representatives from selected suppliers as a group to monitor the overall health of those relationships and help guide their development. Since advisory boards represent the interests of many suppliers, their power depends on the merit of their advice, the respect held by participants, and the ability of customer representatives to implement worthy suggestions.

Motorola's supplier advisory board has been a key instrument in transforming what were once hostile relationships into true alliances. It has done this by raising difficult issues about Motorola conduct—and suggesting changes—to a group of its people who wanted to hear and were empowered to act. Today, the board represents the best interests of the entire preferred supply base to the customer in ways that discussions with individual firms cannot.

By contrast, a senior manufacturing executive at one consumer goods company says that his firm gets valuable insights about supplier attitudes from surveys it conducts, but tough relationship issues usually do not surface that way. He says those concerns tend to come out only after they have festered, and then just between individual firms. There is no easy way to learn whether a particular issue applies to others.

Closely related to supplier boards are other bodies, representing a firm's major customers or distributors, that may be formed to advise the firm on product development, marketing, and related matters. For these, many of the practices are similar to those used with suppliers, with one exception. Supplier advisory boards can be instrumental in the management of alliances across a firm's supply base. Customer boards, which can be a valuable way to get advice and share learnings, are essentially high-level focus groups and not part of a governance process.

Board Membership

An effective supplier advisory board must reflect the customer's objectives and the nature of its business. At Chrysler, 90 percent of the purchasing volume is with 150 large companies, and each of the vehicle platform groups is a major business. Accordingly, Chrysler's advisory council consists of twelve top suppliers, all of which are major firms. GE Plastics is also a member because of the importance of its work for Chrysler. A second council of minority suppliers has the objective of developing that part of the supply base, a task that supports Chrysler's goal of having at least 5 percent of its purchasing volume with minority firms.

Motorola, by contrast, works with a more diverse advisory board. One reason is that the company has several new start-up businesses that are not well covered by high-leverage purchases. Supply practices that ignore these situations can inhibit their growth. A second reason for wide representation is that many key suppliers are smaller firms, and programs that are acceptable to large companies may not work for them. This was Motorola's experience when it introduced EDI and bar coding, which the board helped guide to meet small firms' needs. Another reason is that Motorola has minority suppliers, some of whom have unique needs.

Choose People, Not Just Companies. In the early stages Motorola selected firms to serve on the board. This practice evolved to an emphasis on choosing people who can be candid and open about Motorola practices, are familiar with the methods of other leading firms, and will champion Motorola goals within their companies. Says Tom Slaninka: "Sharper people respond better to new ideas—both in their critiques and in taking chances on new concepts in their firms." Board members are expected to be able to judge whether issues they raise are broad based rather than driven by one person or firm.

People chosen for the board are all senior executives having substantial responsibility for the Motorola account in their firms, which are top performers in areas important to Motorola (including quality and company values). Typically, these firms are more progressive and willing to participate in new initiatives. Another criterion for board membership is to have solid representation for each major commodity group.

By intentionally empowering the board with people who are bright, have broad knowledge, and are from respected firms, Motorola has created a constructive force for continuous improvement. Slaninka notes that when suppliers say at a board meeting that Motorola needs to improve in a particular area, he knows he must face them again in four months at the next meeting, "and they don't forget."

Supplier representatives benefit from their board membership because it helps them stay near the frontiers of best practice in customer–supplier alliances. Most apply what they learn through the board to their own firms.

Serving on the board is seen as a privilege that implies an extra obligation by the member's firm to perform well. In fact, implicit in membership is an understanding that the board is not a vehicle to win more business. During one meeting, a board member said his firm should have a longer-term business commitment because it was contributing to Motorola through his efforts. A Motorola staffer at the meeting responded that board activities do not relieve any supplier of the need to meet its performance objectives.

Any group tends to get stale if it is not supported by new blood. Reflecting this concern, in a brief formal talk toward the end of one board meeting, John Hawkins of Seiko Instruments, who was ending his turn on the board, said it was vital to cycle people on the board to keep fresh ideas flowing. Bruce Bendoff made the same statement in his departing remarks.

Customer Representatives. Customer employees who attend advisory board meetings should be able to contribute as equals with the supplier representatives. They should also be in a position to implement any policy or operating suggestions that make sense. The appropriate individuals depends on the structure of the customer's organization.

For instance, Chrysler, as noted earlier, has a far more centralized structure than Motorola due to differences in the two firms' product lines. Consequently, Chrysler's quarterly council meetings are attended by several top executives. Among these are its president, vice president of purchasing and supply, the executive directors of supplier and platform management, and others depending on the agenda.

At Motorola, where substantial authority has been delegated to middle and lower levels, each board meeting is attended by all sourcing and commodity managers plus others in materials, purchasing, and engineering, depending on the topics to be covered. Business general managers also attend when topics covered require their help in implementing board recommendations. Motorola's suppliers pushed hard for those people to come to board meetings, and their participation has enhanced the board's work.

AT THE START

Craftsman's Bruce Bendoff, an initial member of Motorola's supplier advisory board, says the board was created because people recognized that a healing process was needed to resolve problems between Motorola and its suppliers, and both sides wanted to convert relationships from adversarial to cooperative. Tom Slaninka, director of sector sourcing in Land Mobile Products, who has been on the Motorola side since the board began, adds that his firm wanted policy-level inputs from leading suppliers above the din of the day-to-day interface. A board was also seen as a psychological power balance between Motorola and its suppliers.

Initially, the board's credibility was enhanced by the participation of top Motorola general management executives at meetings. To start on a constructive path, an outside facilitator was brought in to help the firms talk to each other constructively. At the early meetings, says one participant, people felt awkward because there was more promise than results, and the firms' histories together made people wary. During one of these meetings, the board observed that Motorola's desire for new relationships seemed to be more talk than practice. Motorola listened, however, and made needed changes within its organization. Board members say that Bob Becknell, then manager of sector sourcing, championed the process and was the key to making the advisory board work.

The board was created one year after Motorola began reducing its supply base. By then, people invited to be on the board knew their firms had been selected as preferred suppliers. While the board had no role in deciding which suppliers would remain, it was a mirror for Motorola, providing feedback on what it was doing right and wrong. For example, the board did not believe that metrics first proposed by Motorola were fair, and it helped make changes.

MEETING CONDUCT

Board meetings are held three times a year, regardless of economic conditions or changes in Motorola people at the interface. Board members say that is unusual. Many firms do not display as much constant commitment to formal development of supplier relationships.

Each meeting begins with a private visit among the suppliers to identify issues they want to discuss. Often, someone takes notes and later presents the group's views to Motorola so that no firm is exposed unless it wants to be. Newcomers to the board often use the private sessions to raise issues specific to their firms. However, others with longer tenure understand that the greatest value of the board is in raising generic issues. These members use individual firm's complaints as probes to look for broader-based concerns.

Following the private discussion, Motorola representatives join the board for the formal meeting. Agendas reflect inputs from both sides and are designed to create balanced participation and prevent an "us talking to you" attitude. The accepted style is for discussions to focus as much as possible on exploring issues rather than taking positions. For instance, one topic covered was the strengths and weaknesses in Motorola's early design participation process, with participation by Motorola engineers and engineering management.

Board meetings are characterized by considerable trust, and discussions cover many issues that are not raised at operating levels. One board member says Motorola constantly demonstrates by its actions that it wants and takes feedback from suppliers. He observes that few of his firm's other customers will let a supplier give useful feedback that may be painful. However, people on the advisory board feel there will not be retribution if they offer fair and honest feedback to Motorola. New members need some time to become comfortable with that style since it is so different from traditional customer–supplier relationships.

Ron Schubel of Molex, who served on the board for six years, says the board "absolutely gives Motorola better inputs from the supply base than it could otherwise get." He says the board gets beneath the surface of problems to identify and deal with real issues that inhibit Motorola and its suppliers from functioning as effectively as possible together.

Being on the board also facilitates members' access to relevant Motorola executives. This is not to promote their firms, but to raise important issues about supply relationships, in one-on-one contacts, that would be difficult to voice in other settings.

RESULTS

When the board began, its most significant accomplishment was that Motorola and its suppliers learned to communicate with each other. Since then, other contributions have included its proposing that

Motorola use a supplier questionnaire to help it keep abreast of issues across the preferred supply base, championing the development of commodity teams and the early design participation process, and initiating changes in how Motorola purchasing people are evaluated. The board has also had a key role in shaping the Schedule Sharing process to make it more user friendly, contributing to the definition of a preferred supplier and the development of the supplier rating system, defining document communications processes, and introducing bar coding and pay-from-receipt systems.

By the late 1980s board members were comfortable enough with Motorola to ask if some long-established practices worked in the firms' mutual interest. One concern was how buyers were evaluated. The suppliers thought that buyers were pressing too hard on price and not focusing enough on total cost, as Motorola had been saying it wanted to do. Motorola responded by changing the buyer evaluation.

At about the same time, the board also said that Motorola was missing opportunities by not using all of its suppliers' skills: The latter wanted to get involved early in the design process, before plans became rigid. Motorola responded that while the concept had merits, the timing in the development cycle was too early to write contracts. To better understand the situation, Motorola began several pilot projects focused on what it now calls Early Supplier Involvement (ESI). From these projects the firm began to understand the value of involving suppliers in the design process.

Later, during the development of ESI, the board rejected a confidentiality agreement proposed by Motorola as being too long, overly endowed with legalese, and too punitive. All of these characteristics implied a lack of trust; one supplier tore up the document in front of the board to show his displeasure. A board subcommittee consisting of one person from Motorola and three from suppliers then simplified and modified the document, which Motorola's legal staff reviewed and then adopted.

The board also enables Motorola to launch trial balloons on new initiatives and get constructive feedback before the programs are implemented across the supply base. In addition, Motorola uses the board as a vehicle for communicating its future plans regarding suppliers. At one meeting, for instance, Tom Slaninka told the board that in three to four years the company might only use one-third the number of its existing preferred suppliers. A smaller supply base was seen as the only way to reach Motorola's Six Sigma quality objective. A streamlined supply base was also needed to improve ESI performance, which requires closer relationships with suppliers and thus fewer companies in order to work.

11

LEVERAGING THE CORPORATION

This is not a corporate show. We work for the businesses as a team effort.

Kathy Sullivan, vice president and corporate director of supply management, Motorola

Changing the boxes without changing the way you manage the boxes is not going to give you the results you're looking for.

Dick Ogren, director of business strategy for Ford Motor Company, who led Ford's global restructuring team

A company consisting of related businesses can substantially leverage its resources in concert with its suppliers. One way to do this is to promote consistency by sharing audits, parts, and technologies across business units. Another is to share best practices to help the businesses move further ahead. A third is to use central purchasing, services, and resources to benefit from scale economies.

Every company that has more than one business unit must strike an effective balance between each unit's need for sufficient differentiation to compete in its market, and the wider benefits of integration across the units to achieve scale economies and share resources. This balance has to be reflected in the structure of customer–supplier alliances.

Global alliances with customers or suppliers offer the greatest opportunities for achieving economies of scale and resource use, but these must also support needed local differentiation for each business.

Balancing Corporate and Business Unit Interests

Customer–supplier alliances require the customer to use consistent, objectives-based practices such as metrics, audits, and rating systems across its supply base. When more than one of a customer's business units participates in an alliance, these practices must be consistent for all of them to get collective benefits. Without common supplier ratings, for example, different businesses have no way to agree on what they mean by cost. Consistency is also essential for different groups to agree on supplier selection, development, and long-term alignment, as well as to promote problem solving, shared understandings, and trust.

Being a slave to consistency, however, compromises the needs each business has for autonomy. The appropriate amount of differentiation is determined by what best serves the overall strategic interests of the corporation.

In that regard, Motorola, Marks & Spencer, and Chrysler support different degrees of independence among their respective businesses or product groups. Motorola's individual divisions need more autonomy than Marks & Spencer's clothing departments, and considerably more than Chrysler's vehicle platform teams. These contrasts cause variations among the firms in how they interface with suppliers, as discussed in Chapter 10. Each company uses a distinct organizational arrangement that ensures needed differentiation and takes advantage of common interests. How the firms balance differentiation and integration, and the way this balance influences supplier relations for each of them, is illustrated by their product design activities.

DIFFERENTIATION AND INTEGRATION AT MOTOROLA

Individual divisions at Motorola have a high degree of entrepreneurial freedom to compete in their respective markets. Product design is often determined at the division level. Yet, in addition to meeting financial and other targets, such flexibility is expected to serve clear corporate goals for cost, quality, cycle time improvement, and other areas that are consistently—and almost religiously—enforced across the entire firm. These corporate priorities are articulated in Motorola's vision and strategy documents, backed up by constant top management attention and training programs, and embodied in the performance evaluations of every business and employee. Across Motorola, people are constantly being reminded of the need to move ahead in concert with corporate goals.

Motorola's sourcing units and the corporate councils that support integration in metrics, quality audits, and other areas across the company wholly embrace the same goals. Consequently, they are regarded by the individual businesses as vehicles to help them achieve these goals. This view, in turn, facilitates teamwork and consensus building to establish common practices at group or sector and corporate levels. Wide internal acceptance of Motorola's objectives also permits buyers and those in sourcing, engineering, and product design to give clear and consistent signals to every supplier.

Neither a majority of divisions nor a particularly powerful one can dominate the consensus process if the commodity manager holds people to the corporate objective. For example, a long-term preferred supplier had a serious quality problem with one Motorola division, but not with others. To support its drive toward Six Sigma quality, Motorola's practice is to halt new orders to suppliers experiencing serious problems until these are corrected. But this requires a consensus among all divisions that buy from the firm. Automatic "stop orders" do not work, because they do not consider one-time events. In this case, which is typical, the commodity manager's recommendation to stop new orders caused difficulties in a division that wanted to give the supplier new business. The manager then built a consensus around what was best for Motorola, which everyone accepted until the problem was resolved.

As a necessary complement to consensus processes, corporate authority is used to help establish common practices. To illustrate, Motorola's sourcing units had long believed that early design participation by suppliers would, if used widely, deliver more value by shortening development cycle times. Internal resistance, though, stymied their push in that direction. At higher management levels, people realized that new products had to come on line faster, yet an understanding of that need was not spreading fast enough across the company's engineering community. Given serious competitive pressures, there was not enough time to wait for the practice to diffuse across the firm.

From experience, top management knew Motorola's Six Sigma quality program had a tremendous impact on cost and wanted to give cycle time the same emphasis. The CEO's office therefore issued a clear mandate to reduce cycle times across the company. The new mandate was introduced at each major Motorola location through a formal program that included outside speakers from customer firms, other leading firms, and top Motorola executives. Early design participation was a key to the cycle time objective.

In response, a subcommittee of Motorola's supply management council—a consensus body composed of group and sector representatives—developed a set of early design metrics. Management encouraged all Motorola businesses to use the metrics or suffer poor internal assessments. With the metrics, each engineering group is measured on the extent of its work with preferred suppliers early in the design cycle. Suppliers, in turn, are evaluated to see if their participation actually affects their deliverables, including prototype and production part cycle times.

Design at Motorola involves direct ties between suppliers and division designers. Because each division is somewhat independent, aspects of designs created for one division do not automatically spread to others. This inhibits cost cutting that might be achieved if designs were shared across divisions. One role of the sourcing units is to promote such sharing through a consensus process. These efforts are supported by performance measures that assess how well divisions and their designers reduce costs, which is a corporate goal.

In the past, inconsistent commodity management processes across Motorola caused a bias toward custom designs that made it difficult to find opportunities for standardization. In fact, sourcing people say that one of the hardest tasks in supply management has been developing common metrics. And, of course, local design uniqueness may reflect a need for product differentiation that is part of a division's competitive strategy. Nonetheless, reflecting the high degree of delegation and local autonomy at Motorola, there is also an occasional concern that sharing might compromise the independence of individual divisions. Some divisions may also believe their power with suppliers is enhanced by having unique design links. Despite these challenges, Motorola is making consistent progress in adapting standard parts.

As Motorola's organization continues to evolve to support its business needs, the company's sourcing activities have changed as well. Until the early 1990s, the sourcing unit in the Land Mobile Products sector also served what is now the Paging Products Group. But rapid growth—along with mounting differences between LMPS and PPG products, strategies, and technologies, and a need to serve more than twenty manufacturing locations, often with different requirements at various sites—made satisfying everyone increasingly difficult. To support differentiation in each area effectively, the one sourcing unit separated into two parts in 1994. Both units cooperate in all relevant areas to maintain consistency, and they have kept the same advisory board.

DIFFERENTIATION AND INTEGRATION AT MARKS & SPENCER

Like that at Motorola, Marks & Spencer's top management constantly and rigorously enforces a drive toward specific corporate goals, which include better quality and consumer value. Those goals are also a key focus for consensus processes across M&S.

Compared with Motorola, where individual divisions pursue their own product designs, design is far more centralized at Marks & Spencer. To achieve consistency across its clothing products, which M&S sees as critical to its competitive edge, the firm has a central design group and a color standards center. Each season—and with inputs from suppliers that have been doing their own research on color, fabrics, and fashion trends—they produce a coherent, color-coordinated design brief for all clothing groups. This coordination makes it possible, for instance, for a consumer to buy a skirt and blouse in different departments, knowing they will go together. As noted in Chapter 5, this is similar to the practice of Chrysler and Ford, which begin the design process with a centrally developed vehicle platform from which variations are made for different models.

The design brief handed down from the M&S design center is a generic description of all garments to be sold by each group. The brief relates garment silhouettes, colors, and fabrics. It is the start of a more detailed design process led by selectors in each division, who work with suppliers to develop specific garments. Price point suggestions are always initiated by individual departments, with final decisions being made at the board level. Each department has some room to interpret the brief according to what it and its suppliers understand about consumer desires for specific garments.

Once each week, senior selectors from all departments in each group—such as ladies' clothing—meet as the Merchandise Policy

Committee (MPC). The MPC develops a consensus on design compatibility across all group product lines, to avoid the possibility of each department interpreting the brief its own way. Decisions reached by the committee are ratified, but usually not second- guessed, by department and group executives, who have been involved throughout the design process. Other matters discussed by the MPC include photos used to create the right mood for the season, as well as hangers and labeling. M&S wants to be uniform across the corporation.

DIFFERENTIATION AND INTEGRATION AT CHRYSLER

Chrysler's key goals are achieving quality, cost, cycle time, design, and customer satisfaction levels that will make it the industry leader. As at M&S and Motorola, these goals are vigorously reinforced by word and action, starting in the highest ranks of the company and continuing down through the organization.

As with the design process at Marks & Spencer, Chrysler's corporate design office produces a physical design for each of five platforms. Design engineers on each platform team use the design as the starting point for developing different vehicle models.

Chrysler's corporate purchasing and supply group is the strategic locus of all supplier-related activities, including quality, continuous improvement, and overall supplier relationships, as noted in Chapter 10. Another role of the group is to balance a tendency of engineering to add more suppliers.

CONSIDERING THE TRADE-OFFS

As exemplified by Motorola, Marks & Spencer, and Chrysler, for a company to be consistent with its suppliers across more than one business unit requires clear internal uniformity on all relevant goals, practices, and measures. These firms' experiences also suggest that there are limits on how far one can go in adapting standard designs across independent business units, just as there are limits in building flexibility into central designs. So the basic trade-off decision between local and central design initiatives is a key issue in structuring an organization. This decision is also an important factor in supplier relationships, because it guides the supplier's own expectations, resource allocations, and organization planning. Design and other interactions with a customer's independent business units lead to results that are unique for those units, and they require more autonomy within the supply firm at each interface than do interactions where there is more standardization across the customer's firm.

The trade-offs between central and local design are summarized in the table shown. These need not be mutually exclusive alternatives. For example, following the M&S approach, a company may define certain aspects of a design to be common across its businesses, while leaving the rest up to local decision.

Creating Value Across Business Units

A multi-business firm offers scale economies in purchasing and resource use that can add value to the whole enterprise, so long as needed differentiation is maintained. As noted earlier, because of strong commonali-

Comparing Central and Local Design		
	Central Design	**Local Design**
Benefits	More consistency across business, product areas Lower costs through common parts if variations on standard design are modest	More differentiation for each business, product area
Possible disadvantage	Insufficient local differentiation	Unnecessarily high costs
Balancing local and central needs	Use consensus process for overall consistency and to accept needed local differentiation Need consistent goals and metrics across areas to facilitate localization standardization trade-off	Use consensus process with sufficient authority for needed standardization Need consistent goals and metrics across areas to facilitate localization–standardization trade-off
Effect on suppliers	Less autonomy at each customer interface	More autonomy at each customer interface

ties across the different vehicle platforms, corporate purchasing at Chrysler has a central strategic role in supplier relationships. For more diversified companies, supply strategies are developed closer to the individual business units, as Motorola and Marks & Spencer illustrate. In such cases, commonalities above that level are usually sought through consensus processes, supported by central purchasing.

An additional way to create more value from supply alliances is for the customer to share experiences, know-how, and practices across the organization. One more tactic is to help individual business units participate in a broader alliance, which can create more benefits for the corporation.

CORPORATE PURCHASING

Purchasing practices at many companies have cycled between centralized buying (as the best way to get the lowest price) and decentralized buying (which allows local units to meet the unique needs of their markets). Neither approach is adequate for firms competing in markets that demand both best cost and unique value. Again, centralization and differentiation must be balanced to get acceptable results.

Compare how Philips and Motorola buy production equipment. At Philips, those purchases are standardized worldwide, giving it the low costs that come from global scale economies. This centralization, however, inhibits closer local involvement with particular suppliers. By contrast, Motorola's Paging Products Group selectively allies with equipment firms to push those performance frontiers it regards as important. This has been a key contributor to PPG's success, giving it exceptional flexibility to move from one product model to another, plus high responsiveness to its customers' unique desires. These advantages more than offset the occasionally higher prices PPG pays for equipment.

For commodities, Motorola balances central buying with local differentiation by weighing both options in the buying process. To do this, corporate supply management regularly reviews purchases at all locations. Whenever two or more groups or sectors have common interests and share the same supplier, supply management accumulates their requirements and facilitates a negotiation with that company, with each buying group represented at the table. Negotiations include price, lead times, and performance measures. To get cost savings and have distinct specifications on the same basic part for each business, Motorola and the supplier debate and quantify the differences affecting price. The local businesses do the actual purchasing.

Kathy Sullivan, Motorola's vice president and corporate director of supply management, says this process is not imposed on the businesses, because to do so may violate their unique needs. Rather, it is done for them. "This is not a corporate show," Sullivan notes. "We work for the businesses as a team effort."

PROMOTING COMMON STANDARDS AND PRACTICES

To take advantage of scale economies, corporatewide activities can help build common practices across the firm related to supply alliances. What is particularly impressive about these activities at Marks & Spencer and Motorola is not just their number and variety, but their similarity and effectiveness. Chrysler is developing the same kinds of mechanisms as the automaker continues to transform its organization.

To help keep up with accelerating change, facilitate sharing across the company, and build stronger technology links with suppliers, Marks & Spencer created a group of industry specialists in areas such as dying and finishing, cotton, wool, and man-made fibers. Each specialist interfaces with the respective industry across all relevant M&S garments. The specialists' work complements that of technologists who reside in each buying department, focusing on requirements related to the development and manufacture of the department's garments.

A related practice builds on the fact that suppliers to the ladies', men's, and children's clothing groups all use dying and finishing methods that can be usefully shared. To facilitate such sharing, the retailer set up several specialist teams to cross-fertilize information and ideas.

Another technique used by M&S involves weekly meetings of each Merchandise Policy Committee, held to discuss matters of interest to the departments represented. Topics covered include styling, new fabrics and garment concepts, and marketing techniques. Non-proprietary supplier ideas are also shared with all selectors.

Chrysler uses a similar arrangement, known as "technology clubs," to develop common parts and procedures across two or more platforms. The clubs are consensus groups made up of engineering representatives from all five platforms and are organized by commodity group (such as brakes, or steering and suspension). Because the platforms use the same kinds of commodities and often work with the same suppliers, this is a convenient way to build internal bridges in the company. Still, opportunities for common parts are limited by the automaker's desire to maintain differentiation for each model. The clubs have also proven to be useful for sharing ideas across the platform teams.

At Motorola, the corporate supply management office works as a member of three regional supply management councils—one each for Asia-Pacific, Europe, and North America—that complement group and sector sourcing efforts at the corporate level. The councils work for consensus on important topics within their regions, and cooperate on key global matters such as quality and cycle time. Within each region, topics on the council's agenda reflect supplier needs and local cultural characteristics. Council members are representatives of each group or sector, typically from supply management or sourcing; chairmen are from the respective regions and are elected periodically. Meetings are held about twice a year.

Council activities include developing corporatewide agreements on quality audits, supplier metrics, technology road maps, and rating systems. These results provide consistency on supplier selection and management across the firm, and give suppliers a single corporate message on quality, ethics, and other matters. They also help Motorola move toward its goal of being a better customer. Other council tasks include working on global standard parts by finding and eliminating duplicate part numbers on the same item, and avoiding duplicate specifications on such non-custom parts as capacitors and resistors.

Global consistency on metrics is sought where it is relevant to Motorola's corporate goals for quality and cycle time. Common metrics pertinent to those goals are encouraged for use across Motorola. Implementation may vary among individual businesses, which may choose to implement the metrics and may add to them according to their respective needs.

Consistency on quality audits has made it possible for different Motorola businesses to accept each other's audit results. The resulting elimination of multiple audits at the same suppliers saves them and Motorola considerable money. Commonality also supports corporate priority setting on quality initiatives. Additionally, the three councils profit from local initiative and cross-pollination of ideas. When the Asia-Pacific council was formed in the early 1990s, for example, it championed the development of a quality audit course for Motorola and its suppliers. The other councils backed the proposal, and now there is a standard course for the entire company.

Another practice Motorola has found useful with suppliers is managed by the company's technical operations council (TOC). As part of its mission, the TOC benchmarks major equipment and equipment suppliers for all of Motorola worldwide. This work leads to recommendations of what and what not to buy, as well as which firms not to buy from. Individual divisions still make their own purchase decisions, but they adhere to the list most of the time. No one wants to get stuck with bad equipment.

As a member of the TOC, Sunil Lakhani, PPG director of advanced manufacturing technology, says he often get queries via electronic mail from across the firm about equipment and suppliers with which he is familiar. The TOC also helps with supplier problems: For instance, if one division has a particularly good relationship with a given firm, the TOC may use that division to help one that does not.

At the division level, Motorola commodity managers in the United States, Asia, and Europe regard themselves as members of a single commodity management community, and they share information with each other worldwide. Commodity managers responsible for printed circuit boards, for example, see the performance reports for all suppliers of those parts. If one report indicates superior results, that will be noticed. Then, whoever recognized it will make an informal query about whether the relevant supplier's information and practices may be shared with others. While not everything can be shared, satisfied suppliers are more willing to cooperate wherever possible.

CENTRAL DATA COLLECTION

Corporate efforts in marketing research, technology scanning, and collecting internal performance data can complement similar efforts at individual business units. For instance, Motorola's corporate supply management office summarizes the aggregate track record of all suppliers serving each of the company's groups and sectors. Measures include quality, inventory turns, cost savings, and on-time delivery. This information, which is compared across the company, helps spotlight best practices and also influences new course offerings at Motorola University. Because its conduct with suppliers is critical to its own success, Motorola also uses surveys of the suppliers to determine how they compare it with their other customers. This is done for each group or sector, on a number of measures.

Motorola also has a corporate intelligence department that reports on the latest technology developments and its competitors' manufacturing efforts, as gleaned from journals, conferences, rumors, and such. This information helps build the firm's detailed technology road maps, which indicate where changes are likely to occur, when they can be included in new products or processes, how much money their development will cost, and how rivals are doing.[1] "We know where everybody is," comments vice chairman John Mitchell.

FACILITATING LOCAL PARTICIPATION

At times, supply alliances do not reach their full potential because some business units in the customer's firm do not see enough benefits to participate, even though the entire firm would gain if they did.

Kodak and IBM solved this problem by managing their data processing alliance as a whole, rather than treating it as a set of detached parts. This alliance, which involves hundreds of new projects each year, serves six business units in the United States and others around the world. To best serve Kodak corporate interests, the firm's corporate information services (CIS) department uses its resources to adjust the costs and benefits of projects to make them more acceptable to individual business units if doing so benefits Kodak—such as with better scale economies or capacity use. At the same time, IBM has offered more benefits or better costs to specific Kodak businesses to win their acceptance of new projects if that helps both firms in the longer run. The partners jointly manage their activities to be sure that costs and benefits are fairly allocated between them. CIS takes a small percentage of the alliance revenues to pay for its role.

Global and Multi-Site Alliances

In most industries, business is increasingly global, product cycles are shortening, cost pressures are escalating, and markets everywhere expect the best quality and latest technology. Yet very few international companies have rationalized their supply bases or their own operations to keep up. With much of the average firm's costs, quality, timing, and technology dependent on its suppliers, this can be a serious failing.

Consider that many international firms with plants around the world to meet local needs are now finding that, with the fall of trade barriers, their customers can shop around to get better prices, including distribution costs. As a consequence, some major international companies have a large percentage of their plants operating at very low levels, with well under 50 percent capacity use worldwide.[2] In any industry with this problem, whichever firm gets to lowest global cost first will have a tremendous pricing advantage over its rivals.

To illustrate, look at Ball Corp., the Fortune 200 glass and metal packaging company. Ball built a jar plant next door to the baby food factories of its customer, Gerber Products, in Asheville, North Carolina. With that proximity, coordination was easy and the firms kept their inventories low. But Ball served only Gerber's U.S. operations, and the relationship ended in 1994 after Gerber shopped for a lower-cost worldwide source. Ball was forced to shut down the plant and lay off most of the 350 workers.[3]

In general, the scale benefits of globalization are attended by a powerful drive to better meet local needs. This drive creates corresponding demands for the customer to get closer to its suppliers at the local level; create unique designs or better adapt standard ones; adjust processes; support fast responses to new opportunities, and share the resolution of issues regarding quality, forecasts, technology, deliveries, and more. Taken together, the dual forces of globalization and localization create a substantial advantage for customers able to manage their supply relationships in a way that effectively blends and balances those factors on a world scale.

One traditional supply practice has been for a company to continue depending on home-country firms as it expands abroad, shipping their products to its locations around the world. While this practice may be effective for certain standard goods with low transportation costs and tolerably long lead times, it often inhibits the company from differentiating its goods in local markets and makes it less responsive to market needs in these locales. Additionally, for many products transporation costs are not always low. Consider that between 1987 and 1994, the eight major Japanese automakers operating in North America lost between $1.3 billion and $3.6 billion each year in that market, according to one calculation. A key contributor was their lethargy in moving parts manufacturing out of Japan for cars assembled in North America. A second was a poor product mix that did not meet local market needs.[4]

Another traditional practice of international firms, which is the converse of shipping suppliers' goods around the world, has been to give regional or country units the freedom to choose and manage nearby suppliers based chiefly on local factors. Doing this inhibits know-how transfers between units in each firm, however, thereby slowing the customer's global responsiveness. It also drives up costs by duplicating customer and supplier design, engineering, and other resources at each location.

To illustrate, many suppliers to the Ford Motor Company have design capabilities for the parts they make at several locations around the world. Given that Ford buys many thousands of production parts, virtually all of which are custom designed, this practice carries a substantial cost that could not be justified by any benefits of local differentiation in Ford's products. For this and other related reasons, Ford has been moving to global alliances with its suppliers, in which unnecessary duplication by each supplier will be replaced by worldwide sharing within each firm.

The distinction between global and multi-site alliances is a matter of degree and structure. As in the case of balancing corporate and business unit interests, the right emphasis on centralization and local differentiation in both the global and multi-site situations is set by what best serves the strategic interests of the corporation.

The challenge, however, is greater in the global context, where the twin forces of geographic distance and cultural differences work to encourage political independence of local units from one other. Moreover, incomplete thinking about a business as a global entity causes a bias toward overdependence on the corporate center (which inhibits local responsiveness) or too much independence from it (which obstructs global coordination). And while the country or regional units of most corporations have the authority structures needed to manage local alliances, few companies have created the structures required to build global alliances with customers or suppliers.

BALANCING GLOBAL OR MULTI-SITE AND LOCAL INTERESTS

For any business that operates at more than one location (with or without an international dimension), some consistency across different units, coordination at each interface, and an ability to set and support overall priorities are needed to get the most value from a geographically extended relationship.

Horizontal Consistency, Local Coordination, and Authority. For a customer, having an effective supply base requires common metrics, rating systems, audit processes, capacity and technology plans, inventory management systems, and more at all relevant locations. These facilitate supplier selection and management, support quality and service standards, and help suppliers make the best use of their resources.

For a supplier, serving a multi-site customer requires internal linkages that keep all facilities near the same technology frontiers, maintain consistent quality standards, ensure tooling is available for the right products at the right locations, keep an overall picture of the customer's needs and situation, and provide adequate investment streams for the customer across all facilities. To be responsive to its customer, the supplier must give its lead executive enough authority to be sure these tasks are done. For large customers, a supplier may also have someone at each customer site to facilitate local coordination there.

As an example, Molex is moving toward multi-site (often global) alliances with many customers and adapting a global management structure to support those relationships. Two parts of this new organization are quality and business system functions that meet growing customer desires for global coordination and reporting on their worldwide supply relationships. Another aspect is unique interfaces, as necessary, with each customer. To serve such customers, one Molex employee has the lead to develop worldwide programs for each firm. In general, the Molex country or regional unit having the most business with a customer, or where design control resides, takes the lead on such matters.

For customers, like suppliers, having a single authority structure as well as local and horizontal coordination helps ensure that global and local interests are met by extended alliances. For instance, in Motorola's Paging Products Group, both major regions—Pan America/Europe, and the Far East—have their own commodity managers for local supplier relationships. People in those positions are expected to ensure that PPG regional strategies are consistently supported by suppliers. Commodity managers in each region report to regional sourcing managers.

To complement the regional work, a global champion for each commodity is designated from among the commodity managers to provide worldwide direction and consistency. Global management makes certain that quality audits, technology road maps, business reviews, negotiations, and capacity plans link properly everywhere.[5]

Having a global commodity manager at Motorola, with a counterpart in the supplier, helps keep an appropriate balance between local issues and Motorola's global interests. Typical local issues include meeting requirements for Schedule Sharing (Motorola's inventory management system), responding to dramatic volume fluctuations at one location, and creating product designs for local markets.

Recently, both regional sourcing managers began reporting to the same PPG executive. This change, says Neil MacIvor, the PPG strategic sourcing director, has many advantages: It has greatly facilitated setting global supply objectives; helped rationalize the global supply base; and eased the coordination of metrics, performance ratings, and parts standardization compared with when he and his Singapore counterpart reported to different people. Before, MacIvor observes, the different priorities and different suppliers for each regional organization made it difficult to agree on how to manage them.

Local Differentiation Versus Global Integration. In PPG, competitive circumstances favor substantial local design autonomy and close supplier support for its products. These, in turn, call for enough internal delegation to support this independence and local design interfaces with suppliers. Budgets for supplier-related functions like commodity managers are tied to regional budgets, and the job evaluations of these managers reflect regional performance. By contrast, evaluations of the sourcing directors—who have a more strategic role—are heavily weighted toward their global performance. These arrangements, combined with the authority and coordination structures noted above, give PPG local market responsiveness (in terms of short delivery cycles and the ability to create unique product features for each market) while providing the advantages of global scale.

By contrast, Ford's pursuit of a higher degree of global integration, both internally and with its suppliers, has required a stronger central organization. In 1994, Ford merged its European and North American auto operations to pool resources and eliminate turf wars between different country organizations. According to chairman Alex Trotman, the firm is in "an all-out race" to make more efficient use of its engineering and product development money against rapidly globalizing rivals.

To do that, Ford created five vehicle program centers (seemingly modeled on Chrysler's platform organization), each with global responsibility

for such specific product types as small front-wheel-drive cars. This structure is expected to standardize major parts use around the world while
allowing local variations of basically similar final products. Ford's projected cost savings from the new arrangement total $2 billion to $3 billion
annually.[6] The new global structure will take up to five years to deploy
fully. It is being rolled out first in Europe and North America, with
Asia/Pacific and South America to follow at a later date.

In the global structure, the basic platform design for each vehicle is
determined by the corporate product development executive responsible for that vehicle worldwide. Charlie Ross, director of strategic planning in Ford's purchasing organization, says that variations for local
differentiation will be decided centrally by the same people, reflecting a
"voice of the customer" process that will provide an in-depth knowledge of the needs of each market.

Ford's new structure includes a central supply organization, with
people co-located at each of the five major car platform groups. Both
they and employees from the suppliers are on each vehicle team, with
everyone focused on that platform. Ford supply people help with early
supplier participation in design, suppliers' longer-term technology
alignment with Ford, and related activities. Purchasing people on each
platform team have a solid line reporting relationship to Ford's central
purchasing organization, to support and maintain best practices and
consistency across Ford. They also have a solid line relationship to the
executive for each platform, which helps them make the best decision
for the customer.

Within central purchasing, one group works on common processes
regarding suppliers. Another group, in the product development organization, not only seeks common internal processes across all platform
teams, but is also charged with looking at operations companywide. To
facilitate planning and resource allocation, as well as reduce duplication and costs, Ford has a single global budget for each platform.

Global or Regional Efficiency. Having plants around the world may
not be adequate for global effectiveness, unless the locations are part of
a worldwide strategy. As noted earlier, locally based plant decisions can
lead to poor capacity use and vulnerable cost structures, because the
customer may buy wherever manufacturing and distribution costs are
lowest, even if the supplier has plants nearby.

In the past, when few companies planned globally, a new plant could be justified on the basis of local demand. Insulated by trade barriers and protected from outside competition by rivals that also did not think globally, local costs (and thus local pricing) could be higher than those at distant locations. As those barriers drop and customers shop for the best price, capacity use falls at high-cost facilities, making the entire global enterprise less efficient.

The same forces damage local operations in other ways. Consider the case of a Brazilian customer that can get lower prices from a supplier in the United States than from the same supplier's unit in Brazil. The sale benefits the supplier's U.S. unit, but disadvantages its Brazilian operation, since the customer expects the good to be serviced locally even though it was purchased in the United States.

These problems can be avoided by taking two steps. One is to lower total global or regional costs, with the choice between those alternatives being a matter of economics and response times. This cost cutting is done by taking a total system view of plant and customer locations and distribution costs, for the whole world or by geographic region. The second step is world—or regional—pricing for each major customer, based on the new cost structure. This arrangement will not eliminate local cost differentials due to poor distribution networks or other anomalies, but it creates a lowest total cost position that permits using corporate budgets to cross subsidize where necessary.

CHOOSING AND MANAGING GLOBAL SUPPLIERS

For its early overseas suppliers, Motorola chose centrally managed international firms having operations that were often remote from each of its plants. Delays and misunderstandings, though, resulted from the confusion of working with vastly different cultures scattered around the world. The firm next changed to local suppliers, a step that eased cooperation but sacrificed coordination across sites. To serve its needs on a global basis, Motorola more recently has been moving toward single suppliers with multiple locations and strong internal coordination abilities.

With effective coordination, a firm can quickly transfer designs, processes, and technologies between locations as needed. Internal links are also required to ensure that all relevant sites receive and reinforce the same message about customer requirements (such as for quality and cost) and share a single global view of how well the customer is being served. Coordination may also be needed to ship parts between locations to help meet demand swings and optimize plant loadings. Multi-site coordination also facilitates global product launches. Most firms, for example, do not usually begin manufacturing a product around the world at once. The typical pattern is to start at one place, serve the global market from there, and expand to other sites as guided by marketing and economic considerations.

While transferring know-how between locations within a firm can be challenging, it is far easier compared with transfers between independent firms. Single, multi-plant firms are also better at allocating their resources around the world in response to the customer's global business priorities. And having multiple plants helps avoid the problem of different customer business units pulling against each other on capacity or other matters, which can happen when a supplier has just one plant.

Global suppliers are chosen on the basis of each firm's internal coordination skills, plus normal selection criteria for cost, quality, service, technology, delivery, capacity, and other relevant skills. At Motorola, people from the manufacturing and sourcing organizations make multiple site visits to understand a firm's coordination abilities. They also discuss its performance with colleagues who work with the firm around the world. While some large suppliers are already global, in cases where there are no acceptable suppliers (as with cables and chassis) Motorola must work with different firms at each location.

Because relationships are so important for alliances, companies that are large enough to justify plant-scale investments by suppliers should consider inviting their current supply partners to expand abroad. To support its international growth, Marks & Spencer asked its long-term trusted suppliers based in the United Kingdom to open factories overseas. This step has helped speed the retailer's foreign expansion, since the suppliers already understand M&S's needs. When it must work with suppliers that are not based in Britain, the retailer is building new relationships. The rate at which that can be done paces its overseas growth.

As with more local alliances, it is best for a customer not to become dependent on one source for multiple locations. Single sourcing and other backup arrangements are at least as important in global alliances as they are in those situations.

To encourage a supplier's consistency around the world, customer ratings should reflect all purchases from that firm, without regard to volume differences at various locations. For example, poor quality on low-volume deliveries to any site should cause as much concern as quality problems on high volume. Such problems imply slack global management. They also prevent the customer from using that source to balance demand swings at other locations. Further, if left unattended, they also can inhibit the growth of the customer's local business.

For the same reasons, continuous improvement metrics for global suppliers should reflect their global performance rather than compare suppliers at individual locations. To illustrate, PPG used to make volume allocation decisions within each region. Now regional sourcing people work as members of a global team to make these decisions. This change causes each supplier to focus more on responsiveness and global consistency in quality and other key areas, both of which PPG needs for its own global performance. PPG also uses the same team, representing all sites that buy a commodity, to do quality audits on all suppliers of a particular commodity from around the world. This practice permits globally consistent benchmarking across all suppliers of each commodity.

MAKING THE TRANSITION TO A GLOBAL FIRM

Dick Ogren, the director of business strategy at Ford who led his firm's global restructuring team, says the effectiveness of Ford's new organization depends on the firm's own cultural transformation and that of its suppliers. To be effective, he notes, the structure will require a lot of change toward a more process-oriented style and more emphasis on involving suppliers in advanced activities—including the concept stage, which is well before the final vehicle program is defined.

One early step, creating common global standards and specifications, is probably the easiest part of the transformation. While some facilities may have to close or cut back, changing people's attitudes and practices is likely to be the greatest challenge.

Charlie Ross, the strategic planning director in Ford purchasing, adds that to be compatible with its new structure, suppliers will have to change to support it. While most of them are international, Ross says that few have effective coordination links between their various country and regional units. At present, for example, there are different designers at each location for brake systems, radiators, and many other parts. Ford is helping them make the changes.

Ford people expect, but do not require, that suppliers will be more responsive to the automaker's more centralized global structure if they adopt similar structures to interface with it. This development will facilitate resource allocation on a global basis in concert with Ford's needs. Formerly, some suppliers had multiple structures to interface with Ford's numerous structures around the world.

For international companies that intend to build global supply alliances, it is easier to start the process before downsizing each regional or country supply base. Ford began moving toward a global structure only after its regional operations had launched the process for their own supply bases. Charlie Ross says that because the regions did this, it has been harder to effect corporatewide global supply base downsizing than it would have been had Ford taken a global perspective from the beginning.

Another equally vital cultural transformation must happen at each interface within and between firms, to build a global alliance. Compared with traditional commercial links, which require little internal or external or cooperation, alliances involve intense interactions and deep mutual understandings. For a global alliance, this means paying specific attention to cultural compatibility at each interface. Consider that when Motorola first tried to have Western employees discuss issues with Asian suppliers, things did not go well. When the firm put Asian employees in that role, the discussions worked much better.

The tremendous value of global alliances motivates a firm's evolution to such structures, but it should not conceal the challenge of making them happen. Says Dick Ogren: "Changing the boxes without changing the way you manage the boxes is not going to give you the results you're looking for."[7]

The shared vision of the Kodak–IBM alliance is to give Kodak employees all the information they need from anywhere in the world at a moment's notice. Realizing this goal requires a robust computing environment that not only can access whatever data are needed but is also highly standardized. Probably the toughest issue in creating the global alliance has been that traditionally each firm's management system has emphasized country-by-country authority. As a consequence, IBM's Frank Palm and Kodak's Vaughn Hovey have had little control over their respective firm's international activities. Local participation in each facet of the alliance is a consensus process; no executive has been assigned overall authority. Instead, Palm and Hovey coach their staffers in other countries to participate based on whatever serves local interests.

Further, Kodak and IBM people at the country level tend to promote what they see as best for their own unit rather than broader, longer-term corporate global interests; as Frank Palm says: "The guy in Germany who is trying to figure out how to add eastern Germany to his business is naturally more focused on that." At this point, the global alliance has not yet reached the stage where country units are managed as a portfolio for their collective benefit, although that step is clearly on the horizon.

To move the transition along, IBM needs to develop incentives for those people and units whose support is essential to the effort's success. And, while Palm says that having a single organization with global authority on each side of the interface "would absolutely" facilitate global flexibility and coordination, mandating this in either firm might not secure the needed buy-in.

To facilitate the transformation, in 1993 Dennie Welsh—then chairman of the computer firm's Integrated Systems Solutions Corporation service unit— formed a global council of all service managers to coordinate international delivery. The council is using IBM's experience with Kodak as a benchmark for its success. Frank Palm regards this as an interim structure (on the way to having a single executive) that will help gain the needed acceptance of the alliance at each locale.

Selling the alliance to Kodak and IBM units around the world is managed jointly by both firms, with IBM marketing staffers taking the lead for their company. The IBM person with lead responsibility for marketing to Kodak is the co-leader of the alliance-selling effort. He works with the heads of services and marketing at each IBM country unit to encourage it to participate. The basic selling point is the importance of Kodak as a highly visible customer. Still, IBM staffers know that as the alliance goes global, some business will be pulled away from individual country units. Although there is not yet a standard plan for compensating them for such losses, one seems likely given an overall IBM corporate benefit from the alliance.

The alliance will require a single global budget within both Kodak and IBM. Such a budget cannot be created in one step, though, as IBM and Kodak rank-and-file employees have been reluctant to accept directives from headquarters. To get to the stage where a global budget can be implemented, the firms have created regional budgets and organizations.

Another aspect of building a global alliance is that each manager or executive from Kodak or IBM who is at a business unit/corporate interface must learn to function as a facilitator or a line executive, depending on which role furthers local and global objectives. Striking a balance between autonomy and shared authority is seen as an important task on the road ahead.

12

NEGOTIATIONS
BETWEEN PARTNERS

*In an alliance, if things don't go as well as expected, we
spend zero time worrying about that because we know we
have a future together and trust each other to make it
win-win for both firms. By contrast, in a deal-by-deal
relationship, we try to recover any loss from the customer
any way we can—either in future pricing or whatever.*

Ronald L. Schubel, president, commercial products division, Molex

*Doing a pretty good job is never satisfactory for Motorola.
They always want to know why a supplier is not doing
better. . . . Pricing is a tough nut. But no matter how tough
the negotiation is, you always know that you are going to
get together. We sit, we talk, we reason, and we conclude.*

Bruce Bendoff, president, Craftsman Custom Metal Fabricators

In a commercial relationship, discussions about price or
other terms can be adversarial because there is little sense
of mutual need, and neither company has an interest in protecting the
other's well-being. Further, price is the only way to allocate benefits
between firms: Whatever one firm gains in price, the other loses. If an
unexpected issue arises later, the relationship may end if it cannot be
resolved.

To build an alliance, management and organizational factors must be explored to determine each firm's commitment to the same market-beating objective. Here, discussions are less about give-and-take and more about alignment. Further, once formed, alliances require regular negotiations to stay ahead of the market, support continued advances, introduce new items, and reset prices to reflect the partners' work on costs. While the negotiations may sometimes be difficult, they are framed by an understanding that it is not in either firm's interest to damage the other or reduce its commitment. Another moderating force is that price is not the only source of benefits for each firm. Customer–supplier alliances continue to produce more for each partner as they both create more value for the customer's market.

The negotiating process begins with specific market-defined objectives, and joins partners in shared understandings about needed results. The customer may push hard for superior price or performance but logic—rather than bargaining power—is the sole means for reaching agreement. To seal negotiations, agreements are based largely on trust rather than detailed formal contracts.

Setting Stretch Targets

The customer's intent to deliver more value to its market creates the agenda for supply alliances. To be accepted and earn people's commitments, that goal must be specific and realistic.

DEFINING SPECIFIC TARGETS

Desired performances for alliances are based on a clear knowledge of which value frontiers the customer wants to push, and are derived from marketing research, benchmarking, and technological possibilities. Suppliers' understandings of these frontiers are combined with those of the customer, which makes the final decision.

For instance, in the food business at Marks & Spencer, safety is the number one priority. M&S maintains a constant upgrading process that draws on suppliers' expertise, monitors advances in relevant scientific disciplines, and uses these advances to define more stringent safety goals in terms of lower microbiological counts and tighter manufacturing temperature controls. Similarly, Motorola's objective of reaching Six Sigma quality with its suppliers is a key to ongoing price reduction in its products and increasing satisfaction for its customers.

Within the context of such trend-setting objectives, more detailed targets are derived for specific parts and processes. In addition to desired performances, having an objective price target is important to allocate benefits fairly between partners and facilitate joint cost cutting. From a supplier's perspective, Molex's Ron Schubel says having a price target signals the reality of competitive pressures the customer is experiencing. The only way to gauge whether a target is realistic, he adds, is to know prices for the same or a similar part in the marketplace and to understand a customer's economic situation.

At Motorola, price trends for its products, plus its margin requirements, are the starting point for a new product value engineering exercise. The process, which also reflects market price trends for each major commodity, leads to cost and price targets for internal designers and suppliers. Since it seeks to do better than the market, Motorola wants to set ambitious targets yet avoid squeezing its suppliers too hard. To do this, it uses data from the audits and other sources described in Chapter 7, which indicate how each firm is progressing on quality and other cost drivers, as well as from trends in focused competition.

Other inputs for price targets come from a continuing analytic effort to develop better understandings of cost drivers for key parts, and are based on the experience of Motorola and its suppliers. One example is lowering setup costs by going to standard hole sizes for several products. Ron Vocalino, a regional sourcing manager, adds that "a lot of the cost problems in our products come from us. Our suppliers tell us, for example, when we are overspecifying something."

The cost model created by these efforts provides a good idea of direct costs, but not total costs. While one cannot readily know all of another firm's costs, the model has proven to be a useful guide for price negotiations because it recognizes major generic variables that, when changed, reduce costs.

Chrysler's price targets for parts, derived from the total vehicle target price and extensive benchmarking at the piece-part level, are usually realistic. Since suppliers contribute to the target development process, there are relatively few surprises about the final targets. Still, target setting is as much an art as it is a science, so surprises do occur and some negotiation is often needed to reach agreement. For a new piece part, Chrysler always has another supplier in the wings that wants the business if the current supplier cannot meet the target. If no one can meet the target at an acceptable margin, Chrysler must reasses the target.

PRICING ACCORDING TO VALUE

Most firms would like to escape cost-based pricing and win more benefits from a customer if they bring it more value. Clearly, for an alliance to function, suppliers must be rewarded for producing more value for the customer. However, price is just one way that can happen. In highly price-competitive markets such as those in which Motorola participates, suppliers' prices must keep dropping in pace with the market, so there may be little room in their margins for extra benefits. This is why Motorola uses other means to win suppliers' commitment— like giving them training and benchmarking opportunities, which help them earn higher margins from other customers.

Focused competition also limits prices. Unless a supplier delivers unique value—as defined by the customer—it must have competitive prices to keep the business. The CEO of one supplier to Philips Consumer Electronics Company says his firm "is making a very handsome profit" at Philips. He is not looking forward to the day when he will have to compete for its business, he adds, because his most likely rival has comparable goods and services and a cost structure similar to that of his firm.

Most generally, then, there are two paths to healthier supplier margins in alliances: One is to provide unique value to the customer, the other is to have lower costs. PCEC, for example, pays a premium to Motorola for parts like discrete transistors because Motorola always delivers on time, and quality is never an issue. Further, when PCEC has a shortage caused by its own inability to forecast, Motorola always finds a way to solve the problem. The premium, says PCEC's Bill Kennedy, reflects his firm's cost savings from those performances. Similarly, Noel Jervis, CEO of Courtaulds Textiles, says there is little problem getting Marks & Spencer to agree to healthy margins on unique, popular garments supplied by his firm.

Such opportunities, however, are often temporary. High margins invite competition, and customer demands usually change. The only sure way to sustain higher margins through unique value is to continue finding new ways to create more value than one's rivals can offer.

Lower costs—the second route to better margins—may come from unique operating technology or any of the factors described in Chapter 6. Still, given focused competition, other suppliers are likely to be on the same path. Again, the only sure way to maintain better margins is to stay ahead of others.

Reaching Agreement While Avoiding Damage

Alliances typically involve many joint tasks, with numerous issues on which people must concur. In all cases, the most effective decision making uses logic alone, guided by a mutual desire to find the best way to meet the shared objective.

On matters such as price where the customer needs the supplier to stretch, negotiations are one element of a process that includes focused competition, objective performance measures, and cooperation to improve the firms' separate and joint processes. All of these activities are designed to keep each partner committed to continuous improvement. In that context, negotiation for price or performance is done to elicit the supplier's best efforts. Key aspects of this include helping suppliers appreciate the urgency of the task, sharing relevant data with them, and avoiding damage while focusing on underlying forces to reach agreement. Price negotiations are usually conducted at least annually, both to reflect changes in costs and because suppliers usually hold on to any savings until the time of formal discussions.

CUSTOMERS: PUT SUPPLIERS IN YOUR CONTEXT

The more people understand the merits of reaching a difficult objective, the harder they work to achieve it. Such understandings can be powerful motivators in alliances.

In the early 1990s, Motorola began encouraging suppliers to reduce their cycle times as part of its ongoing campaign to lower costs. This initiative passed a key milestone during the September 1993 supplier advisory board meeting, when an executive from one firm presented data showing that Motorola's volume forecasts often varied widely from its ordering practices, forcing his company to carry large inventories. He concluded by asking for better forecasts. In response, a Motorola participant said improved forecasting was not the answer. He showed a chart of his division's sales that indicated wide week-to-week fluctuations, ranging from negative (that is, more sales being removed from the order book than were added) to several thousand units per week. Noting that each unit was built to order on a customer's specification, he explained that Motorola could not warehouse finished products. The only solution for suppliers, he added, was to achieve shorter cycle times—an objective Motorola was vigorously pursuing internally.

Tom Slaninka, the sector sourcing director, who was also at the

meeting, noted that Motorola faces similar problems with its own customers. Sometimes they ask for goods to be delivered before Motorola
can do so. Yet he acknowledged that meeting the customer's desired
date was extremely important. Motorola is often asked to deliver
within two to three days of receiving an order, and customer expectations constantly shrink that time. Slaninka said that if Motorola had
the shortest and most efficient manufacturing and supply chain
processes, so that it could deliver faster than its rivals, it would have a
distinct advantage over them.

Slaninka also observed that Motorola suppliers which were reducing their own cycle times were not complaining about the forecasting
problem. He concluded by saying that shorter cycle times were becoming critical for Motorola's competitive strategies. One supplier executive then spoke up: "We get the message," he said. Another asked to
share the Motorola order book chart with his own sales, manufacturing, and materials people so they could better appreciate the nature of
the problem.

To maintain the critical spirit of shared risk and opportunity,
Motorola also gives its suppliers key price and competitive data. One
item is the rate at which the average selling price is declining for many
of its products. Also described is the cost improvement curve each
product must meet to avoid early obsolescence, which causes lost business for Motorola and its suppliers. Motorola also provides illustrations
of the aggressive global competition it must deal with, as well as product examples of what rivals have accomplished.

Like Motorola, Molex wants suppliers to appreciate the competitive
pressures in its markets. To do that, the connector maker publishes a
booklet that describes trends in its customers' demands, based on data
from those companies. Categories covered include quality, delivery performance, delivery cycle time, customer service, transactions and
related systems requirements, new product cycles, predictive engineering, tool design, and quality assurance complaint resolution times. The
booklet goes to all Molex employees as well as to suppliers.

Pushing Hard While Avoiding Damage

In alliances, the customer depends on its suppliers' health and commitment, and cannot afford to hurt them financially. Still, competitive
forces in the customer's market compel it to get the best possible terms

from suppliers. For that reason, while an alliance involves less conflict than commercial links, that cannot be eliminated. Friction is most common in pricing because any firm, as a supplier, wants solid margins for its own well-being, while customers want better prices for theirs. An effective balance between those interests is found through a combination of pressure from the customer, its knowledge of cost drivers, trust, and the customer's desire not to hurt a supplier.

Sharing Price Targets and Cost Data. "The biggest problem we have in meeting customer price targets is that they [customers] won't tell us what they are," says Larry Groves, president of Targ-It-Tronics, which supplies parts to electronics firms. The practices that frustrate Groves are standard procedure in traditional commercial relationships, where the most competitive bid gets the job. In those situations any price target that is not too low would give the supplier a chance to reduce costs and boost its margins, possibly denying the customer a chance for better prices for its goods or more value creation. If the target is too low, the supplier might not bid. For the customer, these possibilities seem to be ample reason to rely on arm's-length competition and not give a target.

"By contrast," continues Groves, "Motorola is not at all bashful in telling us what they want in price. If you know your price target, that helps surface all relevant issues within and between firms that affect cost. If a customer relationship were based on pure competition, that allows you to work on internal costs but not joint costs. Further, if the customer does not change its ways based on an understanding of our needs—such as level loading our plant— then lowest costs are also not possible."

Chrysler, as noted earlier, involves its suppliers in the target-setting process to help reduce conflict in that area. Similarly, Noel Jervis says that price negotiations with Marks & Spencer are framed by Courtaulds' knowledge of M&S markups and price points, which his designers are always working to meet. Because each supplier also wants to have best sellers in M&S stores, each works hard with the retailer to provide the best prices and values.

Pressing for Best Price. Some firms claim that true partnership behavior requires the supplier to share all cost savings with its customer. While some suppliers occasionally do this, however, most do not, and customers do not assume it. Motorola's Bob Becknell says his firm does not expect to get all of a supplier's internal cost reduction. Similarly, at M&S, Guy McCracken says he hopes suppliers offer to share their internal savings through lower prices, but he recognizes that some of that goes to suppliers' margins. Chrysler shares suppliers' savings with them, which encourages more sharing (see Chapter 8). More generally, a supplier will share as much of its savings with a customer as it judges necessary to remain a priority supplier. The balance is kept for its own health.

For these reasons, Chrysler, Motorola, and Marks & Spencer press hard on pricing in negotiations. At each firm, best practice begins with giving suppliers price targets derived from the desired price for its own final product. In the Paging Products Group, where that analysis is not yet being done, annual negotiations start with a request to all suppliers for a price cut that matches Motorola's price curve, with some firms being given higher targets due to the nature of their cost drivers. That leads to a more detailed discussion of specific costs with each firm.

Obviously, seeking across-the-board price reductions of a given percentage may not be realistic for each firm. Further, a request for such cuts leaves no room to pursue lower pricing on individual items, with an overall balance that is fair to the supplier on the full set of items it is providing. But absent the customer's having full knowledge of each supplier's costs, if a target is generally realistic it conveys a sense of urgency and can be a useful starting point when the customer is facing high price pressures in its own markets. To avoid damaging suppliers, the next step must be a discussion of cost drivers.

Focus on Cost Drivers. To get to a specific price, discussions generally focus on key cost sources and steps taken by the supplier to reduce them. As a rule, more time is allocated for negotiations on items that most strongly leverage the customer's situation. For annual price negotiations on multiyear supplies, topics covered include what the supplier has done to lower costs and where it is on relevant learning curves. To help frame its understandings, the customer compares data from the supplier with known cost drivers and market prices.

Price negotiations are resolved by reason, with an understanding that if the supplier is squeezed too hard it may decline to take the business. One possible outcome is when the customer learns that cost is inherent in a particular design. When that happens, the discussion ends and the firms either look for other ways to lower the cost or pursue a redesign.

Certain costs, such as profits and overhead, should not be disclosed in order to maintain the independence of each business, as discussed in Chapter 3. In fact, most suppliers fear that they may be forced to disclose their margins as they get closer to key customers. Even in alliances with high trust, this is seen as a dangerous step to be avoided except in special circumstances (such as when negotiations break down) and then only in private discussions with trusted individuals.

Still, such information can usually be calculated with some accuracy, based on publicly available data. Both M&S and Motorola have a general sense of margins and overhead for each supplier that is sufficient to make comparisons between firms. Should a supplier appear to have unreasonably high margins or overhead, it may be encouraged to reduce those. Similarly, while suppliers are not expected to share their full cost structure, they must present sufficient evidence for their arguments.

For unique items where price benchmarking in the marketplace is difficult, known cost drivers are the usual basis for discussing costs. For instance, because M&S expects suppliers to share raw material price shifts with it, the company monitors all major raw material prices.

Trust Improves Cost Reduction and Shared Savings. A firm's willingness to share cost data and savings with a customer, as well as the amount shared, depends on the value of the relationship and how much the supplier trusts the customer. In cases of low trust, a supplier fears that customer problems or actions—such as design flaws, failing to disclose key requirements, awarding a lowball bidder, or taking profits at the supplier's expense—could damage its own margins. To protect itself, the supplier may withhold information on costs and the resultant savings, thereby depriving the customer of the best price over the longer term.

By contrast, in an alliance, trust requires sharing. Says Kelly Howell, the Molex sales representative who serves Philips: "You may be able to get away with keeping all savings for a while, but at some point the customer will find out. The supplier should make an acceptable profit, but not more than a fair profit. If I don't have an alliance relationship, I will seek higher profits from the customer because I know that, tomorrow, they will kick the heck out of me. In an alliance, if my customer is under real price pressure, it is not in the spirit of the relationship to make a profit on their back. Part of what I have going for me is my own personal credibility. When I participate in price negotiations, I cannot afford to compromise that."

Suppliers to Motorola and Marks & Spencer do not share all savings, but they give more than in nonalliance relationships. Sharing is most commonly done with high-leverage direct costs that significantly affect the customer's product or service. Molex's Ron Schubel says that even if the savings beat the customer's price target, sharing helps strengthen a long-term relationship by reinforcing trust and building both the customer's and the supplier's confidence in their ability to drive costs down. He also says that sharing creates "psychological credit" in price negotiations so that when the supplier says price cuts have gone far enough, the customer is more likely to accept that position. "It makes negotiations more like a soccer game than a rugby match," Schubel notes. Of course, for a firm to share any savings with a customer, it must know that it is meeting its own profit objectives on the relevant item, which is not always the case.

Similarly, in the Kodak–IBM alliance, Kodak's Vaughn Hovey says that IBM may "take to the bank" any cost savings it achieves beyond the agreed targets. If IBM does significantly better, however, Kodak will know it from benchmarking, and the internal Kodak business units will walk away if the results are not shared.

Another way trust promotes better costs for the customer is when the supplier suggests an alternative that gives the customer lower costs at the supplier's immediate expense. For example, Molex showed Philips how to replace a complex cable assembly with a simpler one. The new assembly required fewer Molex parts and caused the firm to lose about $600,000 in revenue. But Molex benefited from its action in the longer term because it reinforced Philips' commitment to the relationship.

Tactics Vary with Circumstances. While negotiations focus on underlying cost drivers, specific tactics depend on how supplied items leverage the customer's business. In that regard, two key pricing parameters are the magnitude of price competition in the customer's market and whether the supplier's goods are sold directly in that market.

To illustrate, prices are dropping rapidly in the pager market, which makes pricing highly critical for Motorola's Paging Products Group. Accordingly, sourcing people at the Boynton Beach, Florida, facility have found that negotiating with each firm by individual part number yields better prices than developing a single price for a range of parts.

As another example, risk sharing with suppliers depends on their role in the customer's market (see Chapter 3). Since the goods of Marks & Spencer's suppliers sell directly in its market, the suppliers strongly influence sales and are expected to share the marketing risks. When demand is price elastic, discussions with suppliers include the possibilities of their lowering their margins (which are discussed only in qualitative terms) along with those of M&S to make a product line more attractive. At Motorola, suppliers have less influence on its market success. So when Motorola lowers its margins to improve its own pricing, it works with suppliers to reduce their costs, but does not expect them to reduce their margins. For the same reason of appropriate risk sharing, Motorola asks suppliers for quotes at various volumes (called "step pricing"), while M&S expects its suppliers to profit or lose according to whether volume is above or below estimates.

Avoiding Damage. Healthy suppliers are good for the customer's business. Solid margins make them more viable over the long term, support needed new investments, and keep their stockholders and management well motivated. "We both have common objectives," says Clinton Silver. "A drive to offer the best possible combination of value and price to consumers, tempered by the belief that we want our suppliers to make a good profit, because we want them to survive and we want them to be prosperous and invest for the future." That religiously held attitude at Marks & Spencer—and literally identical beliefs at Motorola—guides all aspects of supplier relations, including price negotiations.

In fact, while firms that supply M&S regard it as a hard bargainer, most enjoy average or better profits among all companies in their industries. Listen to Northern Foods' Chris Haskins: "M&S is a tough price negotiator—much more so than their competitors. They make it their business to know more about suppliers' costs, and how we source materials, to push us hard on price. And because they are in our factories all the time, M&S will know if we have spare capacity on a line and will push us to take a narrower margin there." Further, he says, "they are very demanding. You have to build the high service levels they expect into your costing. The fact that they push us hard helps us both create more value for the consumer, which is what this is all about."

To help frame price discussions, M&S merchandisers, who lead the negotiations, have a broad knowledge of the overhead structure for each industry in which they work. Suppliers may disclose their margins to resolve conflict; when this happens, M&S listens to their concerns. Real pricing difficulties are communicated to higher M&S management levels. If there are clear signals from significant segments of the supply base that pricing is hurting them, Marks & Spencer will raise its prices or look more diligently for ways to cut costs or to lower its own margins. Says Haskins: "On almost any issue except quality, one can bang the table at M&S. There are very few areas where, if I thought my case was solid, I would be reluctant to speak my mind with them."

In general, price negotiations on individual items may favor the supplier or M&S. But both firms look at the supplier's average margin over the full range of goods it supplies, to be sure the overall deal is fair and acceptable to both of them.

Each season in each department, M&S usually makes last-minute price adjustments due to an upper management initiative or market responses to a new product. Such changes are always negotiated with suppliers, though they occasionally decline to go along. Any reduction is shared by M&S through lower margins.

Like Marks & Spencer, Motorola is a tough negotiator. "Doing a pretty good job is never satisfactory for Motorola," says Bruce Bendoff, Craftsman Custom Metal Fabricators's president. "They always want to know why a supplier is not doing better. But as tough as they are, they also want to be partners. Pricing is a tough nut. But no matter how tough the negotiation is, you always know that you are going to get together. We sit, we talk, we reason, and we conclude."

As with M&S, Motorola knows when it is pushing suppliers too hard. For instance, a considerable variation in pricing among suppliers implies that there is room for improvement, and some firms may be holding back. Also, if a supplier is well down the learning curve, Motorola knows not to press further. Most price-cutting efforts are thus in the early stages of that curve. And during annual negotiations, the whole package from one supplier is negotiated at the same time, with a concern for overall fairness.

Ron Schubel says that in a real partnership, Molex judges the total relationship and not just terms for one part. If, for example, the customer's price target for a given part seems unreasonable, Schubel says that Molex may tell the firms: "If that target is really important to you we will meet it, because the total package looks acceptable." Schubel also notes that "if you set a higher price and the customer's program dies, no one has gained." Further, he adds, "In a partnership, if things don't go as well as expected, we spend zero time worrying about that because we know we have a future together and trust each other to make it win-win for both firms. Then we accept the ups and downs. By contrast, in a deal-by-deal relationship, we will try to recover any loss from the customer any way we can—either in future pricing or whatever."

Avoiding Lowball Bids

In traditional commercial relationships, suppliers will at times sell below cost by offering unusually low prices, fully expecting to win increases after they get the business. In alliances, doing this amounts to bad faith. Just as suppliers expect customers to keep their promises, suppliers should never commit to unrealistic prices. An equally improper scenario is for a supplier to give a low price and then cut investments in quality, R&D, or service to raise its margins.

Customers can prevent such practices. When Motorola gets a lowball proposal from a firm hoping to buy its way into the business, it simply rejects the offer. With focused competition all bids are compared with others in the same commodity. Further, Motorola has a good sense of costs in each area, so those bids are immediately recognized. Given the same basic cost structure for every firm making a given part, the lowball supplier will later have to raise its price or cut investments to make a profit.

Probably the most effective way to deter lowball bidding is for the customer to recruit and build trusting relationships with suppliers that are committed to the same long-term goals. Few companies will risk such relationships for a short-term advantage.

When Partners Disagree

Some of the most difficult alliance negotiations happen when there is no objective way to set targets or resolve contrasting viewpoints. If differences cannot be reconciled through reasoned discussions, partners may agree to disagree, with independence requiring that each firm makes its own decision. The customer, for example, may choose a different design from what a supplier thinks is best, and the supplier must then decide whether to accept or decline that business. Even so, such disagreements are tolerated due to the long-term value of the alliance to both firms.

To illustrate, Denis Desmond, chairman of Desmond & Sons, says that those aspects of his firm's negotiations with Marks & Spencer that concern price (which focus on cost drivers) can be easier than those concerning design. People in his firm, Desmond says, like to think of themselves as having a lot of experience in the business and want to be seen as design experts by the customer. Further, M&S buyers change jobs over time, while Desmonds is building up its expertise over the years. He says those factors put a large responsibility on his firm for providing intelligent leadership and developing credibility for its own expertise with new buyers. Of course, as a premier marketer, M&S has its own clear ideas about what creates the best value for consumers, and new buyers do bring in new ideas.

These patterns create negotiating issues when the Desmond & Sons representative and the M&S buyer each believes he or she has the best view of how to satisfy the customer. Sometimes, such matters cannot be resolved at all; at other times, they are settled by going over the buyer's head. But that cannot be done often without hurting relationships. Generally, though, such disagreements are sporadic and involve individual products, so there is never a major issue between the firms.

At Marks & Spencer, such events are seen as opportunities to improve mutual understandings and solve any underlying problems. Says Clinton Silver: "We do not want a supplier relationship to be based on the fact that every season he has to pit his judgment against the buying department's judgment, and if there is no consensus he will lose the business. We have both invested in our relationship and expect to keep making it more profitable for both firms."

At both Motorola and Marks & Spencer, suppliers have the right to appeal to higher organizational levels issues that have not been resolved to their satisfaction. Chris Haskins says that with M&S, no games are played in the process. Each firm must recognize whether its case is strong or weak, and it must appreciate the interests of the other side. Bruce Bendoff, of Craftsman, adds that an appeals process for suppliers should be used only in exceptional cases because of the risk of compromising relationships. "More often than not," he says, "you are better off trying to work out an issue with the buyer than pulling rank. You can win the battle and lose the war."

No Room for Bargaining Power

The most effective alliances depend on a spirit of trust and commitment, with a respect for each firm's interests and an understanding that all issues are resolved by logic in the context of a common goal. Power relationships, in which one firm uses a position of leverage to extract harmful concessions from the other, are not consistent with alliances. Such experiences can largely be avoided through a partner selection process that considers how a prospective partner deals with other firms. For a customer, focused competition and limiting each firm's volume also helps deter suppliers' use of power. A supplier can protect itself from a customer's actions by limiting its dependency and, if necessary, reducing any investment that is unique to that customer.

Suppliers that use a position of leverage to extract concessions (such as more favorable terms) are not an issue at Marks & Spencer, simply because such firms would not be chosen as suppliers. "A supplier's most powerful weapon with us," says Clinton Silver, "is its ability to produce high-quality, high-value goods on time and make reliable deliveries. One attribute of our best suppliers is their hit rate in terms of finding successes for the department, rather than pushing the buyer to buy what is not best for M&S. Another attribute is management style regarding candor and relationships. Our suppliers have to know how to work the system. A firm that keeps going to the selector's boss is not popular, especially with the boss."

On rare occasions, a supplier of unique items to Motorola uses its position to gain unfair terms that are damaging to the company's interests. When that happens, Motorola will find another source, and at times has even developed a new supplier to replace the one that was causing problems.

Eliminating Contracts

In customer–supplier alliances, the completion of each negotiation is sealed with agreements based largely on trust. It is not possible to write formal contracts about the extensive interfirm activities required by alliances. There are too many tasks, too many needed adjustments, and too much uncertainty for that.

For instance, when customer and supplier cooperate in early design, a purchase agreement cannot be written, because contracts require definite terms about what the supplier will deliver. Nothing is certain at that early stage; there are no specifications, just an agreement on the objectives. Suppliers involved in early design must thus work on the basis of trust that they will get the order or, if more than one is involved in a design competition, that each firm will get its fair share. Similarly, no contract can ensure a full exchange of information or provide for a flexible response. If a contract were used to define all aspects of an alliance, each change in procedures made to improve how the partners work together would call for a renegotiation. For a customer that has alliances with all of its suppliers, this would have to be done with every firm.

Consider that most activities in the Hewlett-Packard alliance with Reed Personnel Services are agreed upon informally. Says Chris Kelly, group managing director at Reed: "That allows us needed flexibility to work toward improved quality without feeling constrained by some clause regarding what we can or cannot do. With a traditional contract we would have to renegotiate every time we thought of a new way of working together."

Consider also that there are no legal agreements between Marks & Spencer and its suppliers. Says M&S director Barry Morris: "We don't have contracts; the day we write one it can be broken for many reasons—a change of mind, quality problems, or a recognition that we can do better. Instead, the entire relationship is long term and based on trust." Once M&S and its suppliers have concluded price negotiations and M&S has decided on volume allocations, the final understanding is confirmed in writing, but there is no legal contract. With all of its boilerplate, caveats, conditions, and other trappings, says Morris, a contract would weaken trust by saying, in effect, that "we do not believe we can resolve issues together, so we must specify solutions ahead of time."

There is a distinction between the tasks required by legally binding terms and the enthusiastic combined effort of two companies. It is the difference between a relationship with, say, the local gas company and a marriage. A traditional contract is best in one case, but not in the other. Detailed contracts are used in arm's-length relationships because there is little shared understanding beyond the written word to hold firms together. By comparison, an alliance, like a marriage, may involve a legal document, but that does not include the core of the relationship: the many ways the partners will cooperate and adjust together to create more benefits for each of them. Those elements are understood and are enforced by the partners' need to continue together. The same mutual need discourages opportunistic behavior by either firm toward the other, because that would reduce commitments to their relationship.[1]

Most supply contracts at Chrysler are one page long and exist only for the life of a part. Generally, the only legal documents Motorola uses with its suppliers are one-page purchase orders and three-page agreements about invention ownership for supplier participation in early design. Even the purchase orders have limited scope. As blanket orders, they are binding only for the parts produced by the supplier within an agreed lead time. At present, there are no life-of-part contracts for custom items developed through early design participation. Even so, the supplier can expect to have the business for the duration unless it does not meet volume requirements or has a serious quality or other problem. These, however, are rare exceptions.

Comments Molex's Ron Schubel: "With Motorola, it is a long-term relationship with nonbinding agreements. If the relationship is there, a long-term contract is superfluous; it does not add anything. To have a contract one must spend a lot of time focusing on negatives—conditions, contingencies, penalties. In reality, if we have a contract and conditions change, it will always be rewritten—and not just at Motorola."

Alliances do benefit from written understandings that help people remember what they have agreed upon, just as a company uses internal memos and guidelines to help communicate decisions and procedures. For example, Motorola uses letters of intent to purchase that make it easier for suppliers to buy unique raw materials during the design phase, thereby shortening cycle times and limiting the suppliers' risks. The idea is not to have a legally enforceable contract, but to have clear understandings. The firm also maintains written guidelines—often prepared with the advice of its suppliers—describing the rules of conduct for important joint activities like early design participation.

Moving Away from Contracts

Clearly, the ability to rely less on contracts depends on the level of trust between companies, the people involved, the acceptance of nonbinding agreements by a firm's legal and accounting staffs, and people's comfort with a more informal style.

At Philips Consumer Electronics Company, there is no longer any legal paperwork with the top suppliers. Bill Kennedy, the senior vice president, says one key to moving to these alliances was the change from lengthy formal contracts to a reliance on mutual need and commitment. In that regard, his firm's legal department helped pave the way. "While they of course look out for our interests," says Kennedy, "they saw those interests as being in the new direction and were quite willing to look at things in a new light. They understood the central importance of relationships in these situations and were constructive in their approaches. Similarly, our auditors asked how we would know if we would be getting a fair price, and when we showed them they were satisfied. I never lost sleep on these matters: We made the case, and they accepted it."

Another factor in reducing the use of contracts is that trust between companies is a long step away from trust between a few respected individuals. The distinction is important, because alliances require broad support across a company, and people change jobs.

For example, the original contract between Kodak and IBM was just eleven pages long, plus appendices containing various price curves and other reference data. Still, while the alliance has produced substantial value for both firms, traditional attitudes have made it less than totally acceptable to everyone. This doubt made the relationship between Vaughn Hovey and Frank Palm a critical link in their firms' mutual trust. Hovey and Palm were expected to move on to other assignments eventually, though, and there was some discomfort with the brevity of the original document, especially as a basis for expanding the alliance. For these reasons, amendments for additional work have been more detailed than the initial accord.

At Motorola, Tom Slaninka says his firm is moving toward reducing or eliminating legal documents as a basis for doing business. Purchase orders, however, may not be entirely discarded. One reason is that some suppliers, particularly smaller firms, want formal documents to justify hiring and making capital investments. Another is that Motorola plants—which serve government and private sector customers—use the same paperwork for each, and government buyers require environmental and other clauses in purchase documents.

What to Include in Contracts

Aside from legally mandated topics, when contracts are used in alliances they should include major issues of concern to either company, such as each firm's obligations upon termination. But details of implementation, monitoring, penalties, and control should be held to a minimum. There is a difference between defining areas of understanding and concern and putting in all the possibilities. Clause after clause of contingency planning assumes that an understanding will not be implemented fairly, and this assumption affects the tone of a relationship.

Another factor in alliance agreements is that some performances depend on cooperation, and so neither firm can be held accountable alone. For instance, the contract between Kodak and IBM does not include service levels, which require teamwork to achieve. While the document could have specified what each firm would do (the traditional approach), this tactic would reduce flexibility and inhibit cooperation, just as would specifying teamwork within a firm. Also, there are so many service-level parameters the contract would have to be constantly amended. Frank Palm says most customers want service-level requirements in their contracts, with penalties for not achieving them. But because performance depends on both firms, such clauses lead to accusations instead of joint problem solving. With Kodak, cooperation has made it possible to meet the initial targets, after which people have discussed setting higher ones.

The Kodak–IBM agreement does include an elaborate price matrix that reflects various levels of Kodak consumption. This is appropriate, since IBM controls the cost drivers aside from volume. Both companies recognized that a variety of factors, including abrupt changes in the technology/cost curve due to the introduction of new technologies, could invalidate the matrix. But they agreed to develop a future price curve through negotiation when the time comes.

In the process of drafting an alliance contract, any aspect viewed as punitive by either firm can fuel mistrust, weakening the alliance the contract is intended to support. To avoid this, it is worth making sure that the contents and language are acceptable to each partner.

When Motorola began its early design participation program, for example, one of its attorneys wrote a long agreement that included clauses on default, the cost of noncompliance, and more, most of which was at the suppliers' expense. These provisions focused the whole early design effort on the details of the document; people worried about what information to share and what to withhold. After Motorola asked for and listened to its suppliers' comments on the agreement, the contract was reduced to a simple two-part document that spelled out invention ownership in a manner acceptable to everyone.

13

SUCCESSFUL ALLIANCE PRACTITIONERS

We are very self-critical; it is part of the infrastructure of the company to be open to criticism. We always keep stretching—in store design, product design, quality. Many firms say these things, and even put them in mission statements. M&S has no mission statement. We simply live this way.

Carole O'Beirne, senior selector, Marks & Spencer

Motorola gives you tremendous freedom to be creative. Even if you fail, they don't kill you. People don't get fired for taking risks, unless those are thoughtless.

Neil MacIvor, director of strategic sourcing for the Americas, Paging Products Group, Motorola

Before, management directed a lot of the work. In the new Chrysler culture of empowerment, it is a team decision that makes things happen.

Lynn Tilly, engineer, Chrysler

Within every firm, alignment and decision making are guided by a combination of authority, culture, and politics. By contrast, in an alliance there is no single authority, each firm has a unique culture, and there are no shared political processes.

Yet an alliance requires clear direction, ongoing alignment between firms, continued stretching by each of them, and mutually constructive decisions.

Those conditions make shared objectives and understandings about tasks to be done absolutely critical for alliances. Also needed for implementation and to build trust are effective relationships between people, and supporting behavior by their organizations and management.

People, Performance, and Management

Marks & Spencer and its closest suppliers believe that people are one of the few factors that really matter in business. "One of the most important things we do," says Northern Foods chairman Chris Haskins, "is develop people who can establish the kinds of relationships we need with Marks & Spencer. Having outstanding technical skills is not enough, although it can be for some other customers."

At M&S, relationship and teamwork skills are key selection criteria for hiring and promotion, and these are increasingly emphasized as people advance to higher levels in the company. Teamwork, supplier relationships, and negotiating with suppliers are required elements of in-house training programs for all employees. Further, training subordinates in supplier relations is part of the job for every senior executive. One way they do that is by taking more junior people on most supplier visits, to expose them to best practice in managing the relationships.

In the 1920s, when M&S began transforming its supply relationships to alliances, management had to persuade the firms to develop close bonds between people and adopt progressive attitudes about wages, benefits, hiring, and firing. Today, shared values and practices in these areas—along with common attitudes about service, quality, and continuous improvement—are the forces that keep M&S and its suppliers aligned and committed.

While Motorola began its supply alliances more recently than Marks & Spencer, its views on relationships are identical. Tom Slaninka says high levels of interpersonal competence are key criteria in choosing people for sector sourcing. Adds Len de Barros: "A purchasing or materials procurement manager who does not have supplier relationship skills in his or her inventory does not stay here for long. One responsibility in those functions is to create positive relationships. These must be close and productive, just like our customer relations. In a partnership environment you walk a fine line—you must be a skilled negotiator, but at the same time they are your partner."

"Twenty years ago, an effective purchasing agent at Motorola was a person who squeezed suppliers the most for cost reductions," de Barros continues. "That is radically different now. Making the change has meant a revolution in hiring, training, and promoting people for that position."

Although purchasing job descriptions did not change with the advent of supply alliances at Motorola, the purchasing culture did. Training programs were developed to install needed technical and interpersonal skills, including the ability to resolve issues at the interface rather than elevate those to higher levels. Performance feedback from suppliers through the advisory board helped reinforce the transition.

Starting in the early 1990s, Chrysler went through a dramatic metamorphosis, changing from a rigid, near-death company to a flatter, highly nimble, and empowered organization based on cross-functional platform teams. Says Tom Stallkamp, who heads purchasing and supply as well as large car programs: "We've tried to become lean without becoming mean. We didn't reach that overnight. Truth be told, we weren't a particularly friendly bunch in years past."

BUILD RELATIONSHIPS AT EVERY INTERFACE

For the most effective alliances, productive relationships are essential at every value-creating interface between partner firms. Otherwise, joint creativity is lost, trust is weakened, and cooperation slows.

Inside most companies, people who do not agree can appeal to a higher management level to which both sides report. Such appeals weaken relationships between the people who could not resolve their problems. They also slow decision making. These problems exist in alliances as well. But unlike individual firms, there is no single authority above an alliance, and no final referee for any issue. This difference increases the value of resolving issues where they first appear.

For these reasons, says Craftsman's Bruce Bendoff, each designer in his firm who is involved with an alliance customer has first-level responsibility for making the relationship work, and for fixing it when there are problems. At Craftsman, relationship building is discussed all the time. "You have to learn you get a lot more with honey than with vinegar," says Bendoff. "It is critical that personalities do not get in the way. It is imperative for our people to handle themselves in that manner." He places so much importance on this that he personally discusses the matter with everyone who will interface with another firm. At Motorola, Dale Kelsey, a buyer, adds that his job has evolved from focusing on negotiation and order placement to 20 percent orders and 80 percent cooperation and problem solving with suppliers on quality, delivery, and other matters.

With the growth of multifunctional and increasingly multi-firm relationships, M&S people often work as facilitators to help others within the company perform effectively as a team with garment makers and fabric suppliers. With two or more firms involved on a project, group dynamics are more complex; the natural human tendency for finger pointing adds to occasional friction among participants from different firms (and even from the same company). Alan Lambert, an M&S division director, says that for these reasons—and as its continued drive for excellence causes M&S to work even more closely with suppliers—the company is increasingly aware of the need for people who not only have solid technical skills but also can facilitate dynamic relationships.

Alliances do not even begin well without having the right people at key interfaces. In the business of temporary staff recruitment, as in many industries, there has been a history of adversity in customer–supplier relations. The alliance between Reed and Hewlett-Packard became possible only when Mike Haffenden was appointed H-P personnel director for the United Kingdom. Reed's Chris Kelly describes Haffenden as being particularly enlightened with respect to supplier relationships; Haffenden realized he would get better productivity and service if relations were constructive and nonadversarial. "He does not try to screw the supplier into the ground," says Kelly.

Early in the Kodak–IBM alliance, IBM's Frank Palm gave Elmer Beke, who had come from Kodak in the outsourcing process, a key position as chair of the firms' advisory council and made him a visible advocate for better service levels at Kodak. Although Kodak people expected Palm to take that job, he wanted Beke to have it. Well regarded within Kodak, Beke had excellent relationship skills. Says Palm: "I wanted Kodak people to believe I was here to meet their needs, and that I respected them. Giving Elmer a central role was a key to starting relationships on the right track." In looking back, Palm says: "Elmer's role was crucial."

Both Kodak and IBM understood that the effectiveness of their alliance would depend on how well people worked together. Before the deal was signed, the firms each sent ten to twenty people through a training course on alliance negotiating, a process that was repeated with new hires when they came on board. Now Kodak does this at the start of all information systems alliances, after the partner has been picked and before negotiations begin, to help ensure that these negotiations are conducted in a win-win style. In Vaughn Hovey's view, this practice has carried Kodak through some tough negotiations. Still, he notes, the lessons of alliance building are not sustained without regular reinforcement.

Compared with traditional arm's-length relationships, which tend to be relatively fixed situations, alliances involve more disciplines, need more integration, and present more opportunities. These activities require people at the interface who are generalists. This facilitates the integration and helps spot lessons that can be applied elsewhere. Clearly, alliances also require strong team skills and high personal integrity. Without the latter, the greater flexibility people have at alliance interfaces creates opportunities for hidden agendas, which can be destructive.

ENCOURAGING BEST PERFORMANCE

For an alliance to succeed, the partners' objectives must be translated into specific expectations for people and groups who will do the work, and performance must be monitored against these expectations. Relationships with top customers should be included in senior management reviews, and aggregate supplier performance should be part of every operating review. In addition, each person and team making significant contributions to an alliance should be measured against its performance.

Link Performance Evaluations to Objectives. Many efforts to build customer–supplier alliances have failed due to conflicts between purchasing people (and others) who retained traditional short-term views and their companies' need to build long-term relationships with a committed supply base. Those traditional views have caused buyers to emphasize lowest price rather than total cost, and to shop for it outside the supply base.

This cannot happen at Motorola, because buyers' performance measures include their contributions to reducing the supply base, which is compromised if they go outside. Further, each Motorola employee, from top executives down to line operators, is measured in his or her job evaluation on actions that advance the firm's stretch goals of Six Sigma quality and cycle time reduction—the same performances on which suppliers are judged. This means that everyone at Motorola who is involved with or influences its supply alliances has specific incentives to contribute to their performance. In addition, through their words and actions, Motorola executives are constantly beating the drum for quality, cycle time, and other key goals.

On the other side of the interface, people at Motorola's suppliers are measured by the same objectives. At Molex, for instance, the president of the commercial products division, the industrial marketing manager, customer service people, and others are all evaluated on their contributions to Motorola's stretch goals, including Six Sigma quality and cycle time reduction. Additionally, Molex employees who work on early design projects for Motorola are measured specifically for that work.

When people are not held accountable for alliance performance, other pressures within their firms may easily distract them. Since the start of the Kodak–IBM alliance, Frank Palm's annual compensation reflected the level of customer satisfaction at Kodak, which was formally shared with management above him in IBM. Similarly, for the first few years of the alliance, a part of Vaughn Hovey's compensation was tied to IBM's meeting specified service levels. After that, however, his performance measures were changed so that they no longer reflected alliance results. Hovey says that while he evaluates the director of data center services—Kodak's key relationship manager at the operating level—in terms of alliance objectives, the absence of such measures from his own performance has the potential for creating a serious disconnect in the alliance.

Monitor Relationships. Another key measure is how well people work together. Performance reviews of all Marks & Spencer employees who interface with suppliers reflect the quality of their relationships, with more weight given to selectors, who have more leverage on suppliers. Information about these relationships comes from informal discussions with suppliers and observations in meetings (such as watching for candor and respect).

To illustrate, Carole O'Beirne is assessed on her ability to get suppliers to produce for M&S. Part of that regards design and production, and how merchandise in her department meets consumers' needs. Other measures include her team leadership, ability as a team player, communications skills with her peers and higher management levels, and relationships with suppliers. Inputs on O'Beirne's supplier relationships come from discussions with them at management levels above her, just as she discusses with her counterparts within suppliers the quality of relationships at lower levels.

This focus on interpersonal relations gets constant attention. People at Marks & Spencer say it is central to the success of their supply partnerships, and that there is always room to improve communications to avoid or resolve issues about personality conflicts, misunderstandings, and misinterpretations. At each interface there is an ongoing dialogue to assess how things are going with the teams, search for latent issues, and be sure people really understand each other. O'Beirne says part of her regular job, along with that of the merchandiser, is to maintain regular contact with suppliers for that purpose.

At Motorola, supplier relationships are also a major factor in performance evaluations. For Sunil Lakhani, every regular visit with a supplier includes a discussion about how people are working together. Motorola group leaders and section managers bring up this topic at every meeting, both one-on-one and in group settings—not just to find and resolve problems, but also to head off potential difficulties. Says Lakhani: "We even check people's perceptions to be sure there are no misunderstandings."

Suppliers probe for relationship issues as well. Bruce Bendoff says that to evaluate Craftsman people who work on early design projects for customers, he goes to the key customer contact and to others who participated in a meeting, requesting comments on results against expectations. At times, Bendoff learns the chemistry is not right and has to change people.

Maintaining Continuity for Alliances

During the formation of the Kodak–IBM alliance, Harry Beeth, vice president of finance and planning in IBM's service division, established a trusting relationship with Kathy Hudson, chief information officer at Kodak. Frank Palm, who reported to Beeth, says the atmosphere of trust and candor they created made an alliance possible. "Vaughn [Hovey] and I mirrored what they had done," he says. "Fortunately, we had Kathy sitting above us for one and a half years before she took a new assignment. Both she and Harry went on the alliance management board at the start. But Harry rotated away after six months, which increased the challenge of alliance building. When new people come into an alliance, it is difficult for them to have the same understandings others have built."

Personnel discontinuities are a common problem that can wreck alliances. Shortly after an alliance that got a lot of press attention was formed, several senior management people in one of the firms changed; managers at lower levels had to introduce their replacements to the partner. Today, person-to-person relationships are not as strong as they were during the early stages of the alliance, which is being held together by the lower-level people. Even worse, the new executives have not felt bound to keep the original commitments. At the same time, the early visibility catalyzed other firms in the industry to form their own alliances, and some of those have moved farther ahead.

Such events can be avoided through explicit policies, performance reviews that reflect the alliance objectives and the quality of relationships, teamwork on each side of the interface, and coaching in relationships by senior managers. Other useful measures include succession planning that chooses people with high relationship skills for key interface positions and gives them a chance to learn about a relationship before they move those roles. For example, Marks & Spencer has a clear policy against damaging suppliers. Says Barry Morris: "People who do not respect the continuity of supplier relations will not succeed at M&S."

One way to avoid discontinuities is to keep people at the interface for more time than normal job tenure would allow. That, however, can cause people's thinking to become biased toward the partner firm, and thereby damage their own firm's interests. This can be avoided if both firms have a clear agreement on alliance objectives, and if each one uses performance measures on its side of the interface that support those objectives.

Another issue with longer tenure at the interface is that it can compromise career opportunities in firms where rotation is important to people's progress. Motorola avoids this problem for commodity managers in assignments where relationship skills are particularly important by keeping them in their posts longer. To give them more growth opportunities, sourcing units have considerable latitude in job grading, salaries, and responsibilities.

To implement its supply alliances, Motorola ended the customary practice of frequently rotating purchasing agents. This practice had assumed that when an agent and his or her counterpart in a supply firm developed a close relationship, pressures might grow for self-serving behavior that would compromise the interests of either firm. But frequent rotation reinforced a narrow emphasis on price and short-term optimization, because buyers did not have enough time or training to become experts in what they were purchasing. For alliance effectiveness, Motorola needed continuity and well-informed people at the supplier interface.

Ethics problems are avoided with the new approach because people are measured on constant improvement, with benchmarking and focused competition keeping the entire process at the cutting edge. There is no room for self-dealing in that context. Teamwork at the interface also makes it difficult for anyone to take personal advantage of a relationship. Further, suppliers that engage in questionable practices get reputations of dishonesty, which compromise their performance and prevent them from becoming supply partners.

The new arrangement places more emphasis on selecting the right people, and key values are constantly reinforced. Today, both buyer and seller are professionals who place the mutual interests of their firms at the center of their activities. Trust and ethics are at high levels, and only rarely do problems arise. Changes to Motorola's standards of internal conduct now permit considerable leeway in developing purchasing agents by allowing them to specialize in certain commodity groupings.

A related way to have continuity is to keep some interface responsibilities for key people when they move to other positions. Vaughn Hovey and Frank Palm were recently given new assignments in their firms. But Hovey was appointed to IBM's customer executive council for its service business, and Palm stayed on the Kodak–IBM alliance management board. In those roles, each has continued his contact with the alliance.

A similar approach is to ask people to maintain contacts after they have left an alliance interface. Boeing, for example, requests that its employees who worked with Japanese partners periodically call on their former colleagues on trips to Japan. Such visits help spot issues that may not have surfaced in newer relationships.

Because teamwork at the interface also helps continuity, relationships are rarely interrupted when people change at Marks & Spencer. M&S employees share their understandings with each other for internal discussion and decision making, and to bridge discontinuities. Says Barry Morris: "We move people a lot. But we do not move all at once, so continuity remains." Further, Morris notes that like most of his M&S colleagues, he knows the suppliers well. This familiarity makes it easier for him to get up to speed on new issues.

These and other ways to manage continuity are summarized in the following table .

External Alliances Need Internal Alliances

To an important extent, alliance performance depends on each firm's internal style; how people work on the inside largely determines how

Managing Alliance Continuity	
Practice	**Comment**
Dominant shared objectives	Limits destructive opportunism when people change
Limit job rotation	Must add growth opportunities, measure people's performance against alliance objectives
Interface team	Requires reinforcement by management and performance measures; works best in team culture
Relationships in job evaluation	Always necessary, never sufficient
Succession planning	Emphasize team skills for key interface positions Have replacement at interface before taking key role
Coach replacement	Best in coaching culture
Specific policies against damage	Must be enforced
Keep contacts after departure	Either by keeping some responsibility or through informal visits

they work on the outside. If a company treats its employees fairly, honestly, and with trust and dignity, they will be more likely to treat others that way. Also needed are substantial delegation and empowerment, and easy vertical links.

The very best customer–supplier alliances are found in companies that have achieved substantial alignment between people at all organizational levels and the goals of the firm. That condition promotes the wide support of alliance objectives, and it avoids the conflicting priorities that hinder many firms. Further, the multifunctional interfaces needed for alliances are most effective at firms that have mastered teamwork, including horizontal processes that easily span internal boundaries. Says Philips' Bill Kennedy: "Without a consensus, conflict will blossom, and the supplier will be the victim. All you need is a dissenting engineer to upset the apple cart."

Listen to Clifton Reichard, director of business development for Ball Corp., the packaging company, describe a frequent experience of his in selling: "If I succeed in getting a purchasing agent to think of buying from us, I find he has a VP of purchasing who thinks otherwise. And if, over time, I succeed in getting the VP of purchasing to try us, I find there is a VP of manufacturing who says that none of our products are going into his plants until he says so. Then I find that the VP of R&D thinks he is the protector of the family jewels, and none of our products will be accepted until they meet his specifications."[1]

A PASSION FOR TEAMWORK

Teamwork at the customer–supplier interface requires the same practices inside each company. Otherwise, if the rest of an organization is fragmented, interface teams will not get the support they need. The result, then, is like building a bridge across pontoons that are drifting in different directions.

Teamwork at Motorola is imbedded in the firm's culture, and this is one reason for its success with supply alliances. During one recent year, more than 3,000 total customer satisfaction (TCS) teams were at work within the company around the world.[2] The teams, initiated by anyone who is interested, focus on quality (as broadly defined), speed (in terms of removing non-value-added steps), and cost reduction. Such teams have become a stalwart source of constant renewal in every dimension of the firm. In effect, their use is spontaneous process re-engineering, organized around customer needs and requirements. Most teams being formed go through workshops run by Motorola University. Quality tools are used by the teams, and they are judged on the use of those tools.

When the TCS team concept was first proposed, many people doubted that it would work. But, says one executive, "It has been amazing what the teams have done." Not infrequently, people talk about saving a million dollars on an individual project. Now Motorola has been training its suppliers to use TCS teams, and it intends to link their teams with its own. This is a new frontier.[3]

As might be expected, teams are also part of the organizational fabric at Marks & Spencer. Starting in the 1970s, a rising consumer interest in fashion caused the firm to build closer internal ties and adopt consensus processes among designers, merchandisers, selectors, technologists, and others across the company. Before then, weak internal links made it difficult to get design innovations through the system. Now new initiatives receive strong functional support. The change also built closer bonds between M&S and its suppliers, which helped them through the fashion transition.

EMPOWER THE WHOLE ORGANIZATION

"Before, management directed a lot of the work," says Lynn Tilly, a Chrysler engineer. "In the new Chrysler culture of empowerment, it is a team decision that makes things happen." Adds Bob Lutz, Chrysler president: "We really are trying to get the 'boss' to no longer be the wellspring of all wisdom and authority and to stop being the boss, and to start being a teacher and coach, instead of saying, 'Here is what I want you to do.'"

The tremendous ability of customer-supplier alliances to affect cost, quality, design, cycle time, and other value sources comes from the many ways that firms can improve their joint efforts—from cooperation between plants to strategic coordination at policy levels. For best performance, each interfirm link must have room to innovate on its own impetus. Creating such room requires an empowered environment for the entire firm. One obvious reason for this need is that management layers add costs and delays; another is that local initiative is self-reinforcing.

For these reasons, Motorola has constantly worked to delegate more authority to lower levels. Today, shop-floor teams in some plants are making $10,000 decisions for purchases that will streamline or simplify process flows on the production line. Motorola has formal budgets for those contingencies.

Throughout Motorola, people at all levels are strongly encouraged to experiment, guided by the firm's highly visible objectives, participative culture, and performance measures that emphasize constant improvement. Says Neil MacIvor: "Motorola gives you tremendous freedom to be creative. Even if you fail, they don't kill you. People don't get fired for taking risks, unless those are thoughtless." While the buying job in other firms mainly entails paperwork, Motorola's Dale Kelsey, at his initiative, launched a pilot program involving production floor people and a supplier to speed problem identification and resolution. For the same purpose—and also at his initiative—Kelsey arranged to spend five days working at a supplier's plant to learn about its processes.

Motorola's success with supply alliances is usefully seen in the context of its longer-term efforts, begun years earlier, to move toward a highly participative, people-centered management style. Without that, the cooperation and delegation needed for its alliances would not be feasible. Continuing clear signals from top management, plus obvious value coming from cooperation, reinforce people's belief in the process. To illustrate the emphasis Motorola places on human resources, terminating a ten-year employee for performance reasons requires a review by the chairman of the board.

Motorola's internal style, which is formally articulated and communicated within the firm and to suppliers, serves as a model for supplier relationships. In the early days of its alliances, some firms did not know how to resolve problems they had. Motorola's response was to use the same open-door policy with suppliers that it had been using within the firm. An internal document on conflict resolution procedures was shared with all suppliers, who were free to take any problems further into the company if they were not resolved at the interface. Since those days, better issue resolution processes at the interface get virtually all problems resolved there.

EASY VERTICAL LINKS

To sustain alignment between customer and supplier, or to change direction when doing that makes sense, people need easy access to higher organizational levels for quick responses and to resolve matters that require more senior management attention.

For example, to meet Motorola's request that suppliers use bar coding on items they made for it, Molex had to make new investments in forty eight plants worldwide. Each location required a bar code printer, as well as people who were trained to use it. To adopt the system, Molex's Dan Prescott first sold the concept to management by explaining its merits. He then worked with corporate operations, which had to install bar coding at each site. All of these tasks required easy access to people above Prescott. Approval of Prescott's proposal took only a week from the date he first made it to when approval was given.

Building Durable Alliances

The greatest value from customer–supplier alliances comes from ongoing improvement by each company over the long term. That behavior is most likely found in organizations that are constant innovators, have high quality levels, and are consistent in their conduct over many years.

MAKE INNOVATION THE NORM

For alliances to keep producing more value than market transactions, there must be a drive for continuous improvement across each firm. As Francois Castaing, vice president of vehicle engineering at Chrysler, said in addressing an off-site meeting of several hundred employees: "Continuous improvement is, for all of us, wherever we are in the company, an attitude we must all have to keep the company in business."

Listen also to Marks & Spencer's Barry Morris: "What is unique to M&S and rubs off on its suppliers is divine discontent—a constant questioning of what we are doing and can we do better, in terms of price, quality, volume, and profit." Adds Carole O'Beirne: "M&S often wins the first division [large retail chain] championship, but that does not make us complacent. We are very self-critical; it is part of the infrastructure of the company to be open to criticism. We always keep stretching—in store design, product design, quality. We never accept that we offer the perfect product or sell it the best way. Many firms say these things, and even put them in mission statements. M&S has no mission statement. We simply live this way."

For many companies, operating reviews focus on gaps between desired and actual performances. At Marks & Spencer, by contrast, most discussions of current operations—whether they focus on successes or failures—regard how to do things better the next time.

Like M&S, Motorola is constantly reinventing itself through numerous TCS teams, as noted earlier, and in multifunctional meetings that cut across the company, brainstorm for new ideas, and (with top management support) install new practices. In addition to such efforts, and including constant improvement in job evaluations, Motorola keeps pressing its people for advances in many ways. In monthly meetings, for instance, top managers in each business lead reviews of new and current initiatives on cost, quality, delivery, and cycle time; new products and market developments; business performance and projections; and factory and supplier capacity.

At the heart of these constant drives for change is a corporate humility which appreciates that success is always temporary. Says Northern Foods' Chris Haskins: "It takes great self-confidence for an excellent company to say, 'what we have done is not good enough.'"

HAVE A QUALITY MENTALITY

The best way to get high quality and low cost in any activity is to make continuous improvement a way of life, accept long time horizons, and use a root-cause process for problem solving. Constant improvement, which requires an ability to sustain small, ongoing advances and is known by the Japanese term *keizan*, facilitates a steady flow of ideas within and between firms. Similarly, comfort with long time horizons makes incremental change acceptable.

Without a long horizon, there is no patience for the benefits that future improvements bring, and other firms are treated as mere opportunities for the moment. The experience of Bankers Trust illustrates. In 1994, the firm was sued by several major corporate customers for substantial losses they had suffered on financial products (known as derivatives) it had sold them. Although other financial firms also sold derivatives on which customers lost money, Bankers' deal-making culture resulted in fewer long-term customer relationships compared with its rivals. As the *Economist* speculated, that may explain why more customers sued the bank than other institutions.[4]

Similarly, a root-cause attitude—the preference to get to the bottom of problems and eliminate their origins—is needed to resolve issues between firms without animosity, and to build new understandings needed for continuous improvement.

All these behaviors—continuous improvement, long time horizons, root-cause attitudes, and *keizan* cultures—along with teamwork and empowerment—go hand in hand with a constant drive for total quality in all aspects of a business. It is no coincidence that firms like Chrysler, Motorola, and Marks & Spencer excel in these areas, and consequently enjoy excellent supplier alliances. Says Bob Eaton, Chrysler chairman and CEO: "Quality is our number one objective above everything else—profit, productivity, new vehicles, everything."

If quality is defined broadly in terms of customer satisfaction—which is the case at Chrysler, Motorola, and M&S—rather than just manufacturing statistics, then customer–supplier alliances do best when quality improvement is practiced by every part of each firm. Such behavior supports the broadest continuing adjustments for mutual gain. Further, companies in which these attitudes are widely and deeply held are inherently more flexible and responsive to new demands. This has been a major reason why Marks & Spencer has been able to stay with the same suppliers for several decades and through market changes that required major adaptations by everyone.

BE CONSTANT IN RELATIONSHIPS

Persistence pays high dividends. Says Ron Schubel of Molex about his firm's relationship with Motorola: "We know Partnership for Growth [Motorola's supply alliance program] and the behavior it represents are going to be there regardless of changes in the company, so we can count on doing business with them that way. Because we have that confidence, we can sell to all levels of our organization that Motorola can be relied upon. Further, if we behave in a similar way, our relationship with them will grow and prosper."

Now listen to the CEO of another firm: "When [a major customer] launched its supplier partnership program, its first advisory board meeting was attended by high-level people. The second meeting, seven months later, had less attendance. The third, eight months after that, was attended by two low-level customer people. That experience paralleled declining support for promises they had made to be fair and candid with us, listen to our concerns, and get past the old problems. Recently, we decided that we could not safely invest in this relationship to the extent that we have with others."

Like so many other aspects of alliances, what is practiced on the inside determines behavior on the outside. Says Clinton Silver, "Stability breeds stability. A firm with excellent supplier relationships tends to be more stable because the style required for such relationships is one of internal continuity. Further, a supplier having a close relationship with an important customer has strong incentives to ensure stability in its management structure, over time." The most venerable supplier to M&S has served it for more than 100 years; many suppliers have worked with it for forty to fifty years or more.

Reducing Not-Invented-Here Behavior

The problem is as old as cooperation. Other people—or other firms—do not seem to have ideas that are as good as those developed at home. Or, others' competence is recognized, but the opportunities still get low priority. Either way, cooperation is rejected, or at least resisted, as unwise. This aversion to new concepts, popularly known as not-invented-here or NIH, has a number of roots, and there are several specific remedies.

FOCUS ON CORE COMPETENCE

Often NIH comes from wounded pride or a fear of being displaced. People do not want to admit others are equally able, feel their work will be judged inadequate, or worse yet, believe that cooperation will lead to lost jobs.

Concentrating a firm's efforts on its core strengths lowers internal resistance. People in a focused company know that their work is critical to its success, are less likely to feel threatened by cooperation, and have to work more with outsiders to complement their own abilities. Moreover, people who are part of their firm's core competence are near the frontiers of their disciplines, and have more reason to respect each other, which helps break down resistance.

At Philips Consumer Electronics Company, as at many firms, there is some reluctance to working with outsiders due to a concern about job threats. The industry has been cutting costs and reducing head count, and there is a natural concern that relying more on others will accelerate that trend. To combat not-invented-here attitudes, PCEC has devoted fewer resources to product development (including not refilling positions as employees retire). Now when people say they do not have enough resources, they are told to work more with suppliers.

As an example, PCEC supplies TV sets, VCRs, satellite links, and system integration for Whittle Communication's Medical News Network. One part of that network is a sophisticated remote control that physicians use to operate the system. When PCEC asked a supplier to design the entire housing and layout, no one objected, because it was not part of the core business. In fact, the PCEC project team encouraged outsourcing; they could not develop the component internally, since all resources were already committed to other projects.

To focus on core strengths requires a clear understanding of what is and is not included within that scope. Inadvertently cutting core activities in the process of reducing NIH will stifle creativity where that is most needed. Similarly, failing to drop nonessential work may continue resistance to outside ideas.

MANAGE TASK BOUNDARIES

Motorola's Len de Barros says that, like any firm, his company must be constantly aware that not-invented-here lurks on the edge of every activity. For instance, engineers often enjoy doing a design themselves rather than cooperating with others—especially if those people are in another group or firm. One tactic that has been useful in fighting NIH, says de Barros, is to have tasks delineated so clearly that one engineer cannot do an entire design. M&S uses essentially the same practice: By policy, the internally developed design brief stops well short of describing individual garments, leaving ample room for suppliers' designers to be creative.

A related NIH issue is the concern that in the process of sharing with outsiders, some critical know-how will flow to them. Motorola overcomes that by training (and constantly reminding) people about what its critical technologies are. All managers are responsible for exercising controls at their group's outside interfaces.

People who are too busy to do all of a task themselves happily share the work with others. Some firms use this fact to encourage cooperation by keeping the number of people involved in an activity below the number required to do the whole job alone. Then cooperation has no alternative.

EXTEND PEOPLE'S HORIZONS

Often new ideas are rejected because they appear too difficult to implement, or they do not fit patterns in the organization. And, of course, outside ideas have no chance to be accepted if no one is aware of them. Each of these barriers can be lowered by giving people more opportunity to innovate.

One way to reduce creative inhibitions is to delegate more authority to lower organizational levels and break down horizontal boundaries. A related tactic, as illustrated by Dan Prescott's experience at Molex, is to make a firm's vertical channels more open and responsive to communications from below. People are naturally inclined to resist new opportunities if implementation would require either contending with a bureaucracy above them or crossing turf boundaries around them.

Focusing people's attention on outside events makes them more aware of new concepts and what is needed to adapt them. Regular benchmarking and external scanning are important tools in this regard. Motorola, which benchmarks constantly, does not limit its efforts to firms in related businesses. "The further away from our industry we reach for comparisons, the happier we are," says a senior executive. "We are seeking competitive superiority, after all, not just competitive parity."[5] As a companion to benchmarking, Motorola's monthly meetings—which focus on markets, products, and internal activities and are led by top executives—promote a questioning attitude that encourages people to gather and use abundant information.

Another way to expand idea horizons is to promote an atmosphere that keeps concepts alive, even in the face of stiff opposition. For example, each Motorola employee is entitled to file a minority opinion report if he or she feels that suggestions are not being supported. The reports are read by the bosses of the employees' bosses; retribution is considered unacceptable, so people feel free to express their views. The process has unearthed enormous opportunities—including the company's multibillion dollar global satellite project, named Iridium, and its bellwether computer microprocessor, the 68000 series.[6]

Replacing narrow or risk-averse evaluation criteria with more enlightened gauges also helps defeat not-invented-here attitudes. Narrow criteria cause otherwise promising ideas to be rejected. For instance, an emphasis on purchase price rather than lowest total cost discourages suggestions about a wide range of cost drivers. Frequent job rotation is another boon for new ideas, because it regularly exposes people to different ways of thinking.

DEVELOP A CULTURE FOR COOPERATION

Effective teamwork is a natural enemy of a not-invented-here mentality, because the trust it requires fosters idea sharing. Such efforts work best when people start working together well before any ideas have jelled. Also needed for important tasks are formal measures of cooperation that are actively used and reinforced. At Motorola, for example, product designers were slow to involve suppliers on early design participation until cycle time reduction became a formal objective and was built into their performance evaluations. Since early supplier involvement was a key to this objective, the designers then embraced that process.

Many companies talk about treating people as key assets; few, however, actually go far in doing this. Still, how people are managed on the inside critically determines their receptivity to outside new ideas. At the most innovative firms, such as Motorola and Marks & Spencer, human resources really do get top priority. People there are important enough to warrant top management time, are worth continued investments in training, and treat each other with considerable respect at all times. Negative comments about others are virtually never heard. Innovation in these firms is a cooperative process, supported by values that encourage individual initiative, mutual commitment, and risk taking. In those companies people are more action-oriented, and they accept more responsibility for their behavior.

Guided by a shared vision of the future and confidence in their relationships, such employees place their faith in colleagues' competence above loyalty to turf. They feel encouraged to search for and adapt new ideas from all sources, regardless of whether these fit current practices. Innovative cultures are also more cosmopolitan. Their high concern for people and ease of working across internal boundaries make such firms more inclined to scan their environments for opportunities, as well as more adept at responding to them.[7] On the inside, these are high-learning firms, woven together by countless informal networks that build collective understandings with new information from experience, partners, customers, classrooms, and the literature. Invariably, these companies are found on the leading edge of change.

Visible success with outside ideas also thwarts not-invented-here. At Motorola's Paging Products Group, Al Lucas, vice president for strategic alliances, says one of his challenges is encouraging people to want to work more with outside technology sources. Nothing gets past the NIH barrier better than success, he notes.

At Philips, Gordon Couch says past adversity with Molex was overcome in part by joint work to modify a connector, which led to reduced manufacturing failures and improved design flexibility for easier manufacturing. Conceptually, he says, the benefits of cooperation were clear to everyone; resistance was mainly psychological. The openness and sharing that came out of this effort "expanded the comfort zone," he adds.

Philips also rewards joint development by its engineers through recognition. "Every time we hear of a successful effort, we make it visible and make sure everyone understands that is the way to go," says Tom Natale. This constant reinforcement is viewed as essential to help change people's attitudes about working more closely with suppliers.

HAVE CHAMPIONS FOR CHANGE

Many important opportunities can be realized only if someone converts others to the cause. Alliances require constant championing on both sides of the interface, both at the start and to promote continued advances. This is illustrated by Dan Prescott's initiatives for new Motorola programs at Molex, and the role of commodity managers in promoting the health of Motorola's supply base.

Champions should be negotiators and cheerleaders, not owners. The advocate who makes an alliance a personal project breeds resentment and disinterest in others. The job is to advance the project, build a groundswell of support, and give others room to make it theirs as well.

In one well-known alliance between a major retail chain and a consumer goods maker, the supplier's upper management tried to slow the development of the relationship because they were not comfortable with the rapid changes it implied. While the retailer has been flexible and responsive to new ideas, its partner's more rigid style required seemingly countless sign-offs on all new projects.

To cut a path through that internal process, the supplier's alliance leaders developed a flowchart of their firm's internal decision-making processes and got pre-clearances on issues that would have to be resolved quickly. They also involved more headquarters people in the alliance and gave them more information about it. For example, because the alliance had made great strides in inventory management, corporate people who were pushing that frontier within their firm were exposed to this work, which gave them a valuable window on the future. That step eased approvals, because it helped corporate decision makers understand what was happening. The supplier's alliance management team also worked to get its firm's business unit executives involved in relevant alliance decision processes. The team's success further reduced internal resistance and made the supplier more flexible at the interface with its partner.

The practices discussed above, plus other ways to combat internal resistance, are summarized in the table shown.

Top Management Leadership Is Essential

At a recent meeting of top purchasing executives from about sixty large U.S. manufacturers, the topic was supply alliances. While most participants knew the value of those links, skepticism ruled the discussion. Said one executive: "There is an incredible naïveté of top management toward purchasing." Others added that while senior management talks about alliances, the reality is that they drive purchasing to focus on short-term interests. "It's all about 'What are you going to do for me today?'" commented a participant. Several said that in their firms, suppliers were expected to take the brunt of any cutbacks, which prevented a transformation to alliances. "When the crunch comes, the squeeze happens" was a common refrain. No one believed that converting supply relationships to alliances would go far without top management's full commitment.

Still, there is another side to the story. The conversion to supply alliances often permits a large reduction in the number of buying positions, which can make purchasing organizations major barriers to change. One large telecommunications company tried to use such

Reducing Not-Invented-Here Behavior	
Method	**Comments**
Focus on core competence	Promotes sharing by improving job security and expanding need for others
Manage task boundaries	Use scope limits to allow others' creativity; keep people apprised of sensitive items; have fewer people than needed for a task
Extended people's horizons	Frequent scanning, benchmarking; more relevant evaluation criteria; focus discussions on outside events; outside advisory boards; cut bureaucracy, open vertical and horizontal channels; do not let ideas be killed; frequent job rotation
Develop a culture for cooperation	Use teamwork, early participation; performance measures on key tasks; people really are critical assets; become a learning organization; make success visible
Champions for change	Win others' commitments; champion as facilitator, not owner
Top management leadership	Set and reinforce desired patterns

alliances, but the initiative was killed by purchasing, which had the political power to do that and feared a reduction in personnel would mean an erosion of its power base. In the pharmaceutical business, research has traditionally been the key to growth, and research executives have consequently held the reins of political power. Now, with the transformation of the health care industry, alliances between drug firms and health care providers seem essential for the firms' long-term survival. Yet some research executives have resisted those moves—again, because they fear a loss of power.

Regardless of the company or industry, customer–supplier alliances typically require substantial realignment within a firm (including changes at the interface, described earlier) and the adoption of a quality mentality (including long time horizons and root-cause problem-solving methods). None of that is likely to happen without leadership from the top.

Firms with the most productive alliances enjoy ongoing visible support from the highest corporate levels. Motorola made the change with senior executive support; because the company was growing, purchasing people could be reassigned to more productive jobs, which could be redefined to include more strategic tasks like cycle time reduction.

Motorola's Bob Galvin, who was chairman and CEO at the time, drove the transformation and has remained a vocal supporter of supply alliances. Today the various sourcing units derive their authority from many corporate executives who want the process to work. For example, in 1994, when Motorola CEO Gary Tooker gave the prestigious CEO award to the supply management council in Singapore, many vice presidents attended the meeting.

The activities involved in customer–supplier alliances are as complex and demanding as any other aspect of business, and suppliers consume a substantial share of the typical firm's cash flow. To deny them top management attention is equivalent to senior executives ignoring the inner workings of their own firm. In marketing, it is common for a firm's executives to take a lead role in building customer relations. Suppliers typically do not get such attention, although they do get as much as one-half of the average firm's revenues. Somehow customers, as the source of revenue, deserve high-level attention; how a large part of that revenue is used is left to purchasing people to manage in isolation.

Observes Tom Natale: "A management philosophy we are trying to ingrain in the organization is that the executive team running the color TV business is where the real leadership and ownership of the supply partnerships are. We must do that to survive. A substantial percentage of our costs are tied up in our suppliers." At PCEC, Natale and Bill Kennedy had enough authority to get the transformation going. At about the same time, then-CEO Don Johnstone was launching a major quality initiative, which he knew could not succeed without supply alliances. His support accelerated the transformation.

That Marks & Spencer's supply relationships are consistent across the company is due to practices that start at the top. "I know the boss of every company that supplies us," says Clinton Silver. "So does our chairman, Sir Richard Greenbury. Further, we have extremely good communications within M&S—both vertical and horizontal." The highest executives in the company talk to M&S and supplier people all the time, in formal and informal settings. Each executive is regularly briefed on supplier relationships and is easily accessible to any supplier that wants to see him.

Each week, minutes of the executive directors' meeting are circulated to M&S managers throughout the business. These always contain descriptions of visits to suppliers and include comments on the state of each relationship, as well as innovations every firm is bringing to M&S. Further, while the buying departments work hard to get the best possible price from suppliers, Marks & Spencer has a clear policy that one should not damage them. That is actively reinforced by all top executives, who set a standard of conduct for everyone else.

"Due to those factors," says Silver, "people know that excellent supply relationships is our policy. Still, occasionally someone lower down in the organization will attack a supplier. We cannot accept that, because it damages trust and weakens our relationship. To avoid such problems we need constant internal communications to keep people aware of what is important to M&S. Also, there is nothing better than meeting with a supplier and inviting junior levels to participate. In fact, that is one key reason for high level meetings with suppliers. Such meetings cause ownership of our supply relationships by all levels."

These practices were ingrained in Marks & Spencer in the 1920s by Simon Marks and Israel Sieff, who were co-architects of the company, and have become part of its culture.[8] Still, cultures die without continuous renewal. Says Clinton Silver: "The current leaders of the business are the guardians of its culture."

Significantly, the teamwork and values necessary for its supply alliances are patterned at the top. Barry Morris says that everyone in M&S accepts the principles articulated by former president Marcus Seiff: high quality, good value, product development, innovation, good human relations, the development of people, and good relationships with suppliers. Those ideas are kept alive by the firm's top executives, who overtly practice them. Further, the M&S board functions as a team, with the chairman as captain. They know each other well, share the same values, and know what kinds of people should be promoted. With the board reinforcing the model of teamwork, Morris and his peers at his level easily manage as a team, as do people at lower levels.

Similarly, at Craftsman, "Several of us run the company," says Al Krempels, head of quality. "Sure, one is more equal, but that is not how decisions are made. We have real teamwork here. We leave a discussion being comfortable with the decision. For example, we were quoting a part for stamping. Julio Gesklin, our vice president, came to the meeting with a quote, I suggested an alternative, and we revised it together. No one felt stepped on and we got a better result. Most of the time we really get synergy as a management team. You have to have teamwork at the top to get teamwork down below."

Choosing Customers and Suppliers as Alliance Partners

Combining the material in this chapter with the discussion in Chapter 2 provides a set of guidelines for selecting customers and suppliers that have the greatest potential for high-performance alliances. This information is displayed in the table below.

Partner Selection Criteria	
Attractive Company	**Unattractive Company**
Seeks value	Concerned only with price
Effective with cross-functional teams	Suffers from functional isolation
Practices root cause problem solving	Relationships are adversarial
Focuses on trust	Emphasizes rigid contracts
Shares ideas, information	Withholds needed data
Protects others' proprietary data	Others' data leaks to their rivals
Works to earn partners' commitments	No interest in partner benefits
Seeks long-term relationships	Prefers short-term deals
Actively seeks partners' suggestions	Resists others' ideas
Vertically integrated	Vertical isolation
Strong top management support	Top management is indifferent
Excels at quality improvement	Quality gets low priority
Committed to same long-term goals	Goals are different, or change unpredictably

14

VALUE CHAINS AND ALLIANCE NETWORKS

We work as partners in the truest sense.

> Salim Ibrahim, vice president of DuPont, on his firm's fourth-tier
> supplier relationship with Marks & Spencer

*Effective relations with all tiers of our suppliers represent
one of Chrysler's greatest opportunities to add value to our
vehicles.*

> Robert J. Eaton, chairman, Chrysler Corporation

*Fame is a fleeting thing. When the alarm clock rings
tomorrow morning, you'd better get up and understand that
your customers expect more from you than they did the day
before. You'd better find ways to be better.*

> Gary Tooker, vice chairman and CEO, Motorola[1]

When people at Chrysler, Marks & Spencer, and
Motorola talk about their companies' suppliers, they
do not just mean firms whose goods they buy. For instance, materials produced by GE Plastics, a third- or fourth-tier supplier to Chrysler (depending on the items involved), significantly affect the performance of the automaker's vehicles. As a consequence, Chrysler has a direct relationship with GE Plastics and sees this as an important facet of its sourcing strategy. At M&S, the quality, cost, and value of its clothing—as well as

its fast responses to changing demand—depend on the performance of garment makers, fabric producers, fiber sources like DuPont, and many other firms that are one or more companies removed from the retailer. M&S works in various ways with all of them to meet its objectives.

More generally, because suppliers account for about one-half of the average company's costs, *their* suppliers represent one-half of *those* costs, and so on back up the value chain. Further, every company in the chain innovates within its scope of expertise. A customer that effectively manages all of those costs and leverages all of that creativity builds a tremendous competitive advantage for itself, compared to rivals that still regard suppliers as firms whose goods they buy through arm's-length, price-dominated transactions.

Chrysler has embarked upon a remarkable transformation of its entire organization and is well on the way to achieving its quality, cost, cycle time, and other objectives. One key to the company's transformation has been alliances with its suppliers. A critical next step, says purchasing head Tom Stallkamp, is to extend those alliances so that every supplier will see itself as a partner of its customer, and its customer's customer, continuing on to Chrysler and the final consumer. Each member of the chain will have similar views of its suppliers, going back to basic raw materials. Suppliers that do not compete with each other will share best practices to help everyone compete better in the global marketplace. Marks & Spencer, Motorola, Molex, Philips Consumer Electronics Company, and other firms have proven the merits of Stallkamp's vision.

Closely related to value chains, but broader in scope, are networks of companies in which individual links may be alliances or commercial relationships. These arrangements connect customers, suppliers, rivals, and firms in other industries in various ways. Networks provide more ways to create value than individual chains, and they also raise more opportunities for confusion and conflict. Like value chains, their construction and operation are becoming important business practices.

Value Chain Management

With the exception of companies that sell final goods to consumers, every firm may belong to more than one value chain. For example, many suppliers to Motorola, Chrysler, and Marks & Spencer also serve those firms' rivals, increasingly though separate value chains. Each customer's chain is thus an integral part of its competitive strategy.

Because rivals are seeking the same advantages, value chains in effect compete with each other.

For these reasons, value chain management is becoming central to a company's business advantage. The elements of this management process include building alliances with direct customers and suppliers; forming links with others according to what produces more value for the chain's final customer; and continuing innovation by every chain member, guided by a shared desire to better serve that customer.

CHOOSING VALUE CHAINS

While every company may form its own value chain, the performance of that chain depends on two factors. One is the firm's appeal as a customer compared with its suppliers' other customers. The second is the conduct of its own customers and other firms further downstream.

Companies that have significant purchasing power, enjoy rapid growth, and are good innovators and effective alliance practitioners are more attractive to suppliers than firms with fewer of these attributes. Similarly, as appealing as a company may be to its suppliers, the behavior of downstream firms determines the scope of its own opportunities.

In the consumer goods industry, many relationships between retailers and manufacturers remain traditional arm's-length ties that focus mainly on price, shelf space, and features to emphasize in advertising. Little or no consideration is given to finding ways to create more value together, such as through improved product design, and the manufacturer's trade terms are the same for all retailers. In other cases in this industry, some relationships have become focused on value creation, and pricing is based on the economics of each interface.

One effect of these differences is that the manufacturers have fewer opportunities for improvement in the arm's-length relationships than they do in the more enlightened situations. When it is the manufacturers that are rigid, their own suppliers suffer. As a result, many of these suppliers are assigning their best talent and facilities to the higher-value opportunities. Other suppliers seem to be as trapped in the traditional ways as are their more rigid customers, however, and have been slow to consider making the transition. Some value chains and their members are thus gaining strength at the expense of those firms that are locked into the older relationships.

Another consequence of these differences is that the use of standard terms in the traditional relationships reduces the incentive for retailers and manufacturers to improve their joint efficiencies. This, in turn, limits joint cost management. Because most consumer goods are price elastic, this further reduces growth opportunities—in addition to the limits these relationships place on value creation.

Because of the importance of continuous improvement in virtually every market, companies that excel at innovation and alliances can be attractive customers and powerful forces in their value chains. Comments Salim Ibrahim, DuPont's vice president and general manager for Lycra*spandex: "M&S is so energetic about doing things the best way that they've earned tremendous influence in the value chain and respect in the industry. They have far more influence than their size alone would normally have given them. I can only attribute this to solid leadership over time."

MANAGE IN BOTH DIRECTIONS

"We have traditionally thought of ourselves as a supplier," says Molex's Ron Schubel. "But that is not the best perspective. We must also think of ourselves as a customer. We must seek opportunities for improving how we are as a customer. Our suppliers tell us we are not getting as much out of them as we could. Many of us who are working hard to be good suppliers put little effort into trying to be better customers."

In line with this thinking, and following the model of Motorola's Bob Galvin, Schubel and his colleagues (including Molex president John Krehbiel) have had key suppliers assigned to each of them, and they regularly visit these firms to raise the suppliers' visibility at Molex. The company has also developed a supplier management process similar to that at Motorola, although it is not yet as well structured.

Drawing on its experience as a supplier to Motorola, PCEC, Ford, Chrysler, Hewlett-Packard, and others, Molex has reduced its supply base, is adapting single-source relationships, and uses quality audits. The company is giving suppliers clear descriptions of its objectives and those of its own customers, as well as monthly performance reports. It also involves suppliers in early design activities and runs town meetings similar to PCEC's, often with representatives of its customers present. Echoing Molex's message to Motorola, Schubel says his firm's suppliers

---

* Lycra is a registered trademark of E.I. DuPont De Nemours & Co.

have indicated there is much further to go whenever Molex has widened their opportunities for cooperation. Clearly, opening the door to cooperation has meant more value for Motorola, as well as for the connector maker's other customers.

Similarly, one reason Marks & Spencer produces so much value for its customers is that the company leads a value chain in which its suppliers employ many of the same practices it has pioneered. Take one experience at Northern Foods. Until recently, raw milk had to be bought from the British government. After milk retailing was privatized, Northern created alliances with farmers to improve quality, safety, and delivery. It is also working with them on innovations, including finding ways to reduce butterfat.

INNOVATING IN THE VALUE CHAIN

The traditional view of suppliers is one of a hierarchy, in which a firm's direct suppliers rank first and those at lower levels are distant, often unknown companies. In a high-performance value chain, the order of supply links depends on whatever is the best way to create value, reduce costs, and shrink cycle time. Sometimes that looks like a hierarchy, while at other times companies bypass the hierarchy to cooperate on new developments.

Consider that innovation is the lifeblood of Marks & Spencer's business, and it depends on a vast network of relationships between M&S employees and outside companies. Members of the clothing network, for example, include M&S technologists, selectors, designers, and merchandisers. Equally important are links to first-tier garment makers and second-tier suppliers, among them fabric knitters, weavers, and makers of components like buttons, belts, trimming, and linings. Also vital to the network are third-tier firms such as spinners, dyers, finishers, and printers and fourth-tier suppliers like fiber manufacturers. Marks & Spencer's relations with all of these firms are much the same as those with the first-tier suppliers. Joint activities include scanning for and sharing new technologies, pursuing new developments, and discussing market experiences.

For instance, clothing attributes such as garment texture, aesthetics (apart from design), construction, and performance (including stretch and support) all derive from the textile. M&S well understands this and deals directly with textile suppliers and their suppliers to gain the highest possible value and more secure supply. M&S garment makers like Courtaulds Textiles are always involved in these meetings.

In addition to the direct participation of Marks & Spencer in its value chain, suppliers are innovating on their own initiative. They do this sometimes with M&S in mind, and sometimes for wider objectives. In the case of textile machinery, Lycra is a highly technical product that requires custom equipment. DuPont often partners with the machine manufacturers to ensure that textile buyers—including garment makers that sell to M&S—receive the equipment that is best suited for working with Lycra. Similarly, Courtaulds Textiles has close ties to equipment makers in the area of knit stretch fabrics and laces in order to help their product development. Those relationships often give Courtauld an early lead on buying the latest machines.

Marks & Spencer always wants to be an early user of innovations that appear anywhere in its value chain and so encourages such efforts. The retailer constantly works on its relationships with companies in the chain, hoping to be first in line for their new developments. Further, M&S technologists are continually scanning the world, as well as companies in its value chain, for new technical frontiers. Whenever they find opportunities to create unique value, M&S initiates cooperation for that purpose.

Similarly, in its food product line Marks & Spencer and its suppliers review product performances almost continuously, helping each other innovate as they look for ways to create goods that are well ahead of what other retailers are offering. One time, for example, M&S took Northern Foods chairman Chris Haskins to Italy to see a new pasta idea the retailer had heard about. Says Haskins: "When we get it right with Marks & Spencer—when everything jells—we can make more profit than with anyone else. The challenges of innovation and quick response are exciting to our management, and M&S spends a lot of time motivating its suppliers to do what they want them to do." Such attitudes and support are conveyed through conversations and personal contacts—a hallmark of M&S supply relations—as well as more substantive practices.

All of these interactions keep Marks & Spencer's St. Michael brand on a path of continuous improvement and high value. Additionally, as noted in the preface, they have led to important innovations in clothing (such as machine-washable silk blouses, developed with DuPont and Ceiba Geigy) and in its food and home furnishings product areas.

The benefits are also large for suppliers. As a materials producer, DuPont usually must wait for information on new consumer product applications until it has traveled through several layers of the value chain, a delay that can greatly inhibit development work. By contrast, M&S shares weekly sales and related data directly with all relevant suppliers, including DuPont. "This is a remarkable, highly important advantage for any company," says DuPont's Ibrahim. "It gives us a quick reaction capability that is extremely valuable as a competitive edge."

EVERYONE TAKES THE INITIATIVE

Just as M&S keeps pushing its suppliers to keep getting better, they push it as well. For example, at a recent annual review meeting between top managers of M&S and Courtaulds Textiles, Noel Jervis, CEO of the garment maker, challenged M&S to reach out more in two areas.

One was to add more value through improved logistics, lower stocks, and a faster introduction of new products; this was not a new objective, but rather a reemphasis by Jervis. The second area regarded fashion. In some clothing lines, Jervis said, other firms' brands were still the fashion leaders. He suggested that M&S work with its suppliers to become *the* fashion leader in those areas. Jervis pointed out that given the retailer's tremendous strengths, there was every reason not to wait for new ideas to emerge from the brands first. He suggested that M&S and its suppliers form blue-sky teams to pursue both opportunities.

As noted in earlier chapters, Marks & Spencer thrives on such challenges throughout its organization and even invites supplier presentations to its board of directors, an opportunity that is inconceivable for suppliers to most other companies. In a recent presentation to the board, Chris Haskins of Northern Foods praised M&S for its constant drive for more value and better service, its high staff motivation, and a steadfast commitment to its supply base. He also suggested, based on his own knowledge of the market, specific changes in Marks & Spencer's retailing organization that would bring it even closer to the customer.

BUILD DURABLE BONDS

Regardless of the number of companies that are between any two firms in a value chain, the nature of alliances that reach across a chain should be set by mutual opportunity alone. To illustrate, DuPont has worked closely with Marks & Spencer on Lycra for more than two decades, and with Triumph International, the German-based global manufacturer of women's intimate apparel (it owns Lillyette in the United States), since Lycra was introduced in the late 1950s. In each case, cooperation on new fabrics and design ideas has been extensive and has included bonds between the firms at the highest levels. The benefits of the relationship can be seen on the racks in Marks & Spencer stores in every location: Approximately one-quarter of all M&S garments contain DuPont fibers, most of which is Lycra.

In the M&S-DuPont relationship, and in DuPont's links with Triumph and other direct and indirect customers, agendas are set for new developments depending on where the ideas originate. To support these alliances DuPont provides a variety of services, including marketing research on changing consumer values and consumers' receptivity to new concepts. Some research is conducted jointly; other work is shared when it is sponsored independently.[2]

Marks & Spencer and DuPont also share their future plans, just as DuPont does with other major customers. M&S shares its development plans based on its understanding of consumer needs, and DuPont discusses with the retailer its products in the development pipeline. These exchanges help ensure that DuPont's investment in Lycra technology focuses on areas of value to M&S, and give the manufacturer sharper insights on where the market is going.

As with its visits with first-tier suppliers, Marks & Spencer holds a variety of meetings with DuPont. These usually are conducted on a team-to-team basis. For example, DuPont employees meet with each M&S division regarding the status of the relationship, the division's current needs, and its strategic direction. Other meetings involve DuPont and M&S technology people. At higher levels, M&S chairman Sir Richard Greenbury and his team periodically visit DuPont's European headquarters in Geneva to discuss DuPont products, including trends and relevant market experiences, and to exchange ideas on markets and technologies. These meetings often spawn new initiatives and insights, which in turn lead to new joint programs. The meetings are annual at the chairman level and quarterly at the director's level.

"We have launched many products together," recalls DuPont's Ibrahim. "An example was in swimwear, where M&S market data indicated that swimsuits were not performing as well as consumers expected in chlorinated pools. We cooperated and developed an entirely new product and solved the problem together."

Promoting Cooperation Between Suppliers

If a value chain is seen as a set of vertically linked companies, its potential for value creation is limited to that one dimension. By contrast, if a chain is viewed as a network that is composed of as many horizontal, vertical, and other links as members' creativity can produce, its potential adds another dimension. The difference between the two views is like that between a line and a plane, or being restricted to looking for opportunities along a single path versus exploring a vast frontier.

MAKING CONNECTIONS

In January 1993 in Florida, Motorola sponsored its first competition for suppliers' total customer satisfaction teams, intended to promote best practice on that subject. After the event—and at the initiative of several suppliers—a number of their people who were involved in the Schedule Sharing process met to discuss how it might be improved. That meeting led to Motorola's making daily inventory information available on line, which facilitated supplier adjustments to its demand fluctuations. The Florida contest also prompted a group of suppliers to benchmark together in key areas including cycle time reduction, TCS teams, and better ways to manage cost drivers. Ron Schubel of Molex, which sent a TCS team to Florida, says suppliers were attracted to exploring these opportunities because they could benchmark against excellent firms, and because doing so would create an advantage for securing future business with Motorola.

Later in 1993, encouraged by the early efforts, Motorola decided to further promote benchmarking among its preferred suppliers. Bill Hanks, manager of supplier quality programs, says this effort was driven by a desire for faster progress in quality, cycle time reduction, and other key activities. Motorola also recognized, he notes, that preferred suppliers were more apt to be candid with each other than with firms they did not know as well. Another motivation was that firms in the preferred supply base tend to be at or close to best in class in areas of interest to Motorola. Sharing among them seemed to be a good way to spread best practices.

To get started, Motorola chose a small group of firms that were not rivals and discussed with them how best to share their skills. At an open forum, they used the quality audit guidelines to identify topics for discussion, and each firm shared its best practice on specific items. People then began visiting each other's firms and touring best-practice activities at all levels, including plant-to-plant contacts. Once the program was under way, the suppliers took over the leadership. Motorola no longer chairs the meetings and participates only occasionally.

In addition to supplier benefits, the program produces improved feedback to Motorola. For example, two firms involved in early design were using different ways to interface with Motorola. When they compared notes during benchmarking sessions, they developed a better perspective on what worked best. They shared this insight with Motorola, which changed its process.

At Philips Consumer Electronics Company, two complementary practices are used to encourage innovation between suppliers. One tactic, described in Chapter 5, is a series of annual town meetings organized around major subsystems and focused on brainstorming near-term improvements that leverage total TV set performance. All relevant PCEC functions and all suppliers involved in the particular subsystem are included in the meetings. They have been held, for example, with wire and connector suppliers, and with the firms that make PCEC's projection lenses and TV screens.

A related PCEC tactic with a longer-term orientation is the company's annual new product and technology meeting. Once a year, PCEC meets with individual suppliers, which make presentations to a general audience of PCEC people from manufacturing, purchasing, and engineering. Since only high-leverage suppliers are involved, the meetings are a popular attraction. After the presentations, a PCEC component applications engineer—who manages the interface between suppliers and designers—meets with a small group of design, quality, engineering, production, purchasing, and materials control people from PCEC and their counterparts from the supplier. People are chosen on the basis of personal creativity and their ability to implement the results. Suppliers of complementary parts often attend the meetings.

In these meetings, people discuss the direction of their firms over a three- to five-year planning horizon. They review each company's new developments for that time frame, and determine whether those are mutually reinforcing. Much of the discussion focuses on abstract, blue-sky ideas; people look for new and better ways to do things. Says Gordon Couch, a PCEC component applications engineer: "This is one of the best meetings we have with suppliers, because it is a direct, unaffected give-and-take. There are no specific products or prices on the table. At this point anything can be done, and we are building a vision together of product performance and how parts can contribute to that."

These meetings have substantially affected PCEC product costs and performances. One example, a new method of assembling TV sets, reduced part count through an innovative combination of parts and lowered total cost. It also facilitated design.

Drawing on its experience with PCEC, Molex has brought in all suppliers involved in major product proposals to one of its customers for full-day meetings. The agenda for one such meeting was customer expectations, delivery service requirements, and the scope of potential liabilities for material failure. Comments Ron Schubel: "We think all suppliers sometime interact in ways we do not understand. We want to promote better interactions."

At this meeting, morning presentations (followed by questions) were made by the customer's project manager who interfaces with Molex, the Molex project manager, and quality and purchasing people. Topics included expectations for the suppliers and assessments for launch readiness. In the afternoon, breakouts were organized where there was a high potential for interactions leading to desirable changes in product improvement, robustness, and cost reduction. To prepare for the meeting Molex worked with each supplier to get the participation of its relevant top management people, and to make the meeting as open and constructive as possible. Since that meeting, many suppliers have met in groups of two or three to work on improving how their several parts can be integrated to better meet the needs of Molex and its customer.

Motorola has used a similar technique to encourage supplier cooperation. Normally, the company conducts a review of technology road maps separately with each firm; however, it has found significant benefits in doing some reviews jointly. Of course, joint reviews require an alliance atmosphere between suppliers to facilitate their sharing sensitive information. In one case, a Motorola facility held a joint review of technology road maps with three manufacturers of parts that must work together. The meeting helped the firms understand each other's technology and improved their ability to cooperate. It also sharpened Motorola's awareness of how well all three firms were moving in the same direction.

Another way for a customer to link its suppliers is to target specific performances that require collaboration. To illustrate, Motorola's Paging Products Group needed robots equipped with vision systems for its production line, and had concluded that Seiko was best in class for its purposes in robots but did not have the needed vision capabilities. Using the spider charts described in Chapter 5 as an analytic framework, PPG chose Automatix for its vision system and encouraged both firms to combine their products into an integrated system.

While Seiko and Automatix accepted Motorola's plans, they had never explored opportunities for cooperation between them. PPG's Sunil Lakhani told both firms it was crucial for Motorola that they begin working together, and suggested they discuss the potential benefits. He also indicated that if they did not cooperate, their rivals would be invited in. Seiko and Automatix subsequently met and told Lakhani they would be pleased to collaborate.

To set a clear course for the effort, relevant people from PPG, Seiko, and Automatix met. PPG presented its requirements and asked the suppliers to develop a conceptual design to be proposed as the basis for moving ahead. Seiko and Automatix visited each other's facilities, made the appropriate technical people available, and held joint technical meetings to complement parallel work each was doing separately for the same purpose. The system they produced achieved a tenfold improvement in the automated vision systems PPG employs in its manufacturing operations, creating breakthrough opportunities for both suppliers.

Significantly, the entire development effort was based on trust. Until the new system was almost complete, there was no formal contract—just an implied commitment from PPG. Each of the three firms agreed to invest equally; both Seiko and Automatix faced large losses if PPG changed its requirement.

Inherent in the Marks & Spencer supply relationships is an understanding that firms will share ideas on how to improve their business together. That can include meetings with two or more suppliers to discuss common issues in quality, pricing, competitive strategy, or other areas. When M&S bought Kings Supermarkets in the United States, for example, it asked Northern Foods and Cavaghan & Gray to look at the stores together, discuss distribution issues, and get ideas from them.

The techniques for promoting supplier cooperation are summarized in the table shown.

Promoting Cooperation Between Suppliers	
Objective	**Technique**
Make suppliers aware of opportunities	Sponsor events where suppliers can demonstrate their goods and best practices; limit customer attendance so suppliers will focus on each other
Find specific chances for cooperation	In meetings with two or more suppliers, use common frameworks such as quality audits to identify opportunities
Targeted near-term improvement	Joint brainstorming with all relevant suppliers, within defined current scope, such as product function or service offering
Targeted longer-term creativity	Brainstorm with relevant suppliers within defined future scope; jointly review plans or technology road maps with relevant suppliers
Specific advances by chosen suppliers	Customer acts as marriage broker for selected suppliers
More value for specific customer	Presentations and brainstorming by all contributing suppliers

Linking Rival Firms

Rivals have reason to cooperate when the benefits of doing so outweigh the risks. While rival companies cannot share as much information as non-rivals, there is still ample room for cooperation. Typical activities are in areas of common interest that would help the suppliers and their customer move ahead.

For instance, Marks & Spencer encourages its food suppliers to exchange notes on safety. Says Chris Haskins of Northern Foods: "If a rival of ours has a problem, that creates public fears which hurt us. So it is in our interest to work together to keep improving safety in their and our products." Further, adds Haskins, "We visit each other's factories and cooperate on quality, safety, and service issues. Sometimes we exchange safety-related technology." There is, however, no discussion of product innovation, pricing, or profits.

Carole O'Beirne offers that in promoting cooperation among suppliers, one must guard against compromising their technical know-how. Marks & Spencer does encourage sharing that benefits everyone, she says, but if someone at M&S sees a potential benefit from sharing, the supplier is asked for permission before proceeding.

As another example, when Motorola was having a problem with circuit boards (as noted in Chapter 11), the company asked each of its three preferred suppliers if it would be willing to meet with the other two, with Motorola present. If the problem could not be fixed, there was a clear chance that Motorola would have to bring in a new supplier that could solve it. Once assured that successful cooperation would not compromise any of their business with Motorola, the firms shared ideas about how to address the problem, and suggested how Motorola could make changes in its materials and design that would help alleviate the difficulty.

Gaining the Power of a Committed Supply Base

Some companies fear that customer–supplier alliances may become vulnerable during troubled times. Sometimes this happens, such as when the customer squeezes suppliers' profits to protect its own margin in a declining market. In such cases, cooperation declines and years are needed to rebuild the trust, understanding, and commitment that were lost. But another way to go that creates more value for everyone is exemplified by Marks & Spencer's ties to its suppliers. M&S regards the caliber of supplier relationships as so crucial that it goes to great lengths to keep its current suppliers, offering substantial assistance and management guidance when they have problems. Among its clothing suppliers, M&S loses only about one or two a decade.

The efforts M&S makes to help its suppliers may be best illustrated by the retailer's move to become more fashion-oriented, starting in the mid-1980s (see Chapter 7). Many companies, when faced with the need for such major shifts, will abandon any suppliers that cannot keep up. M&S took a different tack. In addition to making a substantial internal investment in design, as well as related organizational changes, the company helped suppliers through the transition in many ways. For those that could not change on their own, M&S gave technical assistance, identifying the needed manufacturing equipment and processes and other necessary skills. When suppliers lacked internal design abilities, M&S provided prototype garments and helped them become proficient in that area. In meetings with supplier executives, M&S constantly reinforced the necessity to invest in design.

This kind of concern for its suppliers' well-being is central to Marks & Spencer's relationships with them. Despite the retailer's relentless challenges to suppliers to produce more value, there is always a concern about their health and a willingness to help when necessary. This style has built a remarkable loyalty among suppliers toward Marks & Spencer. Their commitments yield major benefits through their day-to-day work and, says Clinton Silver, "they enable you to meet difficult times." The retailer's experience in 1992 is illustrative.

In the United Kingdom, 1992 was the third year of a bitter recession. By then, consumers had become financially strapped, and many retailers and their suppliers were suffering from low profits or worse. When M&S saw early signs that the recession was ending, it decided to permanently lower its prices. The company firmly believed that this change, combined with renewed economic growth, would produce a volume increase that would more than compensate for lost profits. By policy, however, M&S does not discount, so price cuts would have to come through reduced costs—without compromising value. Achieving these objectives would not be easy; inflation was higher than usual at the time. Suppliers were the key to the new strategy, which M&S named its "outstanding value campaign."

To avoid the risk of taking writedowns on new items, Marks & Spencer focused on core products. Then, by working closely on those goods with its suppliers, M&S sought ways to lower prices through different garment makeups and other means. To help drive down costs, the retailer consolidated its purchasing, asked suppliers to cut their margins, and told them it would take a smaller margin as well. For example, by going to a different fabric source (but not changing the specification) for boys' jeans, M&S was able to drop the price sufficiently that its volume doubled.

As a matter of policy, M&S never mandates supplier price reductions. When it believes a lower price is in everyone's interest, it negotiates this, as was done in the outstanding value campaign. In this case, Clinton Silver says that negotiations with the suppliers were tough; everything was worked through by individual product. Some suppliers declined to cut their prices because they did not think the expected volume growth would be enough to offset the reduced margins. M&S

accepted those positions, and so some of its prices were not cut. No suppliers walked away.

The combination of lower prices and increased demand following the recession drove volume increases that filled suppliers' factories, making the effort highly successful for everyone. In the first year after the recession, the outstanding value campaign gave M&S record pre-tax profits—higher than the most optimistic forecasts, and in sharp contrast to the experience of other British retailers. M&S and its suppliers also enjoyed significant share price gains for its common stock.[3] None of this could have been done without the suppliers' faith in their relationships with M&S.[4] "I am quite happy to go into the wilderness with Marks & Spencer," says Northern's Haskins, "because I make a lot of money out of it."

Branded Goods and Value Chains

The increased use of value chains has made innovation potentially a more powerful force than ever before. Without these chains, innovation is largely a matter of internal development for any firm; with them, a company can add the resources and expertise of many others to its own. Firms that formerly succeeded as lone innovators but ignore the potential inherent in these new arrangements are vulnerable to rivals that capitalize on them.

Paralleling the rise of value chains is the emergence of a new generation of consumers. As widely reported in the press, today's consumers are better informed and looking for more value. They also have more choices of what and where to buy, including improved private-label goods, more retail stores, and catalog shopping. For these reasons, there has been a decline in consumer loyalty to many established brands.

These factors pose a challenge to firms whose business is based on traditional branded goods. Many of these companies have regarded retailers simply as warehouses for their goods on the way to consumers. Lulled by the security of past successes that rest on their brands, some seem to have grown lethargic. However, the often-predicted death of brands is highly unlikely.

The purpose of brands is to supply information. For some goods, they make a statement about their user's lifestyle or values. Image, for instance, leads some consumers to pay more to have a certain label on their clothing or a particular food item on the shelf—even though the product may be almost identical to its non-branded counterpart. For other goods, brand names connote unique high value attained through innovation.

Clearly, educated consumers who have a variety of choices will always need (and want) information about the goods they buy. Consequently, the concept of brands still has merit. But the rise of value chains is making it harder for single companies to retain the value consumers associate with a brand, and firms that lose this cachet will suffer.

Lycra illustrates this point. DuPont developed the fiber and continues to innovate on its own in many performance areas. But a good part of Lycra's growing success comes from DuPont's alliances with M&S, Triumph, and an array of textile machinery makers, yarn spinners, and other companies in its value chain. Each partner contributes its own technical and market knowledge for the fiber's wider applications and further development.

Marks & Spencer offers another illustration of the growing link between brands and value chains. Because of the retailer's relationship with its value chain, St. Michael is one of the best-known brands in the United Kingdom.[5] Although M&S does not carry any finished goods other than its own brand, it does recognize the power of others' brands and builds on those whenever doing so makes sense. In fact, Marks & Spencer was a pioneer in co-branding. For instance, because of the way Lycra performs and is promoted, the fiber adds unique value to the M&S garments in which it is used. All those goods are clearly labeled as containing Lycra via in-store displays, on the goods themselves, and with hang tags. M&S does the same with other fibers when those same conditions apply.

If brands will not disappear, what will happen in the battle between them and private label? Since value chains are available to makers of both kinds of goods, the competition is certain to grow more intense. That is good news for consumers, because it will create more opportunities for them to buy value.

Frontiers of Value Chain Development

Value chains are a self-reinforcing activity. Just as they contribute to better performances and sharper strategies, chains will continue to evolve and gain importance in response to the heightened competition they help produce. Aspects of that progression include an increased emphasis on technology, more direct ties between chain members, and a greater strategic emphasis.

INCREASED EMPHASIS ON TECHNOLOGY

In most industries, technology is an integral component of value creation, and the pace of that dependency appears to be accelerating. This trend is shaping the role of value chains.

Looking ahead, Tom Slaninka of Motorola expects that his company and its rivals will be getting to the same levels of quality, delivery, and cycle time. He also sees an increasingly competitive marketplace. To continue to leverage its suppliers ahead of others, Slaninka believes that Motorola will emphasize relationships that bring it advanced ideas about design, technology, and product concepts before these are offered to anyone else.

Technical innovation has always been important to Marks & Spencer as well, and is becoming even more vital. In garments, for example, the uses of Lycra are growing rapidly. New formulations of man-made fibers are also appearing with increased frequency, and natural fibers like silk and linen are becoming more important as a result of new manufacturing processes. In addition, technical advances are improving fabric performances (for example, in machine washability). For these reasons, Marks & Spencer is honing its already sharp focus on technology relationships with its value chain. Similarly, when Chrysler's Tom Stallkamp talks about the future of his firm's supply relationships, getting new technologies first is one of his priorities.

MORE DIRECT TIES WITHIN VALUE CHAINS

One inevitable consequence of pressures to reduce cycle time—which is a characteristic of every market—is a growing need to build direct links between everyone who is contributing to an activity, regardless of their positions in firms or value chains. DuPont's ties to Marks & Spencer are illustrative.

A related effect regards organizational behavior. The only way a company can swiftly build and support numerous fast-response ties between its employees and other firms is to make the well-known but often poorly implemented empowered organization a reality. This task involves more than day-to-day decision making in current alliances.

People at lower management levels must be able to recognize and respond to new opportunities quickly, largely on their own initiative. Direct links also require that all participants have outstanding relationship skills.

Consider the cooperation between Northern Foods and Marks & Spencer. Many products Northern makes for M&S are highly perishable and must be sold within a few days of their production. People must continuously solve problems together in a very close hour-by-hour, day-by-day relationship that allows no room for acrimony. During the week before Christmas, for instance, Northern typically ships 1,600 trailer loads of food to M&S. To meet such tight schedules requires an interdependent, integrated logistics system that calls for deep understandings and fast problem solving. There is virtually no time for hierarchies to intervene if something goes wrong.

INCREASING STRATEGIC EMPHASIS

Because value chains help produce distinct value for each member, companies are increasingly including the chains in their strategic thinking and devoting more resources to chain management. To strengthen ties across the company with key technology sources in its value chain, for example, Marks & Spencer recently restructured its technology group, as noted in Chapter 11. Similarly, Motorola's Paging Products Group reorganized its Material Quality Engineering function. Originally, the MQE job was solving technical material problems discovered in PPG factories. Now it focuses on suppliers' process characterizations, supporting early design efforts, root-cause analysis, and other long-term forms of technical assistance.

Another way that value chains become more strategic is through the development of unique joint processes. One example of this is Motorola's Schedule Sharing, which is used with all suppliers to improve inventory management, reduce joint costs, and increase responsiveness.

As another illustration of joint processes, M&S and Northern Foods pioneered a common container that has greatly improved the handling of chilled food. Factories and store systems have been designed around it for better billing and processing efficiency. The container permits computerized order processing, and the full system is hard to duplicate due to its complexity. One must take the value of a container's contents (such as breads versus cooked meats) into account in processing each tray. Also, the contents must be sold within a brief time limit; a sandwich goes stale after two days. Getting the complete mix right for each store is tricky. In the United States, this is done only for milk, but Northern and M&S use it for all chilled food. Compared with the alternatives, the container requires less labor and cardboard, improves hygiene, and saves substantial costs.

Using and Managing Alliance Networks

A company's value chain consists of suppliers and customers linked to each other in various ways to produce more value for the final customer. But customers and suppliers are not a firm's only outside sources of added value. Growing needs for new technologies and opportunities that exceed what is available within a chain are causing firms to build links to others, including rivals and firms in different industries. In this context, a value chain is the core of a more extended network that serves the same objective of more customer value.

These multiple connections, many of which are alliances, create more opportunities for confusion, priority conflict, and destructive information leaks than exist in arm's-length relationships. This friction is magnified because rivals often share value chains.

Consider that Motorola and Hewlett-Packard compete in some markets, are respectively customer and supplier for each other in various markets, share suppliers in many markets, often have the same customer, and have alliances in yet other markets. Consider also that Triumph International is a customer of Courtalds Textiles in fabrics and laces, a branded competitor in lingerie, and a supplier of branded lingerie to Courtalds Textiles' retail lingerie chain. At the same time, Triumph supplies private-label lingerie to M&S, and hence it is a competitor to Courtalds Textiles' own private-label lingerie at M&S.

With appropriate controls, information leaks can be avoided. Some conflicts, such as those over capacity use, can be resolved through better joint planning. Other issues can be prevented through organizational arrangements. To maintain separation between its private label and branded lines, Courtaulds Textiles has built "Chinese walls" between the different businesses, starting at the very top of the company, and typically uses different plants and designers for each line. As an example, the firm's lingerie retail chain is not located in towns having Marks & Spencer stores. Additionally, the chain stores provide a highly personal fitting service, which helps differentiate the M&S and non-M&S businesses. As a consequence, the businesses are fully segregated from each other.[6]

Other conflicts are more challenging. For example, whenever technology helps define a customer's unique value, that company wants to be the first to get new technologies from its suppliers. But its rivals want that as well, often from the same suppliers. One way to resolve this issue, as illustrated by PCEC's shifting from Mitsubishi to Motorola for some chips, is to work with firms where there is no conflict (see Chapter 2). If that is not possible, one may have to develop a new source or become less dependent on the particular technology. Another tactic is to earn the right to get new technologies first, either by being a more attractive customer or by engaging in joint developments before others spot those opportunities.

Probably the most difficult, yet increasingly common area of conflict, is in alliances between rival companies. The number of these relationships is growing because rivals by nature have more resources of a similar kind—and hence more opportunity for synergy—than do non-rivals. Alliances between competitors are also a logical consequence of rising competition, which drives firms to join others to draw on complementary skills and resources. Examples cited in Chapter 2 are alliances between Ford and Nissan, and Coke and Schweppes. Others include Unilever and Procter & Gamble, Labatt and Molson, GE and Pratt & Whitney, Philips and Sony, and Nucor and U.S. Steel.

As discussed in *Partnerships for Profit*, cooperation between rivals requires a shared objective for the venture that dominates any conflict. Also needed is a separation of the people who are expected to cooperate from those who contribute to their firm's rivalry. Related factors include incentives structures that reinforce cooperation where that is desired, and top management actions that help people overcome the political and psychological barriers to cooperating with an adversary. Having an objectives hierarchy within each firm that shows how and where such alliances contribute to its interests further supports such efforts.

These principles, together with material from earlier chapters, are summarized below in a set of guidelines for managing the growing networks of relationships that most companies are now building.

NETWORK DEVELOPMENT GUIDELINES

Have Clear Objectives. Each business unit needs enough clarity about its objectives and priorities so it can identify relationships that will contribute the most value. For companies with more than one business unit, an objectives hierarchy is needed to define how each alliance contributes to the whole, support multi-unit alliances, and help people recognize acceptable conflicts among different alliances.

Rationalize the Supply Base. Conflict among suppliers is reduced, and value and commitments are increased, by reducing the number of suppliers to the minimum needed for focused competition and capacity requirements.

Distinguish between Alliances and Commercial Links. Recognize that alliances, which involve significant information sharing, present more conflicts than commercial ties, which require relatively little sharing.

Use Partner Selection Criteria. For alliances, customer and supplier choice must assess each firm's ability to achieve the agreed-upon market-beating objectives, as well as its partnering skills.

Ensure Dominant Value. Be sure that the merits of cooperation for each alliance significantly exceed the benefits of alternative arrangements, including commercial links, other alliances, acquisitions, and internal development. This is necessary to resolve partner conflicts, work with rivals, and support the extra effort alliances require.

Limit the Initial Scope. The wider the commitment to another firm, the more chance there is for conflicts with other alliances. Broader commitments also reduce opportunities for working with others and make each firm more dependent on its partner's performance. Consequently, alliances should be defined narrowly at first and expanded based only on growing value and success.

Define Information Boundaries. In each relationship, agree on what information will be shared and what will not. Misunderstandings here can weaken trust and damage partner firms.

Restrict Future Technology Sharing. When a company agrees to share future technologies with current partners, that may later prevent it from building alliances with others who want to restrict how their technology is used.

Avoid Quid Pro Quo Deals. Each alliance and commercial link must stand on its own merits. Attempts to make one relationship conditional on another make them all vulnerable to the weakest among them.

Form Direct Links. To ensure clear understandings for innovative activities, contributing companies should interact directly with one another, regardless of their location in a network.

Constantly Scan and Benchmark. To keep up with ongoing change and find new partners, a business must continually refresh its knowledge of best practices and emerging opportunities.

Seek Other Arrangements. When conflicts dominate a relationship, they may be best resolved by ending it.

NETWORK MANAGEMENT GUIDELINES

Empower Every Interface. Each business unit must have sufficient authority to manage its own alliances.

Set Relationship Priorities. A company's most important alliances deserve the most attention in terms of resources and management time.

Use Joint Planning to Reduce Conflict. For important alliances, share future capacity needs and technology plans to identify opportunities, adjust longer-term agendas, and ensure that expectations can be met.

Protect Sensitive Information. Each person involved in an alliance must know what information may be shared and what may not. Use organizational separations and limited access to protect each partner's information.

Clarify People's Roles. Avoid role conflicts by reassigning responsibilities. People who are expected to combat a rival in the marketplace cannot be expected to build trusting relationships with that firm as well. Create incentive structures that encourage desired cooperation.

Hold Alliances to Stretch Goals. Each alliance should continue only as long as it continues to be each partner's best choice for reaching its own objective.

Maintain the Core. Even when core skills are not shared, alliances increase each firm's learning and cash flow, and accelerate change. The growing use of alliances consequently raises the importance of a firm's maintaining its core through investment and learning. Also needed is an ongoing assessment of how the core is defined to ensure that it reflects changing conditions.

Be Each Partner's Best Partner. Manage every relationship to earn the priority commitments of each partner.

The Limit on Alliance Performance

There is just one constraint on the performance of a firm's outside connections—a human one. "Personal chemistry," says Chris Haskins, "which means making sure all relationships between partner firms from top to bottom are working well, defines the limits of what can be done." Adds Motorola's Sunil Lakhani: "Alliances are not based on formal connections between firms. Instead, they critically depend on trust between people, which must be constantly reinforced."

"Attitudes, more than anything else, shape the quality of these relationships," comments Bill Kennedy of Philips Consumer Electronics Company. "If people have the mentality that it is acceptable to harm the other firm, then an alliance is impossible. By contrast, if they believe in doing their best to make everyone happy and make a buck while doing that, then everyone has a chance to prosper." Kennedy illustrates his point with the case of engineers cooperating on joint design, which "only works when the chemistry is great between the people and the organizations. Since firms are always bringing their cultural baggage with them, that does not always happen."

Kennedy is not singling out engineers for criticism; the issue is broader than that. In all disciplines and at all management levels there is a shortage of people who can build the relationships that are essential for alliances. At PCEC, this limits opportunities. To improve its links with major customers, the company is creating a team at each interface. Because team performance depends on personality, Kennedy says progress will be paced by the ability to find the right people to fill these positions. While longer-term sales incentives may be helpful, he says that to an important extent performance is a people issue.

Kraft General Foods is another company that is moving toward team interfaces. Says Joe Durrett, senior vice president of sales: "The biggest difficulty is changing attitudes. You must reengineer what you have because there are no experienced salespeople you can bring into the company who relate to this team approach."[7]

Denis Desmond of Desmond & Sons observes that the ability of his firm and Marks & Spencer to push each other hard as they keep reaching for more value "reflects a high degree of mutual confidence built up over many years. Other retailers are attracted to the M&S results and style, but its relationships with suppliers have matured over so many years that others cannot get to the same level of trust in the short term—especially when their past record is one of jumping among suppliers. M&S is tough, demanding—and fair with its suppliers. We share an emotional atmosphere with a great deal of trust."

NOTES

Introduction

1. G. Christian Hill and Ken Yamada, "Motorola Illustrates How an Aged Giant Can Remain Vibrant," *Wall Street Journal*, December 12, 1992, p. 1; Ronald Henkoff, "Keeping Motorola on a Roll," *Fortune*, April 18, 1994, p. 67.

2. Paul Taylor, "M&S and ABB Head List of Europe's Respected Companies," *Financial Times*, June 27, 1994.

3. Paul Ingrassia and Joseph B. White, *Comeback: The Fall and Rise of the American Automobile Industry*, New York: Simon & Schuster, 1994; "Crunch at Chrysler," *Economist*, November 12, 1994, p. 121.

Chapter 1. CUSTOMER–SUPPLIER ALLIANCES: UNLOCKING THE POTENTIAL

1. ABB quote from Paul Hofheinz, "Europe's Tough New Managers," *Fortune*, September 6, 1993, p. 111.

2. Neil Templin and Jeff Cole, "Manufacturers Use Suppliers to Help Them Develop New Products," *Wall Street Journal*, December 19, 1994, p. 1.

3. For U.S. manufacturers, the cost of purchased materials and equipment averages about 57 percent of the value of shipments (revenues). See Annual Survey of Manufacturers, Washington, D.C., Bureau of the Census, General Summary, Manufacturers—Subject Series, pages 1–2, 1–3, and 1–90. If a typical firm has 10 percent pre-tax earnings, then 33 percent of revenue goes to internal expenses, compared to the 57 percent for suppliers.

4. Closing address delivered to Marks & Spencer's management and management from its leading suppliers, at M&S business conference on September 21, 1994.

5. Data sources: Chrysler Corporation; Kevin Done, "Chrysler to Cut Number of Parts Suppliers," *Financial Times*, October 3, 1994; Alex Taylor III, "The Auto Industry Meets the New Economy," *Fortune*, September 5, 1994, p. 523. Prepared remarks by Thomas T. Stallkamp, vice president for procurement and supply and general manager for large car operations, at the Automotive New World Congress, Detroit, Michigan, January 10, 1994.

6. Joseph A. Heim, "Removing Barriers to World-Class Manufacturing," National Academy of Engineering, Washington, D.C., October 1992.

7. Jordan D. Lewis, "IBM and Apple: Will They Break the Mold?" *Wall Street Journal*, July 29, 1991.

8. See Jordan D. Lewis, *Partnerships for Profit*, New York: Free Press, 1990.

9. Israel Sief, *Memoirs of Israel Sief*, London: Weidenfeld and Nicholson, 1970; Marcus Siet, *Marcus Sief on Management*, London: Weidenfeld & Nicholson, 1990.

10. James P. Womack, Daniel T. Jones, and Daniel Roos, *The Machine That Changed the World*, New York: Macmillan Publishing Company, 1990.

Chapter 2: GETTING STARTED

1. On brands, see Guy de Jonquieres, "Not Just a Question of Price," *Financial Times*, September 9, 1993; "Cheap Thrills Are Not Enough," *Financial Times*, September 11, 1993; Erik Ipsen, "Europe's Food Firms Look Abroad," *International Herald Tribune*, April 23, 1994, p. 7; "Almost the Real Thing," *Financial Times*, April 23, 1994, p. 9; Emiko Terazono, "Japan's Brands Feel the Pinch, Too," *Financial Times*, April 28, 1994, p. 9; Michael Williams, "Japan's Shoppers Bring a New Era to Economy," *Wall Street Journal*, June 20, 1994.

2. *Financial Times*, November 24, 1993, p. 22.

3. Sherwood C. Frey and Michael M. Schlosser, "ABB and Ford: Creating Value Through Cooperation," *Sloan Management Review*, Fall 1993, p. 65.

4. Patricia Sellers, "How to Remake Your Sales Force," *Fortune*, May 4, 1992, p. 98.

5. Charles Batchelor, "Planning Your Future Together," *Financial Times*, August 8, 1993, p. 8.

6. "Is Partnering Being Priced Out of the Marketplace?" *Purchasing*, June 17, 1993, p. 22.

7. For more on finding leading-edge partners, see Lewis, *Partnerships for Profit*, chapter 14.

8. "Crashed," *Economist*, September 25, 1993, p. 94.

9. For more on core competencies and on the drawbacks of vertical integration, see Lewis, *Partnerships for Profit*, chapters 4 and 2, respectively.

10. Charles Handy, "Ex-exuberance," *Economist*, April 24, 1993, p. 131.

11. For details on core competencies and the benefits of focus, see Lewis, *Partnerships for Profit*, chapters 2 and 4.

12. Tom Natale observes that core competence in the consumer TV set business is in the display components (tubes, yokes, etc.). The barrier to entry is relatively small if one can get these components at a reasonable price; thus, to be viable, a firm must have its own display-components manufacturing abilities. Vertical integration beyond that is not critical—if one can get unique world-class skills and designs from supply partners.

13. For more on what to outsource, see Ravi Venkatesan, "Strategic Sourcing: To Make or Not to Make," *Harvard Business Review*, November–December 1992, p. 98; John Stuckey and David White, "When and When Not to Vertically Integrate," *Sloan Management Review*, Spring 1993, p. 71.

14. Tom Steel, "Take Your Partners," *Business Life*, November 1993, p. 44.

15. Hiser and Wahlstedt quotes from Cindy Skrzycki, "Suppliers Under Scrutiny," *Washington Post*, November 26, 1989, p. H1. For difficulties U.S. auto firms have had in transforming their supply relationships, see Susan Helper, "How Much Has Really Changed Between U.S. Automakers and Their Suppliers?" *Sloan Management Review*, Summer 1991.

Chapter 3.   CONDITIONS FOR HIGH PERFORMANCE

1. Oscar Suris, "GM Tries to Heal Supplier Relations, Yet Reduce Costs," *Wall Street Journal*, August 9, 1993, p. B8; Kevin Kelly, Zachary Schiller, and James Treece, "Cut Costs or Else," *Business Week*, March 22, 1993, p. 28; Kevin Kelly and Kathleen Kerwin, "There's Another Side to the Lopez Saga," *Business Week*, August 23, 1993; Erle Norton, "Balking U.S. Automotive Suppliers Talk of Giving Up Business with Car Maker," *Wall Street Journal*, November 2, 1992, p. A6; Oscar Suris, "GM's Auto-Parts Suppliers Hope Speech by Wagoner Will Alter Lopez's Stance," *Wall Street Journal*, August 6, 1993, p. A8; Kathleen Kerwin et al., "Can Jack Smith Fix GM?" *Business Week*, November 1, 1993, p. 126; "General Motors: Europeaniseable?" *Economist*, March 11, 1995, p. 65.

2. Part of the art of defining a commodity group is to identify a close functional relationship to the goods or user behavior for which they will be employed. That helps set the scope for relevant buyers' or purchasing peoples' know-how, creativity and ability to make well-informed trade-offs. Another part of the art is to know the best level for defining a commodity. For example, dealing with printed circuit boards (PCBs) is more effective than PCB laminates; the latter are too far removed from the functionality that characterizes key interactions between the supplied goods and the consumer's product.

3. Different companies report different experiences with a backup strategy that involves moving tooling to new locations. At Ford, says Charlie Ross, that backup strategy has often not worked well. When the need to move tooling arose, moving it and ancillary equipment often took so long that it did not make sense. By contrast, Chrysler's Steve Zimmer says his firm has not had problems moving tooling from one supplier plant to another when that was necessary for backup; it has even done so over a weekend.

4. In the case of Seiko robotics, which are critical to PPG manufacturing, the backup was created within Motorola, which has always developed robots to fill unique needs not met by others. Seiko's awareness of this is a source of pressure on them. Increasingly, the kind of robots Motorola wants do not make business sense for Seiko to produce. Motorola is also working on a robot arm that might replace what it gets from suppliers, out of concern for its own core needs. Similarly, Motorola decided to move into vision as a core competence because no one was close to doing what Motorola needed. Still, Motorola will need some Seiko robots in certain areas.

5. Kevin Done, "A Pyramid of Many Parts," *Financial Times*, August 3, 1994, p. 13.

6. Marks & Spencer believes it has helped its suppliers to be at the leading edge in technical areas such as quality and fabric innovation, such that it would gain little benefit from their experience in serving M&S rivals. M&S would thus be concerned if a supplier used skills gained from it to sell to its rivals. This can be a discussion issue with nondedicated suppliers, and at times it is difficult to reach agreement. In the final analysis, the decision has to be made by the supplier; that firm must determine who is its most important customer.

Chapter 4. PRACTICES FOR JOINT CREATIVITY

1. "Banking on a Bird," *Economist*, March 12, 1994, p. 85.

2. For more on how a firm can protect itself while sharing sensitive information, see Lewis, *Partnerships for Profit*, chapter 4.

3. "Partnering and Team Building Go Hand-In-Hand," *Construction Industry News*, May 1994, p. 3.

4. "Small Car Engineering Group Teams with Dow to Develop Vision Statement," *Chrysler Corporation Supplier*, May–June 1994, p. 3.

5. Kathleen Kerwin et al., "Can Jack Smith Fix GM?" *Business Week*, November 1, 1993, p. 126.

Chapter 5. COOPERATING FOR MORE VALUE

1. For more technical detail about the manufacturing aspects, see Geoffrey Gill and Steven Wheelwright, "Motorola, Inc.: Bandit Pager Project," Harvard Business School case N9-690-043, 1989; "To Each His Own," *Economist*, December 5, 1992, p. 91.

2. The benchmarking–spider chart–road map process also feeds an ongoing redefinition of PPG core capabilities, which evolve with changing technology and the marketplace.

3. People who develop the performance envelopes are directly involved in core manufacturing processes and are able to ensure equipment is available when needed. To appreciate their role it is helpful to place them in a broader context. PPG has three organizational levels, which correspond to the three kinds of road maps:

• *Current portfolio*—technology operations, which maintains and optimizes current operating processes

• *Core development operations*—a unit that solidifies emerging technologies into a defined system (develops processes for new products; mostly applied work)

• *Pure technology shelf*—an advanced manufacturing technology research unit that looks ahead three to five years

Significantly, there is a leap-frogging effect among the groups. For instance, technology operations people become entrenched in a given technology and know its pitfalls; they become a source of improvement ideas with higher-level groups.

Chapter 6. COOPERATING FOR BETTER TIMING AND COSTS

1. Carla Rapoport, "A Tough Swede Invades the U.S.," *Fortune,* June 29, 1992, p. 76.

2. "Partners in Inventory Control," *New York Times,* March 3, 1991, p. G5.

3. The objectives of Schedule Sharing are to lower inventory costs while maintaining desired flexibility. The basic tool is a minimum/maximum window that indicates how much of each kind of part Motorola wants in inventory at a given time.

The overall paradigm for Schedule Sharing is to achieve the lowest combined total cost of Motorola plus its suppliers, without compromising deliveries to Motorola customers. If a supplier's manufacturing cycle time is one week and it has unlimited capacity, then Motorola could set a target of fifty-two cycles a year without forcing overtime or other diseconomies at the supplier. Inventory buffers, however, are needed somewhere, to account for demand uncertainty and capacity limits. Schedule Sharing is a way to do this without causing unnecessary stock holding by customer or supplier.

How Schedule Sharing Works. With Schedule Sharing, Motorola sends forecasts to its suppliers of how many parts will be consumed over specific time periods. Every Monday, each supplier receives a detailed updated annual demand forecast by kit number for each week for the next eight weeks, the five weeks after that, the thirteen weeks after that, and the final twenty-six weeks. Actual inventory levels at the end of each week are also reported to suppliers the following Monday morning, directly from Motorola's manufacturing information system. Recently, to be more responsive to demand fluctuations (and encouraged by its suppliers), Motorola began making daily inventory information available; this permits even better supplier adjustments.

If inventories are within the stipulated window, demand fluctuations do not require supply changes. Whether they occur is up to the supplier to determine, based on how it can best manage its resources. For instance, if the window is three weeks maximum and one week minimum with an average of two weeks, and a supplier targets for the average, it will produce twenty-six annual turns at Motorola.

Motorola defines minimum and maximum inventory levels for each facility. Those levels are derived from experience regarding how much inventory is needed to buffer its forecasting, given the cost of carrying each part. More specifically, parts are first classified using the traditional ABC analysis: For each part, weighted consumption is calculated by multiplying the cost per part by the projected consumption of that part. Next, all parts are ranked according to descending total dollar value, with the highest value parts being classified as "A" parts. Typically, these may represent 80 percent of total production material expenditures and involve perhaps 10 percent of the total number of parts. These parts deserve the most attention in terms of cost management.

To illustrate, consider that a two-week average inventory target is to be established on "A" parts, with a minimum of one week and a maximum of three weeks, for a given Motorola facility. Similarly, "B" parts could be assigned a four-week average inventory target, and "C" parts ten weeks. Next Motorola computes the forecast average weekly consumption of each "A" part for the next thirteen weeks, then multiplies that by the minimum and maximum weeks (one and three, respectively) to get the minimum and maximum inventory number for each part. A similar analysis is done for "B" and "C" parts.

Depending on demand fluctuations, the actual quantity of parts held in inventory will change. Note that window limits are numbers of weeks, not quantities, so the windows can change weekly. While Motorola does not yet have quantitative measures of Schedule Sharing benefits, those are known to be so substantial that this practice will have to be used to get the total annual cost reductions it must have.

Supplier Management. When it began using Schedule Sharing, Motorola defined on-time delivery in terms of early and stockout, with early receipt putting inventories over the upper limit, and stockout defined as 10 percent or less of minimum requirement (which is typically one week of parts). More recently, Motorola stopped tracking "overs" and began following total number of inventory turns of each supplier's parts, plus stockouts. A focus on turns gives a better handle on the whole process.

For inventory turns, each week the number of annual turns is computed for the middle of the window for all parts in the aggregate. While the actual number of turns varies by part, that level of detail is not sought in supplier management. To get the aggregate turns number, the arithmetic average between the minimum and maximum is calculated for every part, weighted by dollar value, from each supplier. In that way, the turns target weighs the highest-value "A" items more than others.

Window width is not negotiated with suppliers, except for low-volume parts or for parts where the minimum lot size and Motorola consumption are in conflict (that is, Motorola needs relatively few parts, but the supplier has to make a large number for economic reasons). Then, window width is computed to be a multiple of the lot size added to the minimum, with the multiple reflecting how much stock Motorola wants and economic production runs for the supplier. As an example, consider the case of a reel of parts that is most economically made with 500 parts per reel, yet Motorola only needs 100 parts per week. In that case, a window width of one lot size—that is, 100 parts minimum and 600 maximum—might not suffice, because if there were 300 parts in inventory at a given time, the next shipment of one reel with 500 parts would exceed the maximum. To compensate for that, the window width could be two lots.

Schedule Sharing also accounts for parts that take a lot of storage space, such as cabinets. Then, min and max windows are established by part number, and the inventory balance is sent to suppliers every day. This methods used mostly with local suppliers of relatively large, low-value items that cannot be economically shipped very far and, relatedly, cost a great deal more.

Requirements on Suppliers. With Schedule Sharing, a supplier must analyze when to place an order to its factory to replenish the customer. Jerry Deutsch of Molex describes this as a very simple process. Molex gets its planning information electronically from Motorola each Monday, although it could get current information daily, which would allow it to see closer-in fluctuations. Molex software takes the Schedule Sharing data and automatically integrates that into an MPR-style report for easy analysis and planning product replenishment orders.

Motorola expects its suppliers to reduce their manufacturing cycle times and helps them improve in that area if they take the initiative. Since Motorola states its requirements once a week, if a supplier can get its manufacturing cycle under the one week re-forecast time, then it is not possible to be delinquent. That also keeps the supplier's work-in-process inventory as low as possible. It further allows the supplier to react to a new window without becoming delinquent. The farther out in time a supplier must accommodate variations in demand, the more complex is the management of the schedule.

Schedule Sharing is not used in all cases. For example, if a supplier has a nearby plant, it may prefer to physically observe daily consumption to keep Motorola at appropriate levels. It also does not apply to distributors, which should be able to respond much faster.

4. Kevin Kelly et al., "Cut Costs or Else," *Business Week*, March 22, 1993, p. 28.

5. Another circumstance when the customer might pay for tooling is when that is changing regularly. Motorola pays for plastics tooling for this reason. If the supplier paid, it would be coming back for price negotiations each time it bought new tooling.

6. Fred R. Bleakley, "Some Companies Let Suppliers Work on Site and Even Place Orders," *Wall Street Journal*, January 13, 1995, p. 1.

Chapter 7. SUPPLY BASE MANAGEMENT

1. See, for example, "Elastic Brands," *Economist*, November 19, 1994, p. 75.

2. For the data systems business, independent organizations provide a useful benchmarking service regarding standard costs, typically by performing a standard data run on different systems. Beyond that, however, it is difficult to develop a total cost picture that allows a comparison of large-scale alliances, each of which involves many unique activities. Further, outside benchmarking organizations do not deal with all of the various activities in these alliances.

Chapter 8. MANAGING CONTINUOUS IMPROVEMENT

1. Suppliers get monthly reports on their ratings and are told of their relative standing compared to others in their commodity group in quarterly meetings, where development and other issues are also discussed. Suppliers do not yet see others' ratings, but Chrysler expects to share those (appropriately masked) in the future as its supplier program advances.

2. Chrysler does not quantitatively define the meaning of "slip," but suppliers that are having problems go on a "watch list," an event that initiates dialogue.

3. As a complementary effort, Motorola and other firms (including Texas Instruments) have cooperated through an organization known as the Six Sigma Institute to develop a "cookbook" that characterizes key processes that drive quality, cost, and cycle time on commodities shared across many firms. Motorola is doing the same on commodities important to it that are not of interest to other Six Sigma firms; an example is motors that make pagers vibrate. Motorola has some advantages in making cost projections because it has internal supply units in some of the same commodities.

Some firms avoid life-of-part agreements by seeking "most favored customer" pricing, in which a supplier agrees to a price as good as that given to any other customer; however, Motorola will not do that. Due to its substantial investment in supplier development, cost driver characterization, and joint cost reduction, Motorola expects to get lower costs—and prices—from its suppliers than what they give other customers, unless those customers use similar practices with the suppliers.

4. Consistent with auto industry practice, and due to substantial integration between different auto parts, suppliers must submit all ideas regarding design or material changes—and any process changes that could affect fit, functionality, or packaging—for approval by Chrysler before these can be implemented. Each proposed change includes an estimate of the cost savings involved, as well as estimated effects on weight, investment, and other Chrysler objectives. In deciding how it will use each suggestion, Chrysler considers the consequences for each of its objectives and adapts the suggestions accordingly.

At first, the SCORE system was managed manually, but a communications network is now being used that flows the ideas directly from suppliers to the implementers within Chrysler. There is no bureaucracy in the idea-sharing process because only four or five people are needed to monitor the whole process.

Ideas from second-tier suppliers are submitted to first-tier firms, which are responsible for implementing those ideas, unless the second-tier firm has direct ties to Chrysler. Ideas within the scope of that relationship go directly to Chrysler. The practice is essentially the same with third- and fourth-tier suppliers, and so on. Chrysler discusses with its first-tier suppliers how well they are doing with the ideas submitted to them, but does not yet measure their performance. Steve Zimmer says this is an area where there is a lot of room for improvement, and Chrysler expects to pursue that. The SCORE network does not yet show Chrysler the flow of ideas between second- and first-tier suppliers, or between lower tiers, but the system is moving in that direction as a means of better monitoring and managing its full supply chain.

Chapter 9.   BUILDING TRUST AND HIGH PERFORMANCE

1. Ihle's experience is buttressed by recent surveys conducted by Hyatt Hotels Corp., and by Arthur D. Little, reported in the *International Herald Tribune*, November 11, 1994, p. 9.

Chapter 10.   ORGANIZING THE INTERFACE

1. Patricia Sellers, "How to Remake Your Sales Force," *Fortune*, May 4, 1992, p. 98.

2. For Compaq and Ryder, see Ronald Henkoff, "Delivering the Goods," *Fortune*, November 28, 1994, p. 64.

Chapter 11.   LEVERAGING THE CORPORATION

1. "Motorola Tunes Up the Volume," *Economist*, August 28, 1993, p. 61; G. Christian Hill and Ken Yamada, "Motorola Illustrates How an Aged Giant Can Remain Vibrant," *Wall Street Journal*, December 9, 1992, p. 1.

2. Based on interviews with several American and European firms in late 1994, a period described by the companies as being one of general economic well-being for them.

3. Fred R. Bleakley, "Some Companies Let Suppliers Work on Site and Even Place Orders," *Wall Street Journal*, January 13, 1995, p. 1.

4. Woodworth Holdings, as reported by Alex Taylor III, "Japan's Car Crash in North America," *Fortune*, December 12, 1994, p. 20.

5. Champions are selected in discussions between the regional sourcing managers serving Boynton and Singapore. Depending on the key tasks, selection is based on experience, knowledge, proximity to the supplier, and leadership skills.

6. John A. Byrne et al., "Borderless Management," *Business Week*, May 23, 1994, p. 24; Robert Keatley, "Ford Reorganizes to Stay Competitive and Reach New Markets in the World," *Wall Street Journal*, July 22, 1994, p. A5.

7. Robert Keatley, "Ford Reorganizes to Stay Competitive and Reach New Markets in the World," *Wall Street Journal*, July 22, 1994, p. A5.

Chapter 12.   NEGOTIATIONS BETWEEN PARTNERS

1. For an excellent discussion of these concepts, see John Kay, *Foundations of Corporate Success*, New York: Oxford University Press, 1993.

Chapter 13.   SUCCESSFUL ALLIANCE PRACTITIONERS

1. Clifton J. Reichard, "Salesmen Shouldn't Sell; Buyers Shouldn't Buy," *Wall Street Journal*, August 6, 1993, p. A16.

2. Number of TCS teams from Tom Slaninka, "Supplier TCS Teams— Making a Difference," *Partnership for Growth Newsletter*, April 1993, p. 1.

3. For a description of internal TCS competition at Motorola, see Barnaby J. Feder, "At Motorola, Quality Is a Team Sport," *New York Times*, January 21, 1993, p. D1.

4. "Bankers Mistrust," *The Economist*, November 19, 1994, p. 87.

5. A. Steven Walleck, "A Backstage View of World-Class Performers," *Wall Street Journal*, August 26, 1991, p. A10.

6. G. Christian Hill and Ken Yamada, "Motorola Illustrates How an Aged Giant Can Remain Vibrant," *Wall Street Journal*, December 9, 1992, p. 1.

7. There is good evidence that outward-looking cultures adopt innovations more quickly than inward focused ones. See Everett M. Rogers and F. Floyd Shoemaker, *Communication of Innovations*, New York: Free Press, 1971. For evidence that innovative firms scan more than less innovative firms, see Donald C. Hambrick, "Environmental Scanning and Organizational Strategy," *Strategic Management Journal*, Vol. 3, 1982, p. 159.

8. K. K. Tse, *Marks & Spencer*, New York: Pergamon Press, 1984.

Chapter 14.   VALUE CHAINS AND ALLIANCE NETWORKS

1. Ronald Henkoff, "Keeping Motorola on a Roll," *Fortune*, April 18, 1994, p. 67.

2. DuPont also has extensive fashion services that monitor trends, fabric, and garment innovations in nearly all developed countries. The company shares its market scans in presentations, fashion shows, and video conferences connecting other regions of the world, as well as through informal communications by many DuPont professionals who routinely interface with customers, including M&S. DuPont trains the M&S sales staff (frequently holding seminars on garment performance), helps M&S develop positioning strategies for new offerings, and develops point-of-purchase merchandising tools. Other DuPont services include purchasing garments with and without Lycra to show M&S what is selling well around the world. The company's extensive network of couturiers also makes collections to demonstrate ways of combining fabrics containing Lycra. Highly regarded fashion consultants help identify trends in colors and fabrics.

3. Neil Buckley, "M&S Up 21% As Price Freeze Pays," *Financial Times*, November 4, 1993.

4. As another example of the same practice, in early 1992 M&S became highly dissatisfied with the prices and quality of its men's footwear line. In response, it decided to take whole product lines off display and return them to the manufacturers. It also reduced prices on remaining lines. Out of the ashes arose a phoenix: By working together, M&S and its suppliers improved the quality and achieved lower costs of the shoes. Since then, sales have been running 20 percent higher on a cash basis.

5. At low price points, products have limited design and there is less differentiation between private and branded goods, so conflict is more of an issue. Noel Jervis of Courtaulds Textiles says that conflicts are avoided when both sides see the potential sensitivity. As in any business, one has to manage the differentiation between customers. In the case of hosiery, where product differentiation is low his firm uses the same plant to supply both kinds of customers, using different specifications for each. That is because the scale needed for lowest-cost production exceeds what any one customer buys, and hosiery manufacturing equipment has the flexibility to accommodate different specifications. By contrast, Courtaulds Textiles can afford to run brassiere factories exclusively for M&S, because capital requirements are low.

6. Patricia Sellers, "How to Remake Your Sales Force," *Fortune*, May 4, 1992, p. 98.

INDEX

A NOTE OF THANKS

One of my great pleasures in writing this book was meeting the wonderful people who helped with the research. By the time it was done, I had known some of them for four years and visited with several of them many times. Several have become my friends; I look forward to being with each of them again soon.

It has been an enlightening experience. Each company where I did my research is on the cutting edge of customer–supplier alliances, and virtually every person with whom I worked has been a key contributor to those efforts. All of them continue to advance best practice in their firms. As a consequence, they have had a keen interest in better understanding the methods that contribute to alliance success. Their curiosity made our meetings mutual explorations rather than just one-way interviews. Over the months and years, our discussions increasingly probed all aspects of these alliances, with each of us wanting to understand more about why and how things work.

To illustrate the depths of their interest, several people set up telephone conversations with me from their homes so we could have more time to talk than would be possible in their offices. Some took vacation time for our visits. Virtually everyone responded to my calls on short notice when I was getting close to the deadline. One person, a top executive at a well-known global company, arranged for us to talk in the middle of the 1995 Rose Bowl game, even though he had invited twenty friends to his home to watch the game.

My debt to these people is tremendous. Their insights and experiences compose much of the text. Even so, listing them in a long roster of names would dilute the contribution each made. The best way I know to thank them is to acknowledge their help first.

Within this larger group, eight individuals stand out. First and foremost, I am indebted to Neil MacIvor of Motorola, who shared with me his remarkable breadth of understanding of the topic, which was critical to my own learning. That he made himself constantly available throughout much of my research helped advance my knowledge base and fill in missing pieces as the work progressed. Thanks to Neil's kindness, I ran out of questions before he ran out of patience.

Others who were particularly helpful (all are identified in the text) include Bruce Bendoff of Craftsman Custom Metal Fabricators, Vaughn Hovey of Kodak, Carole O'Beirne and Barry Morris of Marks & Spencer, Frank Palm of IBM, Ron Schubel of Molex, and Sunil Lakhani and Tom Slaninka of Motorola. I am especially grateful to them not only because they tolerated my many visits, but because they often went beyond my questions to offer additional insights and avenues for further research that they believed would be useful.

One person—the only individual I never met face-to-face—gave me many telephone hours over almost two years. Because of the sensitivities of the alliance we were discussing, he asked that I not mention his name or that of his company. It was he who interrupted his Rose Bowl guests to visit with me. That he shared his most difficult experiences, and trusted me to use this information constructively, was immensely valuable to me.

Special thanks are due to five people who opened their companies' doors for me and shared their valuable time. They are George Fisher, chairman and CEO of Motorola when I began my research, and now chairman and CEO of Kodak (my Kodak research began long before he arrived); Tom Natale, vice president of operations, Philips Consumer Electronics Company; Ron Schubel of Molex; Clinton Silver, then vice chairman and managing director of Marks & Spencer; and Tom Stallkamp, vice president for procurement and supply and general manager of large car operations at Chrysler.

Many other people shared their time and insights with me during two or more—some as many as twenty—visits. (I have indicated the positions of people not identified in the text.) At Chrysler, they included Stephen Zimmer and Russ Jacobs (manager, supplier quality planning and implementation); at Courtaulds Textiles, Noel Jervis; at Desmond & Sons, Denis Desmond; at DuPont, Salim Ibrahim; at Ford, Richard Ogren and Charlie Ross; at Hewlett-Packard (U.K.), Mike Haffenden; at Insul Reps, Kelly Howell; at Marks & Spencer, Alan Lambert and Guy McCracken; at McCann-Erickson Worldwide, Stewart Pierce Brown (senior vice president); at Molex, Richard Black, Jerry Deutsch, and Dan Prescott; at Motorola, Len deBarros, Bob Becknell, Rob Conway (associate general attorney), Bill Hanks, John Ihle, Dale Kelsey, Tom Koch (director, strategic sourcing and manufacturing planning, Paging Products Group), Jerry Leonard, Al Lucas, Isao Shirai, Kathy Sullivan, and Ron Vocalino; at

Philips Consumer Electronics Company, Gordon Couch and Bill Kennedy; at Northern Foods, Christopher Haskins; at Reed Personnel Services, Chris Kelly; and at Targ-It-Tronics, Larry Groves.

Special thanks are also due to the wonderful people I met at Motorola. I began my research there, and I took a lot of time asking questions that helped build my basic framework of understanding. They graciously tolerated many queries that led nowhere other than to help me understand the boundaries and dimensions of customer–supplier alliances.

Senior public relations professionals Karen Stewart at Chrysler; Margot Brown, Ken Countess, and Pat Schod at Motorola; and Brian Hudspith and Sue Sadler at Marks & Spencer were a tremendous help to me in arranging initial meetings, suggesting people to meet, gathering background data I wanted, and speeding the approval of my interview notes. Their willing support greatly eased my work. In fact, Ken's suggestion that I visit with Tom Slaninka, made when I was contemplating this book, was a critical early factor in my decision to proceed.

My thanks also to Bob Smith, until recently vice chancellor at the University of Maryland, and to his wife, Ginny, also a top executive in the university world. Their encouragement to write this book was an important early boost. José Salibi Neto, of HMS Brazil, suggested research strategies for this book and also encouraged me to write it. Joanna Brown, my secretary, assistant, and friend, managed the challenging tasks of scheduling meetings, arranging travel, retyping interview notes, protecting me from the telephone during my final writing days, and keeping me organized through the entire process. Her efforts made a huge difference for me. I am also grateful to John Bell, who was always available on a moment's notice, often by long-distance telephone to help fix my laptop computer when it had problems.

Most significantly, this book is a product of a very special alliance I have long enjoyed with Lynn Lopata Lewis, an accomplished editor and writer as well as my best friend. Without her tolerance of my seemingly endless work on this book, it could not have been done; without her expert and detailed comments on my writing, it would not make much sense; and without her constant encouragement, it would not have been possible. That we met thirty-one years ago today, and married soon after that, makes this date particularly meaningful for me.

Washington, D.C.
January 20, 1995

ABOUT THE AUTHOR

Jordan D. Lewis, an international consultant, author, and speaker, advises many of the world's leading firms and is a well-known expert on strategic alliances. A Fellow of the World Economic Forum, he has been profiled on CNN "Business Day," in the *Wall Street Journal*, the *Financial Times*, and the *Japan Times*.

Dr. Lewis is a former lecturer at the Wharton School of the University of Pennsylvania, where he taught courses that integrated strategy, technology, and organizational behavior. His last book, *Partnerships for Profit: Structuring and Managing Strategic Alliances*, is also published by The Free Press (1990). He lives in Washington, D.C.